HILARY WATSON

Complete & Balanced

101 Healthy Home-made Meals for Dogs

SECOND EDITION

HW VETERINARY NUTRITION INC.
Guelph, Ontario

The dietary recommendations provided in this book are based on current nutritional research at the time of publication. Veterinary nutrition is an evolving science and new research may change dietary recommendations. Readers are advised to consult their veterinarians regarding the nutritional care of their dogs. The publisher and author assume no liability for any injury and/or damage arising from this book.

Note for librarians: A cataloguing record for this book is available from Libray and Archives Canada at www.collectionscanada.ca/amicus/index-e.html

SECOND EDITION

ISBN 978-0-9812267-0-5

Book cover design and illustration by John Fraser
Book interiorDesign and composition by John Reinhardt Book Design

To my parents, Jack and Audrey, with much love and appreciation.

Contents

Acknowledgments

MY THANKS TO:

- Master Chefs Ann Vossen and Lynda Rumney, and their discerning taste-testers Sunny, Kailly, Layla, and Lily.
- John Reinhardt of John Reinhardt Book Design (www.bookdesign.com) for the professional interior page layout and for guiding this project from inception to completion.
- John Fraser (www.johnfraser.creativesource.ca) for the book cover design and cover illustration

PHOTO CREDITS

There is no happier dog than one working at a job he was bred to do. To the talented photographers who have so brilliantly captured the working dog in action, my thanks for allowing me to feature your photos in my book:

Opposite Page 1—Labrador Retriever, Field work. © Cindy Noland (www.nolanddogart.com)

Page 12 and title page—Basenji, Lure coursing. © Daniel Gauss, Shot On Site Photography (www.shotonsite.us)

Page 18—Doberman Pinscher, Tracking. © Cindy Noland (www.nolanddogart.com)

Page 26—Airedale Terrier, Search & Rescue (SAR). © Belyaeva Ekaterina (http://rescuedogs.ru)

Page 32—Papillon, Agility. © Cindy Noland (www.nolanddogart.com)

Page 36—Husky crosses, Skijor. © Joy Martinson, Joy's Sled Dog Photos (www.joymartinson.com)

Page 42—Australian Shepherd, Herding. © Jeff Jaquish, ZingPix Photography (www.zingpix.com)

Page 62—Belgian Malinois, Obedience. © Cindy Noland (www.nolanddogart.com)

Page 170—Belgian Shepherd and Australian Shepherd, Hiking. © Hilary Watson

Back cover—© Frank Vossen

Foreword

VIRTUALLY ALL COMMERCIAL canned and dry pet foods offer "complete and balanced" nutrition. Critics of home-prepared pet foods claim that home-made meals are inferior because they don't provide complete and balanced nutrition. While this is often the case, it doesn't need to be. Properly formulated homemade recipes can provide the same complete and balanced nutrition as traditional commercial pet foods.

I have worked as a pet nutritionist for more than 20 years. During that time, I have formulated many complete and balanced pet food products. Formulating complete and balanced recipes is a straightforward, three-step process. First, all potential ingredients are analyzed to determine their protein, fat, vitamin and mineral content. Next, the nutrient targets for the finished pet food are defined. In most cases, pet food companies use the dog and cat nutrient profiles published by the Association of American Feed Control Officials (AAFCO). Finally, all the ingredients' nutrient contents and the final pet food's nutrient targets are entered into a food formulation software program and a complete and balanced recipe is generated.

The same process can be applied to home-made recipes. Rather than entering the nutrient content of commercial pet food ingredients, such as poultry meal or brewers rice, the values for human food ingredients, such as chicken breast meat or cooked brown rice, are entered instead. The nutrient targets for the complete recipe are the same (following the AAFCO nutrient profiles for dogs or cats). The formulation software can then generate a complete and balanced recipe based on human food ingredients.

There are 37 essential nutrients for dogs. Not only must these nutrients be delivered in sufficient quantities to meet a dog's daily needs, but the entire recipe must be correctly "balanced" to ensure the adequate uptake of all nutrients. By far the greatest challenge in developing complete and balanced recipes is ensuring that all essential vitamins and minerals are present at adequate levels and that all micro-nutrients are properly balanced.

Almost all home-made recipes for pets recommend feeding a vitamin mineral supplement in conjunction with the home-made meal. In developing the recipes in this book, I discovered that commercial vitamin mineral supplements cannot be used to balance a home-made recipe. In Chapter 5, I explain why this is the case. Using food formulation software, I developed HILARY'S BLEND™ supplement, the first and only vitamin mineral prebiotic supplement specifically designed to balance home-made recipes.

This book is divided into two sections. The first section provides information on complete and balanced nutrition (Chapters 1 and 2), assessing the nutritional content of a recipe or ingredient (Chapter 3), balancing the vitamins and minerals in homemade recipes (Chapter 4 and 5), and homemade meal preparation (Chapter 6). Chapter 7 provides recipe rationales and recipe summary tables, while Chapter 8 gives instructions for calculating feeding guides for dogs of various ages. The second section of this book provides 101 complete and balanced recipes, along with their nutritional content, their metabolizable energy, as well as general feeding guides.

The recipes in this book offer the best of two worlds. They combine the nutritious goodness of fresh, human-grade ingredients with the scientific rigor of complete and balanced nutrition.

Your dog can do no better.

New in the Second Edition

The most significant change in this second edition is the introduction of my new brand name and logo: HILARY'S BLEND™. The ingredients and recipe for my supplement have not changed. It is exactly the same product in the jar, there's just a new brand name on the label. My supplement is uniquely formulated to balance the recipes in this book. The new brand name strengthens the connection between the recipes in this book and the supplement that balances them.

There are three significant changes to the book contents.

First, the eight Vegetarian Recipes are now grouped into three categories: Vegetarian Adult (R65-R68), Vegetarian Diabetic (R69, R70) and Vegetarian Urate (R71, R72). The two Vegetarian Diabetic recipes are new. Section 7.8 has been updated to explain the rationale for these new recipes.

Second, the six Low Phosphorus/Low Protein recipes (R91-96) have been reformulated to lower their fat and calorie content. Although the new recipes still provide most of their calories from fat, they all contain more fruits and vegetables to increase the percentage of calories coming from carbohydrate and to lower their total calorie content.

Finally, in response to questions about salmon oil, I've added Section 6.7 "About Salmon Oil" on page 41.

"Complete and Balanced" Defined

1

1.1

Complete Nutrition

THERE ARE SIX CATEGORIES of essential nutrients: water, protein, fat, carbohydrate, vitamins and minerals. Within these six categories, the Association of American Feed Control Officials (AAFCO) lists 36 nutrients (plus water) which are considered essential for dogs (see Table 1). A diet is said to be "complete" if it contains all essential nutrients (except water) at levels adequate to meet a dog's daily requirements. It is assumed that fresh water is available separately to the dog at all times.

PROTEIN

General Overview and Essentiality

The word protein comes from the Greek word *proteos* meaning primary or taking first place. Of the six categories of nutrients, only protein supplies the body with nitrogen, an essential constituent of all cells and tissues.

Proteins are composed of 20 different amino acids. Think of amino acids as letters and proteins as words. How many different words can be built using the 26 letters of the alphabet? The body can construct hundreds of different proteins by stringing together different combinations of these 20 unique amino acid building blocks.

Of the 20 different amino acids that make up proteins, 10 are considered "essential" meaning that they must be provided in a dog's diet (Table 2). The other 10 are "non-essential" because the cells in a dog's body can build them from other dietary constituents so it is not essential that they be provided in the diet.

There are two amino acids which are considered "conditionally essential": cystine and tyrosine. These two amino acids are precursors for the es-

FOOD							
Moisture	Dry Matter (all of the food that is not water)						
Water	Protein	Fat	Carbohydrate	Vitamins		Minerals	
Water is essential for dogs.	Amino acids are the building blocks of proteins. Ten amino acids are essential for dogs.	One fatty acid is essential for dogs.	No carbohydrates are essential for dogs.	Three fat-soluble vitamins are essential for dogs.	Eight water-soluble vitamins are essential for dogs.	Six macro-minerals are essential for dogs.	Six micro-minerals are essential for dogs.

Water	Arginine
	Histidine
	Isoleucine
	Leucine
	Lysine
	Methionine/Cystine
	Phenylalanine/
	  Tyrosine
	Threonine
	Tryptophan
	Valine
		Linoleic acid		Vitamin A
				Vitamin D
				Vitamin E
					Thiamin
					Riboflavin
					Niacin
					Pantothenic
					  acid
					Pyridoxine
					Folic acid
					Choline
					Vitamin B12
						Calcium
						Phosphorus
						Potassium
						Sodium
						Chloride
						Magnesium
							Iron
							Copper
							Manganese
							Zinc
							Iodine
							Selenium

TABLE 1

36 nutrients (plus water) are essential for dogs

TABLE 2

Ten amino acids are essential for dogs and two more are "conditionally" essential.

sential amino acids methionine and phenylalanine, respectively. Cystine and tyrosine are not essential in the diet. However, if the levels of methionine or phenylalanine are below a dog's requirements, the presence of cystine or phenylalanine in the diet can make up the shortfall.

The Role of Protein in the Body

Protein has three main functions in the body:

1. Dietary protein provides energy.
2. Dietary protein supplies the amino acids needed to build body proteins.
3. Certain amino acids are precursors for biologically important molecules in the body.

Arginine	Methionine
Histidine	Phenylalanine
Isoleucine	Threonine
Leucine	Tryptophan
Lysine	Valine
Cystine (conditionally)	Tyrosine (conditionally)

The first function of dietary protein is to provide the body with energy. The amino acids in proteins can be burned by the body as fuel. This energy is used for all cellular functions, for breathing, heart muscle contraction and all physical activity. It is only after a dog's energy requirements are met that amino acids can be used to build body proteins.

Amino acids are the building blocks of proteins. There are five main types of body proteins: structural proteins, peptide hormones, enzymes, transport proteins and immunoproteins (see "The Five Main Types of Body Proteins" below).

The third function of dietary protein is to supply amino acids that act as precursors for several important molecules in the body. For example, phenylalanine and tyrosine are precursors of thyroid hormone. Tryptophan is the precursor of serotonin, an important neurotransmitter. Histidine is the precursor of histamine, the inflammatory mediator that is the target of anti-histamines. The amino acids lysine and methionine combine to form carnitine, a molecule that is important for fatty acid transport and energy production. There are many other examples of biologically important molecules that are produced exclusively from amino acid precursors.

Protein Quality

Protein quality is dependent on the **digestibility** of the protein and its **amino acid score**. Digestibility refers to how easily the protein is broken down into its constituent amino acids in the digestive tract. Eggs, meat, poultry and fish all contain highly digestible protein, especially if these foods are cooked with steam or water. Rawhide, pigs' hooves and leather are examples of poorly digestible protein.

A protein's amino acid score reflects how closely the amino acids that make up the protein match the amino acids required by a dog. Gelatin has

THE 5 MAIN TYPES OF BODY PROTEINS

1. **Structural proteins** provide structural support to the body. This group includes the primary constituents of muscle tissue (actin and myosin); the proteins found in tendons, ligaments and other cartilage (collagen and elastin); and the primary constituent of hair, skin and nails (keratin).

2. **Peptide hormones** are protein-containing hormones that control many body functions. Some examples include insulin, growth hormone and thyroid hormone.

3. **Enzymes** are largely composed of protein. There are hundreds of different enzymes in the body that drive all essential cellular reactions. Some examples of processes that are dependent on protein enzymes include food digestion, energy production, blood clotting and nerve transmission.

4. **Transport proteins** carry substances in a dog's blood. Some examples include albumin, hemoglobin, transferrin and ceruloplasmin. Albumin is the principal protein in blood. It carries many different nutrients to cells throughout the body. Hemoglobin is a transport protein that carries oxygen in the blood. Transferrin and ceruloplasmin bind to iron and copper respectively, allowing these metals to be safely carried around the body.

5. **Immunoproteins**, also called antibodies or immunoglobulins, are proteins of the immune system. These proteins attack and neutralize infectious bacteria and other foreign antigens that have infiltrated the body. These proteins are important for self-defense and disease resistance.

an amino acid score of zero because it contains no tryptophan, an essential amino acid for a dog. The protein in eggs has a perfect amino acid score of 100 because it contains all essential amino acids in a balance that closely matches the requirements of a dog. Eggs, meat, poultry and fish all have high amino acid scores. Plant proteins have lower amino acid scores because they often lack one or more of the essential amino acids. Vegetarian diets must be carefully balanced to ensure that all essential amino acids are present in sufficient quantity to meet the dog's needs.

When protein intake is normal, a dog's amino acid requirements are invariably met with high quality human-grade meat, poultry and fish ingredients. When protein intake is restricted, as for example in diets for dogs with kidney disease, amino acid balance becomes more important. It is not enough to provide adequate protein to meet the dog's daily needs; the diet must also contain adequate levels of all essential amino acids.

FATS (LIPIDS)

General Overview and Essentiality

Fats in foods consist mainly of triglycerides. Triglycerides are molecules that contain three fatty acids attached to a glycerol backbone. The properties of different fats depend on the types of fatty acids contained in their triglycerides.

Fatty acids are classified according to the number of double bonds they contain. Fatty acids with no double bonds are called saturated fatty acids. Saturated fats are typically solid or semi-solid at room temperature. Some examples of fats that are predominantly saturated include pork lard, beef tallow and butter.

Fatty acids that contain double bonds are called unsaturated fatty acids. Those with one double bond are monounsaturated fatty acids while those with more than one double bond are polyunsaturated fatty acids. Unsaturated fatty acids are liquids at room temperature. Some examples include safflower oil and cod liver oil.

Polyunsaturated fatty acids can be further categorized by their omega number, which refers to the position of their first double bond. Omega-6 and omega-3 fatty acids have their first double bonds at their sixth and third carbons, respectively.

Essential fatty acids are fatty acids which cannot be synthesized by the body and must therefore be provided in the diet. There is only one essential fatty acid for dogs: linoleic acid, a polyunsaturated omega-6 fatty acid.

The Role of Fat in the Body

Fat provides the most concentrated source of energy, containing more than twice as many calories per gram as protein or carbohydrate. Fat gives texture and flavor to a food and enhances its palatability. The essential fatty acid linoleic acid is important for skin and coat health, for kidney function and for reproduction. Linoleic acid is also a constituent of cell membranes throughout the body and it can be metabolized in a series of reactions to produce molecules that are important for immune function.

Although omega-3 fatty acids are not considered essential, they may be beneficial in the diet. The metabolism of omega-6 and omega-3 fatty acids depends on the same enzymes (see Figure 1). A high intake of omega-3 fatty acids can therefore inhibit the metabolism of omega-6 fatty acids and vice versa.

The end products of the omega-6 fatty acid metabolism are 4-series leukotrienes, 2-series prostaglandins and 2-series thromboxanes. These molecules are pro-inflammatory and pro-aggregatory mediators. Pro-inflammatory mediators stimulate inflammation, while pro-aggregatory mediators stimulate blood clotting and tissue repair. These mediators play an important role in normal immune function. For example, when a dog contracts a bacterial infection, 4-series leukotrienes and 2-series prostaglandins mobilize immune cells to the site of infection and the inflammatory response is used to destroy the invading bacteria. The 2-series thromboxanes help repair damaged tissue and stop any bleeding. Under normal circumstances, these mediators are helpful. However, some dogs over-produce these molecules or produce them when there is no infection to fight, and this can lead to chronic inflammatory conditions such as allergic skin disease and colitis.

The end products of the omega-3 pathway are 5-series leukotrienes, 3-series prostaglandins and 3-series thromboxanes. These molecules are much less inflammatory and aggregatory than their 4-series and 2-series counterparts. Increasing the level of omega-3 fatty acids in the diet can promote the production of these less harmful mediators and block the production of pro-inflammatory omega-6 mediators.

Increasing the intake of omega-3 fatty acids is recommended for dogs with a number of different diseases. In kidney disease, omega-3 fatty acids can help to improve blood flow to the kidneys. In dogs with cancer or heart disease, omega-3 fatty acids may help delay the onset of cachexia, the muscle wasting condition associated with the terminal stages of these diseases. Omega-3 fatty acids may enhance cognitive function in senior dogs and growing puppies

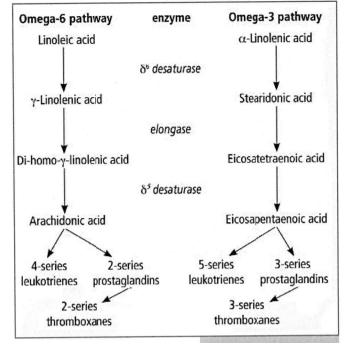

FIGURE 1

Omega-6 & omega-3 fatty acid metabolic pathways share the same enzymes.

CARBOHYDRATES

General Overview and Essentiality

Besides water, the main constituent of plants is carbohydrate in the form of polysaccharides such as starch and fiber. Animal tissues contain very little carbohydrate. Glucose and glycogen, the main carbohydrates in animal tissues, make up less than 1% of a dog's body.

Carbohydrate is not an essential nutrient for dogs, but it does represent a major source of calories for most dogs. Commercial dry pet foods are typically 30%–50% carbohydrate because high starch content is required for the dry pet food extrusion (manufacturing) process. Cereals (such as rice, barley and oatmeal) and tubers (such as potatoes and yams) are high in starch. Fruits and vegetables are also high in carbohydrate but they are typically lower in starch and higher in moisture. This gives fruits and vegetables a lower calorie concentration (Table 3).

In Table 3, the starchy ingredients are listed as cooked, whereas the fruit and vegetables are listed raw. Uncooked starch is poorly digested by dogs. Feeding raw starch to dogs generally leads to diarrhea. Low starch fruits and vegetables can be served raw, but starchy foods should always be cooked prior to serving.

One vegetable that should be occasionally served cooked is the tomato. Although raw tomatoes are healthy for dogs, cooking helps to release lycopene, an antioxidant found in high concentrations in tomato seeds. Many of the recipes in this book include tomato sauce, a concentrated source of this powerful antioxidant (Table 4).

TABLE 3

The calorie content of some high and low starch plant ingredients

	Calories per 100 g (as fed)
High starch cereals/tubers	
Barley (cooked)	123 kcal
Rice (cooked)	111 kcal
Potatoes (cooked)	87 kcal
Low starch vegetables/fruits	
Carrots (raw)	41 kcal
Broccoli (raw)	34 kcal
Strawberries (raw)	32 kcal

TABLE 4

Concentration of lycopene in 100g of raw tomatoes versus 100g of tomato sauce

	Lycopene per 100 g (as fed)
Raw tomatoes	2,573 µg
Tomato sauce (canned)	15,152 µg

VITAMINS

General Overview and Essentiality

Vitamins can be defined as essential organic compounds that are required in very minute amounts for normal body function. Vitamins do not share a common structure or function. They each have a unique structure and an equally unique function in the body.

Vitamins are broadly grouped according to their solubility. Vitamins A, D, E, and K are fat-soluble, while vitamin C and the B-complex vitamins are water-soluble. There are 11 essential vitamins for dogs, three fat-soluble (A, D and E) and eight water-soluble (thiamin, riboflavin, niacin, pyridoxine, pantothenic acid, folic acid, vitamin B12 (cobalamin) and choline) (Table 5). Vitamin C is not considered essential for dogs since dogs can make this vitamin in their bodies. However, providing vitamin C can help to boost immune function and so it may be beneficial to include it in a dog's diet. Vitamins K and biotin are two other vitamins that are not considered essential for dogs. These vitamins are both produced by bacteria in the dog's intestines and pass freely from the digestive tract into the dog's body.

Fat-soluble essential vitamins	Water-soluble essential vitamins
Vitamin A	Thiamin (B1)
Vitamin D	Riboflavin (B2)
Vitamin E	Niacin (B3)
	Pyridoxine (B6)
	Pantothenic acid
	Folic acid
	Vitamin B12
	Choline

TABLE 5

Three fat-soluble and eight water-soluble vitamins are essential for dogs.

Fat-soluble vitamins are carried in fat and absorbed from the digestive tract into a dog's body in association with dietary fat. These vitamins can be stored in fatty tissues within the dog's body. Most water-soluble vitamins on the other hand, mix freely with the digestive secretions in the intestines and pass easily on their own from the digestive tract into a dog's blood stream. With the exception of vitamin B12, water-soluble vitamins are not stored to a significant degree in body tissues.

The solubility characteristics of each vitamin affect the relative risk of toxicity or deficiency. Since fat-soluble vitamins can be stored in the body, risks of deficiency are low but they can become toxic if consumed at high levels. With water-soluble vitamins, the risks are reversed. The risks of toxicity are low because excesses are lost in the urine. However, because these

vitamins are not stored in the body, they must be consumed regularly in order to prevent deficiencies. Water-soluble vitamins are more likely to be destroyed in cooking, or lost in the water drained from boiled foods.

The Role of Vitamins in the Body

Although vitamins themselves do not contain energy, five B-complex vitamins (thiamin, riboflavin, niacin, pantothenic acid and pyridoxine) are all components of the enzyme systems that turn food into energy within the body. B-vitamin deficiency can cause lethargy and a general loss of stamina and vitality. Folic acid, vitamin B12, pyridoxine and pantothenic acid are all required for the production of red blood cells. A deficiency of any one of these vitamins causes anemia. Vitamin D is a regulator of calcium and phosphorus metabolism in the body. Excesses or deficiencies in this vitamin cause skeletal abnormalities, especially in growing puppies.

Each vitamin plays a unique and essential role in the body. Inadequate intake of any vitamin will impair a dog's health. Over-consumption of the fat-soluble vitamins may be equally harmful.

MINERALS

General Overview and Essentiality

Minerals are the only essential nutrients that are inorganic (i.e., they do not contain carbon). Minerals are classified according to the level of their requirement. Macro-minerals are typically included in diets at 100–1000 times the level of micro-minerals. There are six macro-minerals and six micro-minerals that are essential for dogs (Table 6).

The Role of Minerals in the Body

Minerals play a variety of important roles in the body. Calcium, phosphorus and magnesium give structural strength to bones and teeth. Calcium is also involved in muscle contraction, blood clotting and cell division. Phosphorus is important for energy transport, is a constituent of DNA, and is a co-enzyme for several vitamins (niacin, riboflavin, thiamin and pyridoxine).

TABLE 6

Six macro-minerals and six micro-minerals are essential for dogs.

Essential macro-minerals	Essential micro-minerals
Calcium	Iron
Phosphorus	Zinc
Potassium	Copper
Sodium	Iodine
Magnesium	Manganese
Chloride	Selenium

Potassium is important for nerve transmission, muscle contraction, acid-base balance and enzyme regulation. Seventy percent of the body's iron is found inside red blood cells as part of hemoglobin. Zinc is a component of more than 200 different enzymes in the body. It plays an important role in skin and footpad health and wound healing. Selenium is a component of glutathione peroxidase, an antioxidant enzyme that protects cell membranes from damage by free radicals.

Almost all minerals are toxic at high intakes. AAFCO has defined a maximum safe mineral level for all minerals except potassium, sodium, chloride and manganese.

1.2

Balanced Nutrition

The term "balanced" refers to the levels of nutrients in a food *relative to each other*. A diet is said to be balanced when the levels of all nutrients are at the correct level relative to each other such that optimal uptake of all nutrients is ensured.

An example of an important nutrient balance is the ratio between calcium and phosphorus in a diet. For dogs, the calcium-to-phosphorus ratio should always be 1–2:1, meaning that for every gram of phosphorus in the food, there should be between 1 and 2 grams of calcium. For growing puppies, the ideal ratio is narrower: 1–1.5:1. A calcium-to-phosphorus ratio that is too low can cause abnormal bone metabolism and osteoporosis. A high calcium-to-phosphorus ratio is equally harmful and is one of the leading causes of skeletal defects in growing puppies. If a diet contains adequate levels of these two minerals but they are not present in the correct ratio, the diet may be "complete" but it's not "balanced".

There are many other important nutrient balances. Copper is closely linked to iron. A deficiency of copper can impair the absorption and transport of iron, but an excess of copper can have the same effect by competing with and blocking the uptake of iron from the digestive tract. High zinc intake can interfere with the absorption of both copper and iron but zinc absorption can be blocked by high calcium intake. Selenium requirements depend on vitamin E intake while vitamin E requirements depend on the polyunsaturated fatty acid content of a food.

Figure 2 shows the mineral competition wheel. An arrow pointing from one mineral to another indicates that the mineral at the base of the arrow interferes with the uptake of the mineral at the tip of the arrow. For example, there is an arrow pointing from phosphorus (P) to sodium (Na). This indicates that high phosphorus content can interfere with the absorption of sodium. Note that the reverse relationship is not true. There is no

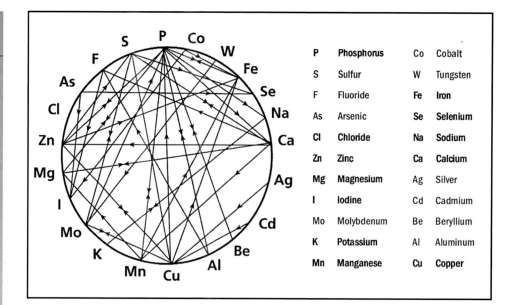

P	Phosphorus	Co	Cobalt
S	Sulfur	W	Tungsten
F	Fluoride	**Fe**	**Iron**
As	Arsenic	**Se**	**Selenium**
Cl	**Chloride**	**Na**	**Sodium**
Zn	**Zinc**	**Ca**	**Calcium**
Mg	**Magnesium**	Ag	Silver
I	**Iodine**	Cd	Cadmium
Mo	Molybdenum	Be	Beryllium
K	**Potassium**	Al	Aluminum
Mn	**Manganese**	**Cu**	**Copper**

arrow pointing from sodium to phosphorus, so high sodium intake does not interfere with phosphorus uptake.

Although "balanced" usually refers to the minerals in a food, it can also refer to amino acids and fatty acids. Certain amino acids use the same enzyme pathways for metabolism or compete with each other for uptake or transport. Although amino acid competition is not a concern with normal protein intake, it may become important when protein intake is restricted. In the case of low protein diets for dogs with kidney disease, proper amino acid balance is critical.

Omega-6 and omega-3 fatty acids use the same enzyme pathways for their metabolism (see Figure 1). High levels of omega-3 fatty acids can inhibit the metabolism of omega-6 fatty acids and vice versa. With healthy dogs, the ratio between omega-6 and omega-3 fatty acids is generally at least 5:1, meaning that for every gram of omega-3 fatty acids, there are at least five grams of omega-6 fatty acids. Many diets contain very high omega-6 to omega-3 ratios, i.e. over 30 times more omega-6 than omega-3. This is fine for healthy dogs. Remember, the only essential fatty acid for dogs is the omega-6 fatty acid, linoleic acid. However, in certain disease conditions, such as kidney disease, allergic skin disease, inflammatory bowel disease, cardiac disease, and cancer, increasing the level of omega-3 relative to omega-6 fatty acids (i.e., *lowering* the omega-6 to omega-3 ratio) may be beneficial.

The Importance of Complete and Balanced Nutrition

2

2.1

Should Dog Owners Be Concerned About Complete and Balanced Nutrition?

Is complete and balanced nutrition really that important? Some might argue that humans don't eat complete and balanced diets and neither do animals in the wild, so why should owners worry about feeding their dogs complete and balanced diets?

Registered human dietitians do strive to deliver complete and balanced nutrition to their patients, and zoo nutritionists know that feeding complete and balanced diets to captive animals helps them live longer, healthier lives. Nutrition has a significant impact on health, longevity, vitality, immune function and disease resistance.

Nutrient deficiencies, excesses and imbalances are far more common in humans than most people realize and they have far more serious consequences. The typical North American diet contains much more phosphorus than calcium and this contributes to the high incidence of osteoporosis in seniors. Vitamin B deficiencies have been linked to numerous diseases, from *spina bifida* in infants to heart disease and cancer in older people. Replacing saturated fatty acids with polyunsaturated fatty acids significantly reduces the risk of heart disease and stroke in humans. Dietary antioxidants have been shown to have numerous health benefits. Obesity, a growing concern in both humans and pets, shortens life expectancy and increases the risks of diabetes, arthritis, cardiovascular disease and cancer.

The World Health Organization estimates that more than 70% of human diseases are preventable with wise lifestyle choices, including healthy nutrition. If the goal is to provide your dog with the best nutrition possible, then it is important to prepare tasty meals that offer complete and balanced nutrition.

2.2

Eating a Variety of Foods Does Not Ensure Complete and Balanced Nutrition

While it is true that eating a variety of healthy foods is better than following a more limited menu, eating a wide variety of foods does not necessarily prevent nutritional deficiencies or imbalances. Complete and balanced nutrition is not necessarily achieved through eating varied meals. Most humans eat a wide variety of foods but nutrient deficiencies and imbalances are still relatively common.

2.3

Nutrient Deficiencies and Imbalances Are Not Necessarily Apparent

Marginal deficiencies and imbalances often go undiagnosed. An iron or copper deficiency can cause mild anemia and fatigue. Calcium-to-phosphorus imbalances alter bone metabolism but it takes years for the signs of osteoporosis to become obvious. Vitamin B deficiencies affect nutrient metabolism and energy production. Optimal health depends on optimal nutrition. Feeding a complete and balanced diet is the best way to promote optimal health, vitality and longevity in people and pets.

2.4

Complete and Balanced Recipes Can Be Produced Using Human Foods Despite Their Natural Variability

All natural foods are somewhat variable in composition. This is as true for commercial pet food ingredients as it is for human foods. There is as much variability in poultry meal or brewers rice as there is in chicken breast meat or brown rice. In fact, it could be argued that pet food ingredients are more variable since they are by-products of human food processing. For example, chicken breast meat is relatively consistent compared to poultry meal which may contain more turkey by-products following Easter, Thanksgiving or Christmas.

The food formulation software used to develop the recipes in this book contains a database of nutrient analyses. For each food ingredient, more than 50 individual nutrients are stored. These include macronutrients such as protein, fat, and carbohydrate, as well as micronutrients such as vitamins, minerals, amino acids, fatty acids, and antioxidants.

Each nutrient value in the database is the average of hundreds of food samples analyzed. Not only does the database store the mean (i.e. average) value for each nutrient, it also stores the standard deviation around that mean. Standard deviation is a measure of the spread or dispersion of individual samples relative to the average of the group. A large standard deviation indicates wide variability between samples. By using both mean values and standard deviations, the formulation software is able to predict the nutrient content of the final recipe with greater than 80% accuracy.

There are two additional steps that have been taken to ensure that the nutrient content of each recipe in this book meets the nutrient requirements of a dog. First, ingredient definitions take food preparation method into account. For example, in the database used to create the recipes in this book, raw peas and boiled peas are two separate ingredients. So are baked potatoes and boiled potatoes. The recipes in this book indicate how each ingredient should be prepared for that particular recipe.

Second, nutrient targets for each recipe can be set to provide a margin of safety. For example, all recipes in this book target nutrient levels well above the AAFCO minimums but well below any AAFCO-defined maximums (see Appendix 9).

The comprehensive and well-defined nutrient database used to formulate the recipes in this book, combined with appropriate nutrient targets that offer a clear margin of safety, ensure that the recipes in this book will meet the dog's nutrient requirements despite any natural variability in ingredient composition.

2.5

Will Treats Upset a Complete and Balanced Home-made Meal?

Most commercial pet food companies suggest that as long as treats are kept to no more than 10%–15% of a dog's calorie intake, they will not interfere with a complete and balanced diet. Above this level of feeding, treats can lead to weight gain and can upset the nutrient balance of the regular diet. These recommendations apply to home-made meals as well. Treats fed in moderation are no risk to a dog. However, if treats become a major component of a dog's daily food intake, then there is an increased risk of nutrient imbalances.

In virtually all recipes in this book, there are some ingredients such as carrots, cheese, fruits and/or nuts that dogs enjoy to eat on their own. Owners can remove these ingredients from a recipe and feed them separately as treats. However, it is important to remember that each recipe represents one kilogram of food when all ingredients are combined. If a recipe calls for

100 grams of carrots, that means that 100 grams of carrots belong in one kilogram of the prepared recipe. If a dog needs to be fed 250 grams of that recipe each day, then if the carrots are fed separately as treats, the 100 grams of carrots need to be fed to the dog over four days.

2.6

Can Home-made Recipes Be Mixed with Commercial Dog Food (Kibble)?

If two complete and balanced foods are mixed, the mixture also delivers complete and balanced nutrition. Dry and canned commercial dog foods are often mixed. Similarly, dry or canned commercial dog foods can be mixed with complete and balanced home-made recipes to provide complete and balanced nutrition.

For owners who wish to mix fresh human ingredients with commercial dog foods, it is recommended that a home-made recipe be prepared as described in this book, using all ingredients including HILARY'S BLEND™ supplement. This complete recipe can then be mixed with commercial dog food in any proportion and it will deliver complete and balanced nutrition.

Assessing the Nutrient Content of a Recipe or an Ingredient

3

THERE ARE MANY REASONS why a dog owner might want to assess the nutrient content of a recipe or an ingredient. Owners might want to compare the nutrient content of a recipe to the nutrient requirements of their dog. They might want to compare the nutrient content of two different recipes. They might want to restrict or increase the intake of a particular nutrient. In these situations, the owner needs to be able to correctly assess the nutrient content of one or more foods.

This section involves numbers and calculations, and some new terminology. One way to work through the concepts is to compare two simple ingredients. Table 7 shows the partial nutrient content of two human foods: cooked salmon and cheddar cheese. The numbers in the table represent the values you could expect to see if you sent a sample of these foods to a laboratory for analysis.

	In 100 grams of cooked salmon	In 100 grams of cheddar cheese
Moisture	65 grams	37 grams
Protein	22 grams	25 grams
Fat	12 grams	33 grams
Calories	206 calories	403 calories

TABLE 7

The composition of cooked salmon and cheddar cheese (as fed basis).

3.1

As Fed Analysis

As illustrated in Table 7, cooked salmon and cheddar cheese have very similar protein contents. On an as fed basis, their protein contents are 22% and 25% respectively. The term "as fed" refers to the nutrient content of a food as you feed it. If you fed 100 grams of cooked salmon to a dog, the dog would be consuming 22 grams of protein. Cooked salmon is 22% protein on an as fed basis.

Dry Matter Analysis

Cooked salmon contains almost twice as much water as cheddar cheese (65 grams versus 37 grams). Since moisture does not contribute essential nutrients or energy, it is sometimes useful to factor out the food's moisture content and compare two foods' nutrients on a dry matter basis. Dry matter refers to the entire portion of the food which is not water.

$$\text{Dry Matter} = 100\% - \%\ \text{Moisture}$$

Dry matter analysis gives the nutrient content of the food as if the food were completely dehydrated. Dry matter values can be calculated using the as fed analysis and the food's moisture content. Calculate nutrient content on a dry matter basis from as fed values, as follows:

$$\%\ \text{Nutrient (dry matter)} = \frac{\%\ \text{Nutrient (as fed)}}{(100 - \%\ \text{Moisture})} \times 100\%$$

For example, for cheddar cheese:

$$\%\ \text{Protein (DM basis)} = \frac{25}{(100 - 37)} \times 100\% = 39.7\%$$

In other words, 39.7% of cheddar cheese's dry matter is protein. Cheddar cheese is 39.7% protein on a dry matter basis.

Table 8 shows the protein and fat analyses for cooked salmon and cheddar cheese expressed on a dry matter basis.

Although salmon and cheese have approximately the same protein content on an as fed basis, salmon has a much higher protein content on a dry matter basis (62.9 g versus 39.7 g respectively).

TABLE 8

The composition of cooked salmon and cheddar cheese (dry matter basis).

	For cooked salmon in 100 grams of dry matter	For cheddar cheese in 100 grams of dry matter
Moisture	0 grams	0 grams
Protein	62.9 grams	39.7 grams
Fat	34.3 grams	52.4 grams

Dry matter analysis is most commonly used to compare foods that have very different moisture contents. For example, it may be used to compare high moisture fresh or canned foods to low moisture dry kibble.

Consider the two pet foods in Table 9. On an as fed basis, the dry food contains 2.5 times more protein than the canned food. However, these values are misleading because there is a significant difference in the foods' moisture contents. If you factor out the moisture and consider only the food's dry matter (Table 10), the canned food is shown to have higher protein content on a dry matter basis.

	Dry food A (as fed basis)	Canned food B (as fed basis)
Protein	25%	10%
Fat	18%	5%
Moisture	10%	75%

TABLE 9

Analyses for two pet foods (one dry, one canned) on an as fed basis.

	Dry food A (Dry matter basis)	Canned food B (Dry matter basis)
Protein	27.8%	40%
Fat	20%	20%
Moisture	0%	0%

TABLE 10

Analyses for Dry food A and Canned food B on a dry matter basis.

3.3

Nutrients Expressed on an Energy Basis (Per 1000 Kilocalories)

In comparing the nutrient content of two foods, there is one final factor that must be taken into consideration: the calorie density of the food.

Dogs should always be fed to meet their energy requirements. If a dog consumes more energy (calories) than he needs, he will gain weight. If a dog consumes fewer calories than he needs, he will lose weight. The energy density of a food therefore determines how much of that food the dog should eat. If a food is high in calories, the dog will need to eat less of that food to meet his energy requirements than he needs to eat of a lower energy food.

In the example in Table 7, cooked salmon contains 203 calories per 100 grams, whereas cheddar cheese contains 403 calories per 100 grams. Suppose a dog needs 800 calories a day to maintain his ideal body weight. That dog could eat either 400 grams of salmon or 200 grams of cheese to meet his daily energy needs. In eating the 200 grams of cheese, the dog is consuming 50 grams of protein (25 grams of protein in 100 grams of cheese, so 50 grams of protein in 200 grams of cheese). In eating 400 grams of salmon, the dog is consuming 88 grams of protein. Therefore, if the dog is fed to meet

his energy needs, he will consume more protein if he is fed salmon than if he is fed cheddar cheese. Expressing nutrients relative to the calories in a diet is the best way of assessing nutrient intake.

Nutrient values are expressed on an energy basis as grams of nutrient per 1000 calories. Salmon has 108 grams of protein per 1000 calories (see calculations below), while cheese has 62 grams of protein per 1000 calories. So even though salmon contains less protein on an as fed basis, it has a higher protein content on an energy basis, reflecting the fact that salmon provides more protein to a dog if that dog is fed to meet his energy requirements.

Calculate nutrient content on an energy basis from as fed values, as follows:

$$\text{Nutrient (g/1000 kcal)} = \frac{\% \text{ Nutrient (as fed)} \times 1000}{(\text{kcal/100g})}$$

For example, for cooked salmon:

There are 22 g of protein in 100 g of salmon.
There are 203 calories in 100 g of salmon.
Therefore, there are 22 g of protein in 203 calories worth of salmon.
Calculate grams of protein per 1000 kcal, as follows:

$$\text{Protein (g/calorie)} = \frac{22 \text{ g of protein}}{203 \text{ calories}} = 0.108$$

Protein (g/1000 kcal) = 0.108 x 1000 = 108 g/1000 kcal

These examples may seem silly since no dog is going to be exclusively fed salmon or cheese. But the same concept applies to complete and balanced pet foods. A dog needs to eat less of a high calorie food than of a low calorie food. The vitamin and mineral concentrations in the high calorie food must be increased to compensate for the dog's lower food intake. In weight loss diets, all essential nutrients must be increased relative to calories to ensure that when calories are restricted, all nutrient requirements are still being met. In evaluating the nutritional content of a food, nutrient levels on an energy basis most closely represent a dog's nutrient intake. For this reason, it is important to assess a food's nutrient content expressed on an energy basis.

These concepts may seem complicated. They are included in this book for two reasons. First, owners may be interested in feeding a food that is similar in nutrient composition to the commercial pet food they are currently feeding. Second, owners may want to compare a recipe in this book to the AAFCO nutrient profiles or select a recipe that provides a specific nutrient profile. In these cases, owners need to choose the best method for comparing the nutrient content of different foods.

Comparing Home-made Meals to Commercial Dog Foods

Most ingredients used in home-made meals are high in moisture, and home-made recipes are therefore much higher in moisture than commercial dry kibble. For this reason, comparisons between home-made recipes and commercial dry kibble should not be made on an as fed basis. Dry matter analysis is a better way to compare high moisture and low moisture diets. Comparing diets on an energy basis is the best way to compare nutrient intake.

Suppose a home-made recipe has a nutrient content of 9% protein, 6% fat and 70% moisture. This recipe appears to have a low protein and fat content, but when you factor out the moisture, its nutrient content on a dry matter basis is much higher (Table 11).

Note that a dry commercial dog food that is 27% protein, 18% fat and 10% moisture, has the same nutrient content on a dry matter basis (Table 12). In other words, the two foods in Table 13 are equivalent if they are compared on a dry matter basis.

Dry matter comparison is more useful than as fed comparison when high moisture and low moisture foods are being compared. However, the best way of comparing two foods is on an energy basis (nutrients per 1000 kcal).

	Homemade recipe (as fed basis)	Homemade recipe (Dry matter basis)
Protein	9%	30%
Fat	6%	20%
Moisture	70%	0%

TABLE 11

Analyses for the same home-made recipe, on an as fed and dry matter basis.

	Commercial dry food (as fed basis)	Commercial dry food (Dry matter basis)
Protein	27%	30%
Fat	18%	20%
Moisture	10%	0%

TABLE 12

Analyses of a typical dry kibble dog food on as fed and dry matter basis.

	Homemade recipe (as fed basis)	Commercial dry food (as fed basis)
Protein	9%	27%
Fat	6%	18%
Moisture	70%	10%

TABLE 13

The two foods at left are equivalent when compared on a dry matter basis.

Since energy density determines food intake, nutrient content on an energy basis (i.e. nutrient per 1000 kcal) reflects how much of that nutrient the dog will be consuming.

Recipes in this book provide nutrient contents on both a dry matter and energy (per 1000 kcal) basis.

3.5

Comparing Home-made Recipes to AAFCO Nutrient Profiles

In defining the nutrient targets for a finished pet food, reputable pet food companies use the dog and cat nutrient profiles published by the Association of American Feed Control Officials. AAFCO publishes these values on a dry matter and also on an energy (per 1000 kcal) basis.

A complete nutrient profile is provided for each recipe in this book, listing all key nutrients on an as fed, a dry matter and on an energy basis. This allows the reader to compare each recipe to the AAFCO recommendations. The AAFCO nutrient profiles for dogs and puppies are reprinted with permission in Appendix 9 at the end of this book.

3.6

Should AAFCO Be the Standard for Home-made Recipes?

There is an important assumption behind the AAFCO minimum guidelines. AAFCO states: "The AAFCO Dog and Cat Food Nutrient Profiles were designed to establish practical minimum and maximum nutrient levels for dog and cat foods formulated from nonpurified, complex ingredients." AAFCO further states: "The values were also modified based on various known effects of ingredients and processing and the potential for lower digestibility in some products."

The AAFCO values were developed for commercial pet food companies and reflect the ingredients commonly used in commercial pet foods. AAFCO (and pet food companies) assume that the digestibility of a pet food's protein, fat, and carbohydrate are 80%, 90% and 85% respectively. Human nutritionists on the other hand assume that the protein, fat and carbohydrate in human foods are more than 90% digestible. When AAFCO states that an adult dog food should contain at least 18 grams of protein per 100 gram of food (dry matter basis), AAFCO is assuming that that protein is 80% digestible. If the protein is more than 80% digestible, then it is possible for a food to contain less than 18 grams of protein and still meet a dog's protein requirements. In other words, if high quality human ingredients are used to create a home-made meal, a recipe that meets AAFCO guidelines will more than meet the daily nutrient requirements of a dog.

Although AAFCO guidelines are exaggerated to compensate for ingredients of lower digestibility, they are not exaggerated to compensate for nutrient losses during processing. The nutrient levels published by AAFCO represent the levels that must be present in the finished pet food after processing has occurred. For example, when AAFCO states that the minimum level of thiamin in a commercial dog food is 0.1 milligrams per 100 grams of food (dry matter basis), this is the level that must be present in the food after processing. Manufacturers will formulate recipes with much higher levels of this nutrient to compensate for losses that occur during processing. AAFCO guidelines represent the nutrient levels that a dog needs to consume to meet his daily requirements.

The recipes in this book use the AAFCO nutrient profiles as the basis for defining complete and balanced nutrition. AAFCO may overestimate a dog's requirements when highly digestible human food ingredients are fed and so it could be argued that AAFCO minimums are higher than necessary for home-made meals. While this is likely true, using AAFCO guidelines provides a margin of error and follows the established standard of the pet food industry.

The home-made recipes in this book meet AAFCO minimum requirements for all essential nutrients, on both a dry matter and on an energy basis, unless otherwise stated (i.e. some Low Protein Recipes do not meet AAFCO requirements because they are not designed to be fed to normal healthy dogs). For nutrients where AAFCO has defined maximum tolerances, the recipes in this book deliver well below these safe upper limits.

Balancing Vitamins and Minerals in Home-made Recipes

4

THE GREATEST CHALLENGE in creating complete and balanced recipes is balancing the recipe's vitamins and minerals. It is easy to produce a diet that contains an acceptable level of protein, fat, energy and fiber. It is far more difficult to create a recipe that delivers all 36 essential nutrients, including all essential vitamins and minerals, at the correct level and in the proper balance to ensure adequate uptake from the digestive tract. This challenge is greater for home-made meals than it is for commercial pet foods because the range of potential ingredients for home-made meals is much wider.

4.1

Every Ingredient Has a Unique Nutrient Profile

Table 14 shows the nutrient content (on an as fed basis) of five high quality protein sources. For simplicity, the table lists only six of the 36 essential nutrients for dogs: protein, calcium, phosphorus, potassium, zinc, and vitamin A. Although these foods all have similar protein content, they have very different vitamin and mineral contents. Beef has 15 times more zinc than salmon. Chicken liver contains 600 times more vitamin A than chicken breast meat. Note that all five ingredients have inverted calcium-to-phosphorus ratios (at least 10 times more phosphorus than calcium). Chicken liver has 37 times more phosphorus than calcium.

If the goal is to provide all essential nutrients in a complete and balanced recipe, meats are not interchangeable. Beef is not equivalent to salmon. Chicken liver is not equivalent to chicken breast meat. Each meat has a unique nutrient profile. Interchanging one meat for another does not produce the same nutrient balance in the final recipe.

Table 15 shows the nutrient content of six raw vegetables. Here again we see considerable differences between vegetables. Calcium ranges from 16 to 99 mg (more than a six-fold difference), potassium from 147 to 558 mg (al-

	Units	Cooked salmon	Cooked ground beef	Cooked ground pork	Cooked chicken breast	Cooked chicken liver
Protein	g	22	28	26	31	24
Calcium	mg	15	16	22	15	11
Phosphorus	mg	252	250	226	228	405
Ca:P ratio		1:17	1:16	1:10	1:15	1:37
Potassium	mg	384	433	362	256	263
Zinc	mg	0.43	6.84	3.21	1.00	3.98
Vitamin A	IU	50	0	8	20	13,328

	Units	Raw carrots	Raw cucumber	Raw spinach	Raw peas	Raw beans	Raw celery
Protein	g	0.93	0.65	2.86	5.42	1.82	0.69
Calcium	mg	33	16	99	25	37	40
Phosphorus	mg	35	24	49	108	38	24
Ca:P ratio		1:1.1	1:1.5	2:1	1:4	1:1	1.6:1
Potassium	mg	320	147	558	244	209	260
Zinc	mg	0.24	0.20	0.53	1.24	0.24	0.13
Vitamin A	IU	16811	105	9377	765	690	449

most a four-fold difference), zinc from 0.13 mg to 1.24 mg (almost a 10-fold difference) and vitamin A from 105 to 16,811 IU (more than a 160-fold difference) per 100 g as fed. For some vegetables, the calcium-to-phosphorus ratio is inverted; for others it is close to ideal.

Every meat, vegetable, fruit and oil has a unique nutrient profile. Substituting beef for chicken or peas for beans does not produce the same vitamin and mineral profile in the final recipe. These tables show values for only six nutrients (protein, calcium, phosphorus, potassium, zinc and vitamin A). There are 36 nutrients (plus water) that are essential for dogs. All 36 essential nutrients need to be present at the right level, and in the right balance relative to each other for a diet to provide complete and balanced nutrition. This is why balancing home-made recipes is not an easy or straight forward task. It is only truly possible to create a 100% complete and balanced recipe using food formulation software designed for this purpose.

4.2

Balancing Home-made Recipes with a Vitamin Mineral Pet Supplement

Almost all home-made recipes for dogs recommend feeding some type of vitamin mineral supplement in addition to the home-made food. Many also advocate feeding a calcium supplement such a Tums® or ground egg shells. In fact, commercial vitamin mineral supplements, even if fed with additional calcium, cannot balance a home-made recipe.

4.3

The Levels of Vitamins and Minerals in Commercial Pet Supplements Are Too Low

Commercial "complete" vitamin and mineral pet supplements are intended to be fed to pets that are consuming commercial pet foods. Virtually all commercial pet foods are formulated to meet AAFCO minimum requirements. Any dog consuming a commercial pet food is therefore already consuming adequate vitamins and minerals to meet his daily requirements. A vitamin mineral supplement that can be safely fed in conjunction with any complete and balanced pet food must contain vitamins and minerals at low enough concentrations to not create risks of toxicity. The level of vitamins and minerals in commercial pet supplements is too low to balance home-made recipes.

4.4

Some Vitamins and Minerals Are Too High in Commercial Pet Supplements

A few vitamins and minerals in commercial supplements are at levels that are too high to balance home-made recipes. Two examples are vitamin A and phosphorus.

Vitamin A is a fat-soluble vitamin that can be toxic at high intakes. Some meats, particularly liver, contain high levels of this vitamin. As well, many vegetables are rich in vitamin A or its precursor, beta-carotene. Home-made recipes typically provide more than adequate levels of this vitamin. Additional supplementation is not only unnecessary, it is potentially harmful.

Commercial pet supplements typically contain calcium and phosphorus in close to a 1:1 ratio. Again, because these supplements are intended to be fed in association with complete and balanced commercial pet foods, they

provide calcium and phosphorus in a ratio that will not upset the calcium and phosphorus balance found in commercial pet foods. Home-made recipes contain meats which have 10 to 30 times more phosphorus than calcium (Table 14) and fruits and vegetables are not high enough in calcium to offset this excess phosphorus. Although home-made recipes do need to be supplemented with both calcium and phosphorus, they typically need at least three times more calcium than phosphorus, rather than the 1:1 ratio found in most commercial pet supplements.

4.5

Complete and Balanced Recipes Are Not Easy to Achieve

If nothing else, this section demonstrates that formulating complete and balanced home-made recipes is not a simple process. Critics of home-made recipes are justified in claiming that home-made meals often don't provide complete and balanced nutrition. However, developing complete and balanced home-made recipes is possible using food formulation software and a vitamin mineral supplement that is specifically designed to balance home-made recipes.

The Need for a Specialized Supplement: HILARY'S BLEND™

5

IS IT POSSIBLE TO CREATE complete and balanced recipes based on human foods when they are so unique and different in terms of their nutrient content? In fact, this is exactly what food formulation software is designed to do. The formulation software database contains each individual ingredient's complete nutrient profile (including all 36 nutrients that are essential for dogs). The target specifications for the finished recipe (AAFCO nutrient profiles) are entered. The software can then mix and match different ingredients to generate an optimal nutrient balance. For example, the software program will automatically avoid using carrots and liver in the same recipe since these ingredients are both high in vitamin A. Similarly, it will include vegetables and dairy products to partially offset the high phosphorus content of meats.

5.1

How I Developed the Recipes in This Book

When I first set out to develop complete and balanced recipes, I began by creating several recipes that did not include a vitamin mineral supplement. I wanted to assess the typical nutrient content of recipes based strictly on human food ingredients. From these recipes, I identified the vitamins and minerals that generally needed supplementation and those that did not. I then formulated a supplement that specifically balanced these home-made recipes. I called this supplement HILARY'S BLEND™ supplement for home-made meals.

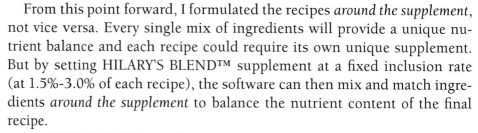

From this point forward, I formulated the recipes *around the supplement*, not vice versa. Every single mix of ingredients will provide a unique nutrient balance and each recipe could require its own unique supplement. But by setting HILARY'S BLEND™ supplement at a fixed inclusion rate (at 1.5%-3.0% of each recipe), the software can then mix and match ingredients *around the supplement* to balance the nutrient content of the final recipe.

HILARY'S BLEND™ supplement is unique. It contains 20 essential vitamins and minerals, carefully blended with a pre-biotic carrier according to a proprietary formula. Uniquely designed to balance home-made recipes, this supplement is made from 100% human-grade ingredients, and is packaged in a government-approved, cGMP-certified human nutraceutical facility.

5.2

HILARY'S BLEND™ Supplement Is Unique

1. HILARY'S BLEND™ supplement is the first and only vitamin mineral supplement specifically balanced for home-made recipes.
2. Its unique proprietary formula provides a concentrated blend of 20 essential vitamins and minerals in a pre-biotic carrier.
3. Its calcium:phosphorus ratio of 3:1 offsets the 1:10 to 1:35 calcium: phosphorus ratio of meats, poultry and fish.
4. Its carrier, chicory root extract, is more than 75% inulin, a natural pre-biotic fiber.
5. It is highly concentrated for great value (typically use only 15–30 g of HILARY'S BLEND™ supplement for every kilogram of prepared food; 300g makes 10–20 kg of food).
6. It is made from 100% human-grade ingredients, produced in a government-approved human nutraceutical facility.

5.3

Pre-biotics Promote the Growth of Healthy Bacteria in the Gut

Pre-biotics are natural plant fibers that promote the growth of healthy bacteria in the gut, at the expense of harmful bacteria. The digestive tract is home to more than 100 trillion bacteria, representing over 400 different species. The microbes in the colon have a very important function. They complete the digestion process, breaking down nutrients that were not completely digested and absorbed in a dog's small intestine. All dietary fiber bypasses digestion in the small intestines and is therefore available for fermentation by bacteria in the colon.

The bacteria in the gut can be helpful, harmful or neutral. Bacteria that are potentially harmful include *Escherichia coli* (E.coli), *Clostridium* (which produces botulism toxin), *Camplyobacter*, *Yersinia* and *Salmonella*. On the list of "good" bacteria are *Bifidobacteria*, *Lactobacillus acidophilus* and other *Lactobacilli* strains. These bacteria exert many beneficial effects on health, both by their direct interaction with the cells lining the intestinal tract, as well as by producing beneficial products through metabolism.

Pre-biotics, such as chicory root extract, support the growth of *Bifidobacteria* and *Lactobacilli* strains but do not support the growth of harmful bacteria. By providing a substrate that only healthy bacteria can use, pre-biotics allow good bacteria to thrive, crowding out the bad species. This is known as "competitive exclusion". As well, the short chain fatty acids produced by bacterial fermentation lower the pH within the colon which makes the gut environment more unfavorable to harmful bacterial strains.

Whenever you feed fresh foods, you increase the risks of harmful bacteria being ingested by the dog. The higher moisture content of fresh food provides a favorable environment for bacterial growth. While kibble can be left on a kitchen counter for weeks without spoiling, fresh foods begin to deteriorate as soon as they are exposed to room temperature. Preparing fresh foods carefully will minimize the risks of bacterial contamination, but an added measure of protection can be achieved by feeding pre-biotic fiber with every meal. The first ingredient in HILARY'S BLEND™ supplement is chicory root extract, an expensive and potent pre-biotic fiber. The chicory root extract in the supplement encourages the growth of beneficial bacteria at the expense of harmful bacteria and promotes digestive tract health in dogs.

Home-Made Meal Preparation

6

6.1

The Importance of Following the Recipe

The recipes in this book provide complete and balanced nutrition. Many of the ingredients are included in the recipes at low inclusion rates and it may be tempting to leave them out or replace them with something else. However, to achieve a complete and balanced meal, it is important to include all ingredients as they are listed in the recipe. To illustrate the significance of small changes, consider two oils included in most recipes: cod liver oil and safflower oil. Cod liver oil is a concentrated source of vitamins A and D, and the omega-3 fatty acids eicosapentaenoic acid (EPA) and docosahexaenoic acid (DHA). Safflower oil is an excellent source of the essential omega-6 fatty acid, linoleic acid. Table 16 compares the nutrient content of cod liver oil and safflower oil. It is important to follow the recipes as they are presented in this book. Each ingredient is included for a reason and each provides a unique blend of essential nutrients to the dog.

6.2

Weights and Measures

Each recipe in this book produces one kilogram of food. The calorie density

	Units	Cod liver oil	Safflower oil
Vitamin A	IU	100,000	0
Vitamin D	IU	10,000	0
Linoleic acid	mg	935	74,600
EPA	mg	6,898	0
DHA	mg	10,968	0

TABLE 16

Nutrient content of cod liver oil and safflower oil (all values per 100 grams as fed)

of each recipe is different and the amount to feed will vary accordingly. A kilogram of a calorie-dense recipe will last longer than a kilogram of a less calorie-dense recipe.

Each recipe lists its ingredients in alphabetical order and indicates the amount to include in grams. Using a scale to weigh the ingredients is the most accurate way of preparing each recipe. It is recommended that owners purchase a scale for this purpose. Using a weight scale offers the additional advantage of being able to correctly measure out the amount of food to feed the dog each day.

Recognizing that some owners may not wish to weigh ingredients, approximate volume equivalents (cups, tablespoons etc) are also provided. Volume measurements are not as accurate as weighing in grams. If volume measurements are carefully made however, the final recipe should be close in nutrient content to the values presented in the charts.

6.3

Blending and Mixing

In preparing these recipes, it is recommended that cooked ingredients be prepared first and allowed to cool to at least body temperature. These ingredients can then be chopped, mixed or blended with the raw ingredients to make a homogeneous mixture. Although most dogs enjoy eating a variety of foods, there are certain foods they may not wish to eat, such as spinach or cauliflower. Mixing less tasty foods with more appealing foods will encourage the dog to eat the entire meal.

The final step in recipe preparation is the addition of HILARY'S BLEND™ supplement for home-made meals. Since this supplement is highly concentrated, care should be taken in measuring out the correct amount according to the recipe. Sprinkle HILARY'S BLEND™ supplement over the entire mixture then blend to ensure that it is evenly distributed throughout the food.

6.4

Temperature and Storage

The recipes in this book can be doubled or tripled so that they can be prepared in large batches and fed over several days. Blended foods can be stored in the refrigerator for several days, but they should be frozen if they need to be stored for longer periods.

Foods are most palatable for dogs when they are served at body temperature (around 98°F/37°C). Humans generally prefer foods served at higher temperatures. When re-heating refrigerated foods, take care to not overheat as this will not only reduce the palatability of the meal, it may also reduce its nutritional value. If foods are re-heated in a microwave, check to make sure that the foods has been evenly heated throughout.

6.5

Cooked Versus Raw

The recipes in this book include both cooked and raw ingredients. Some foods are more nutritious raw, while others are better served cooked. Most fruits and vegetables are best fed raw, while meats and starchy foods, such as potatoes and cereals, are better served cooked.

Uncooked starch is very poorly digested by a dog. Raw potatoes and uncooked cereals such as rice, corn and oatmeal will pass through a dog's digestive tract largely unabsorbed, frequently resulting in diarrhea. Cooking starchy ingredients improves their digestibility from almost zero to approaching 100%, so these ingredients should always be cooked.

There are many benefits to cooking meat, poultry and fish ingredients. In 2004, the US Food and Drug Administration issued a guidance paper[1] which stated the "FDA does not believe raw meat foods for animals are consistent with the goal of protecting the public from significant health risks, particularly when such products are brought into the home and/or used to feed domestic pets." The risks of feeding raw meats are not limited to the pet. Humans handling the food and any people in contact with the dog are also at risk of food poisoning. In 2002, a research study[2] examined the food and stools of dogs fed home-made, raw chicken diets, and those of dogs fed commercial pet foods. This study found that 80% of the home-made raw foods contained *Salmonella* bacteria and 30% of the dogs fed these raw foods also had *Salmonella* in their stools. None of the commercial diets contained *Salmonella* and none of the dogs fed commercial diets had *Salmonella* in their stools. While the researchers did not report any adverse symptoms in any of the dogs in this study, they did, however, suggest that the presence of harmful bacteria could be a risk for both the dog and the dog owner.

The second advantage of cooking meats relates to their nutritional value. There are several anti-nutritional factors in raw meats that are rendered inactive by cooking. Trypsin is a digestive enzyme produced by a dog's pancreas and secreted into the small intestines to help digest proteins. Certain raw foods contain trypsin inhibitors which inactivate this digestive enzyme. Many types of raw fish, including whitefish, cod, herring, carp, pike, floun-

[1] U.S. Department of Health and Human Services, Food and Drug Administration, Center for Veterinary Medicine. Manufacture and labeling of raw meat foods for companion and captive noncompanion carnivores and omnivores. *Guidance for Industry*. #122. May 18, 2004; Revised November 9, 2004.

[2] Joffe DJ & Schlesinger DP. Preliminary assessment of the risk of Salmonella infection in dogs fed raw chicken diets. *Canadian Veterinary Journal*. 2002;43:441-442.

der and others, contain an enzyme called thiaminase which destroys thiamin (vitamin B1). Heating destroys thiaminase. Biotin is a B-complex vitamin produced by the microbes in the dog's digestive tract. Avidin, a glycoprotein in raw egg whites, irreversibly binds to biotin, preventing its absorption into the dog's body. Cooked avidin is not able to bind to biotin. Cooking inactivates anti-nutritional factors in foods and increases their nutritional value.

Cooking (especially with water or steam) contributes to food digestion in much the same way that acid in the stomach does. By opening up the coiled and folded structures of proteins, cooking allows digestive enzymes easier access to their interiors, facilitating digestion. Cooking improves the digestibility of meats, makes them more nutritious by inactivating anti-nutritional factors, and kills harmful bacteria. For these reasons, I recommend that meat, poultry and fish ingredients be cooked before serving.

6.6

Feeding Raw

A growing number of owners are choosing to feed all raw diets to their dogs, and many of these owners are reporting success with this method of feeding. By paying close attention to hygiene and the safe handling of raw meats, these owners have been able to manage the risks associated with feeding raw meats. For owners wishing to feed all raw diets, many of the recipes in this book may be suitable. Most of the recipes in this book will deliver complete and balanced nutrition whether the meats are served cooked or raw. Although the protein digestibility may be slightly lower with uncooked meats, most recipes contain more than sufficient protein to meet the dog's protein requirements if the meat is served raw. The exceptions are:

- low protein recipes (which are marginal in protein by design)
- recipes containing fish of the species listed above (which, if fed raw, may result in thiamin deficiency)
- recipes containing eggs (since feeding raw eggs may cause a biotin deficiency)

It is highly recommended that all starchy ingredients such as rice, oatmeal, potatoes or pasta, be cooked before serving. Feeding raw starch can lead to diarrhea and digestive upset. Dogs suffering from diseases which impair immune function should not be fed raw meats. The bacteria present in raw meats could seriously harm immune-compromised dogs. This is especially true for dogs with gastrointestinal disease where a damaged digestive tract lining could allow the passage of harmful bacteria into the dog's body.

About Salmon Oil

Many of the recipes in this book contain salmon oil. Salmon oil is rich in the omega-3 fatty acids EPA and DHA. An increased intake of omega-3 fatty acids is recommended for dogs with many different diseases. For example, omega-3 fatty acids can help to improve blood flow to the kidneys in dogs with kidney disease. In dogs with cancer or heart disease, omega-3 fatty acids may help delay the onset of cachexia, the muscle wasting condition associated with the terminal stages of these diseases. Omega-3 fatty acids may enhance cognitive function in senior dogs and growing puppies.

Depending on the recipe, you may be able to use salmon oil gel caps that are sold in drug or grocery stores. Gel caps generally contain 1000mg (1g) of salmon oil. So if the recipe calls for 1-10g of salmon oil, gel caps may be a viable option.

If the recipe calls for more than 10g, it becomes impractical to use gel caps. In this case, I recommend a liquid fish oil product called *DermaPet® EicosaDerm®*. Like salmon oil, *EicosaDerm* is very rich in the two important omega-3 fatty acids EPA and DHA. One pump of *EicosaDerm* is equivalent to approximately 1.8 grams of salmon oil. *EicosaDerm* is distributed by Aventix Animal Health and is available from your veterinarian.

Depending on the dog, you may also choose to substitute an equivalent amount of safflower oil, flaxseed oil or hemp oil for salmon oil in a recipe. Flaxseed oil and hemp oil are both rich in omega-3 fatty acids, but primarily as ALA (alpha-linolenic acid) rather than as EPA or DHA. Safflower contains only omega-6 fatty acids. While these three oils are all healthy for dogs, they do not provide the same omega-3 fatty acids found in salmon oil and *EicosaDerm*.

Omega-3 fatty acids are not considered essential for the dog. If you partially or entirely substitute salmon oil with safflower oil, flaxseed oil, or hemp oil in a recipe, the only effect will be to increase the omega-6 to omega-3 ratio. If you have a healthy dog, this will not cause any problems. If your dog has allergies, inflammatory bowel disease, skin disease, joint disease, kidney disease or heart disease, it is recommended that substitutions not be made and that the recipe be prepared as written using salmon oil or *EicosaDerm*.

Recipe Rationales: Indications for Use

THERE ARE 101 RECIPES in this book, grouped according to their type (see Table 17). The 12 sections in this chapter provide the rationales for each recipe type. Recipe summary charts are provided at the end of this chapter in section 7.13.

Recipes	Recipe Type	Purpose	Rationale
R1–R10	Transitioning	Easy to prepare, easy to digest	Section 7.1
R11–R25	For Adult Dogs	Wholesome foods dogs love to eat	Section 7.2
R26–R35	For Puppies	Healthy growth (including large/giant breeds)	Section 7.3
R36–R45	For Senior Dogs	Gentle aging and longevity	Section 7.4
R46–R55	Low Calorie	Healthy weight loss	Section 7.5
R56–R60	High Calorie	Athletic endurance or weight gain	Section 7.6
R61–R64	Low Oxalate	Dogs at risk of calcium oxalate urolithiasis	Section 7.7
R65–R68	Vegetarian Adult	Sound nutrition without the meat	Section 7.8
R69–R70	Vegetarian Diabetic	Dogs with diabetes mellitus	Section 7.8
R71-R72	Vegetarian Urate	Dogs at risk of urate urolithiasis	Section 7.8
R73–R84	Limited Antigen	Dietary hypersensitivities, allergic skin disease, chronic colitis, and other chronic inflammatory conditions	Section 7.9
R85–R90	Low Fat	Dogs with gastrointestinal or pancreatic disease	Section 7.10
R91–R96	Low Phosphorus/ Low Protein	Dogs with chronic renal (kidney) disease	Section 7.11
R97–R101	Low Sodium	Dogs with cardiac (heart) disease	Section 7.12

TABLE 17

Summary of 12 recipe types

7.1

Transitioning Recipes: Easy to Prepare, Easy to Digest

Transitioning recipes are highly palatable and use ingredients that are easily digested by most dogs. They are easy to prepare because they use only a few ingredients. Use transitioning recipes to introduce a dog to home-made meals or feed these recipes indefinitely. These recipes provide 100% complete and balanced nutrition for healthy adult dogs.

Many of the transitioning recipes contain ingredients similar to those found in commercial pet foods. The starch in commercial dog foods usually comes from cereal ingredients such as corn, rice or wheat. Poultry is generally used as the primary source of protein. Poultry fat and vegetable oils supply essential fatty acids. It is possible for home-made recipes to mimic commercial dry diets by using similar ingredients and targeting similar nutrient content.

All recipes in this section contain one or two high quality proteins (chicken, eggs, meat or fish), a single source of digestible starch (rice, pasta or oatmeal), and two oils (safflower oil and cod liver oil) to supply omega-6 and omega-3 fatty acids respectively. Vitamins, minerals and pre-biotic fibers are supplied by HILARY'S BLEND™ supplement for home-made meals.

Note: many of the Limited Antigen and Low Fat recipes are also good choices for transitioning to home-made meals.

7.2

Recipes for Healthy Adult Dogs: Wholesome Foods Dogs Love to Eat

The recipes in this section contain a balance of all essential nutrients to support normal adult canine maintenance. Eggs, meat, fish and/or poultry provide high quality protein. A starchy ingredient such as rice, oatmeal, pasta or potatoes, provides dietary energy. Safflower oil and cod liver oil supply essential fatty acids. Vegetables and/or fruits supply vitamins, fiber and antioxidants. HILARY'S BLEND™ supplement for home-made meals balances each recipe with all essential vitamins and minerals, as well as supplying pre-biotic plant fibers to enhance digestion and gut health.

Because these recipes include vegetables and fruits, they contain more dietary fiber than the transitioning recipes. Fiber, by definition, is plant material that cannot be digested by the enzymes in the dog's small intestines. Fiber passes through the upper digestive tract and arrives in the large intestine largely intact. In the large intestine, bacteria ferment the fiber, producing short chain fatty acids. These short chain fatty acids lower the pH in the colon, which helps to inhibit the growth of harmful bacteria such as *clostridium*. Short chain fatty acids nourish the cells of the large intestines and this may help to prevent colitis.

The soluble fibers in fruits and vegetables are typically more fermentable than the fiber found in commercial pet foods. Dogs that are not used to eating soluble fiber will need time to adjust to the recipes in this section. Larger, softer stools are to be expected, but diarrhea indicates a health issue that requires veterinary attention.

Note: healthy adult dogs may also be fed:

Transitioning Recipes
High Calorie Recipes
Limited Antigen Recipes
Low Oxalate Recipes
Vegetarian Recipes
Low Fat Recipes

7.3

Recipes for Puppies: Healthy Growth and Normal Skeletal Development

The recipes in this section are specifically formulated for growing puppies, including those of large and giant breeds. All recipes in this section meet the AAFCO nutrient requirements for growth. They provide high quality protein to meet the increased protein requirements during growth. Their tightly controlled calcium and phosphorus levels promote normal skeletal development. These recipes contain fish or fish oils as sources of the omega-3 fatty acids EPA (eicosapentaenoic acid) and DHA (docosahexaenoic acid) to enhance cognitive development.

Feeding appropriate calories for optimal growth is the biggest challenge in feeding puppies. The more calories you feed a growing puppy, the faster the puppy will grow. The faster the puppy grows, the greater the risk of skeletal defects. Feeding too many calories does not make a puppy look fat. In fact, the opposite is true. Rapid growth often results in a tall, lanky puppy and the tendency of the owner may be to feed even more to try to "bulk up" the puppy.

The calorie density of a puppy food is not as important as the calorie intake of the puppy. High calorie puppy foods will support normal growth if the puppy is fed the correct calories. However, lower calorie puppy foods are less risky since the puppy can eat more without over-consuming calories. In order to ensure optimal growth rate, owners should take care to feed puppies according to the calorie tables provided in Appendices 5-7 at the end

of this book. See Chapter 8, section 8.2 for directions on how to calculate feeding guides for your puppy.

Excess calcium intake, insufficient calcium intake, or imbalances in the ratio of calcium to phosphorus can all lead to skeletal defects. Large breed puppies are far more sensitive to improper mineral balance than smaller breed puppies. Recipes in this section should be followed very carefully to ensure the proper intake of essential nutrients.

It is VERY important that HILARY'S BLEND™ supplement for home-made meals be carefully measured out according to the recipe directions. Take care to evenly disperse the supplement throughout the food. Supplementation with additional vitamins and minerals is not only unnecessary, it is potentially harmful.

7.4

Recipes for Senior Dogs: Gentle Aging and Longevity

Feeding home-made meals is a great way to promote healthy nutrition in older dogs. Senior dogs often have reduced food intake due to failing taste or smell and this can lead to weight loss and dehydration. The senior recipes in this book are highly palatable and their high moisture content helps to maintain hydration. They contain increased antioxidants and the omega-3 fatty acids EPA and DHA to enhance cognitive function.

Senior dogs benefit from diets which are lower in calories, contain moderate levels of highly digestible protein and have slightly restricted mineral levels, particularly phosphorus and sodium. The energy requirements of senior dogs are significantly lower than those of younger, adult dogs. This is due in part to a lower activity level, but also due to the loss of body muscle. As a dog ages, muscle mass is lost and this lowers the dog's basal metabolic rate. The combination of lowered activity and lower metabolic rate can reduce a senior dog's energy requirements by up to 40% as compared to a younger dog of the same body weight. See Chapter 8 for information on calculating the feeding guides for senior dogs.

7.5

Low Calorie Recipes: For Healthy Weight Loss

The recipes in this section are specifically designed to induce healthy weight loss in overweight dogs. When fed according to the feeding guides, these recipes typically induce a 1% loss in body weight each week.

Low Calorie recipes have higher protein content to promote the maintenance of lean muscle tissue during weight loss. Their lower fat content reduces calorie density while still maintaining adequate levels of the essential fatty acid linoleic acid. Higher vitamin and mineral levels (relative to calories) ensure that essential nutrient requirements are met when calories are restricted. Starchy carbohydrates, such as oatmeal and rice, are replaced with lower calorie vegetables and fruits. The higher dietary fiber content of these recipes may result in larger, softer stools. Take care to transition to these diets over several days. Low Calorie recipes should be fed as part of a veterinary-supervised weight loss program.

7.6

High Calorie Recipes: For Athletic Endurance

These recipes provide more calories for dogs who perform endurance activities, such as hunting, herding or sled dog racing. These recipes are high in fat and contain moderate levels of high quality protein. All recipes deliver at least 2.0 grams of protein per kilogram of body weight per day when fed according to the feeding guides.

Recipe R60 can be used to promote weight gain in non-working dogs. Its high calorie content comes from digestible carbohydrate rather than fat.

7.7

Low Oxalate Recipes: For Dogs at Risk of Calcium Oxalate Urolithiasis

Recipes in this section are designed for dogs at risk of calcium oxalate urolithiasis. Calcium oxalate urolithiasis is a condition in which calcium oxalate stones form in the bladder of the dog. This is a very painful condition that can be life-threatening. Dogs of certain breeds (i.e. Miniature Schnauzer, Yorkshire Terrier, Shih Tzu, Lhasa Apso, and others) may be genetically predisposed to this condition.

Many human foods, including some vegetables and nuts, are very high in oxalate. These foods (see Table 18) should be avoided. Oxalate consumed in food contributes up to 50% of the oxalate excreted in urine[1]. The remainder comes from endogenous oxalate production. For example, oxalate is a by-product of vitamin C metabolism in the body.

The recipes in this section contain only ingredients that are recommended for humans at risk of calcium oxalate urolithiasis (Table 20). These recipes are all high in moisture which helps to promote body water turnover (keeping the bladder flushed).

[1] Holmes RP, Goodman HO, Assimos DG. Contribution of dietary oxalate to urinary oxalate excretion. *Kidney Int*. 2001;59:270–276.

Almonds	Garlic	Sesame seeds
Beans	Lettuce	Soybeans
Brussels sprouts	Parsley	Spinach
Carrots	Peanut butter	Sweet potatoes
Collards	Rhubarb	Vitamin C

Apples	Celery	Ice cream
Baked beans	Cheese	Meat
Beef	Corn	Milk
Blueberries	Cucumber	Tomato
Broccoli	Fish	Yogurt

Bananas	Grapefruit	Oils & fats
Cabbage	Macaroni	Potatoes
Cauliflower	Melons	Poultry
Eggs	Peas	Rice

Research has shown that high sodium intake does not increase the risk of calcium oxalate stone formation in dogs[2]. Owners may therefore choose to further increase water consumption and urine output by adding a pinch of salt to these recipes.

Dogs at risk of calcium oxalate urolithiasis should be fed these recipes under the supervision of a veterinarian.

7.8

Vegetarian Recipes: Sound Nutrition without the Meat

Dogs are omnivores so vegetarian diets can meet all the nutritional requirements of a dog. Vegetarian recipes use pulses (such as soybeans, kidney beans and chickpeas) and nuts (such as peanuts and almonds) as sources of protein. Unfortunately, these ingredients are low in several essential nutrients, particularly methionine, tryptophan, and selenium. Eggs and dairy products can help to balance the nutrients found in plant ingredients and improve the digestibility and palatability of the entire recipe.

[2] Stevenson AE, Hynds W, Markwell PJ. Effect of dietary sodium on urine composition of healthy Miniature Schnauzers. J *Vet Intern Med*. 2001;15(3):300.

High fiber diets are recommended for dogs with diabetes mellitus. Vegetarian recipes generally contain more dietary fiber than meat-based recipes. Vegetarian Diabetic 1 (R69) and Vegetarian Diabetic 2 (R70) not only provide increased dietary fiber, they also contain only foods that have a low glycemic index. Glycemic index reflects how quickly a starch is broken down into glucose. Starches with low glycemic index break down more slowly and therefore require less insulin for their metabolism.

Dogs at risk of urate urolithiasis (some Dalmatians for example) may benefit from being fed a vegetarian diet. Urinary risk factors for uric stone formation are lowest in humans fed vegetarian diets[3]. However, dairy products also help to decrease the risks of uric acid stones in humans. A 2005 study showed that while meat or seafood consumption increased uric acid levels in human serum, the consumption of dairy products was associated with lower serum uric acid concentrations[4]. Vegetarian Urate 1 (R71) and Vegetarian Urate 2 (R72) both include cottage cheese, a high quality dairy protein.

7.9

Limited Antigen Recipes: Dietary Support for Dietary Hypersensitivities, Allergic Skin Disease, Colitis, and Other Chronic Inflammatory Conditions

Limited Antigen Recipes contain only a few ingredients in order to limit the dog's exposure to potential allergens. These recipes use ingredients that are unlikely to have been previously consumed by a dog. The recipes in this section can be fed as part of a 12-week diagnostic elimination feeding trial or they can be fed long term to dogs that are not able to tolerate more common ingredients.

The five Limited Antigen fish recipes contain high levels of the anti-inflammatory omega-3 fatty acids and so are recommended as first choice for dogs with chronic inflammatory conditions. Dogs that do not tolerate fish ingredients may be fed one of the seven non-fish Limited Antigen recipes.

Some of the recipes in this section use common human foods that are rarely used in pet foods, such as pork and trout. Others use more exotic ingredients such as rabbit and venison. Depending on the dietary history of the dog, some of the Transitioning recipes may also be suitable elimination diets for dogs with chronic inflammatory conditions.

[3] Siener R, Hesse A. The effect of a vegetarian and different omnivorous diets on urinary risk factors for uric acid stone formation. *Eur J Nutr* 2003;42:332–337.

[4] Choi HK, Liu SM, Curhan G. Intake of purine-rich foods, protein, and dairy products and relationship to serum levels of uric acid—The Third National Health and Nutrition Examination Survey. *Arthritis Rheum.* 2005;52:283–289.

All dogs with chronic inflammatory conditions should be fed Limited Antigen recipes under the supervision of a veterinarian.

7.10

Low Fat Recipes: Support for Dogs with Gastrointestinal or Pancreatic Disease

The recipes in this section all contain less than 20 grams of fat per 1000 kcal. These recipes are not low in calories and are not designed for weight loss (see instead Low Calorie Recipes, section 7.5). Low Fat Recipes are designed for dogs with pancreatic disease or gastrointestinal disease. A restricted fat intake is recommended for dogs with pancreatitis, exocrine pancreatic insufficiency, small intestinal bacterial overgrowth (SIBO), malabsorption syndrome, dietary indiscretion (scavenging), lymphangiectasia, gastroenteritis, hyperlipidemia, intestinal parasites, motility disorders, as well as chronic or acute diarrhea or vomiting of unknown origin.

Many recipes in this section include yogurt which helps to normalize intestinal microflora, especially when fed in association with the natural prebiotic fibers in HILARY'S BLEND™ supplement for home-made meals. Peas are also included in many of these recipes. Pea fiber contains a unique blend of soluble and insoluble fibers which helps to promote gut health. Vitamin and mineral levels are elevated in these recipes to compensate for losses that have occurred due to diarrhea and/or vomiting.

All recipes in this section are complete and balanced for canine maintenance and are safe for long term feeding to adult dogs. Low Fat Recipes 1 (R85), 2 (R86) and 3 (R87) are highly digestible and most suitable for acute gastrointestinal cases. Recipes 4 (R88) and 5 (R89) contain more vegetables and so may require a longer transition time. These latter two are more suitable for long term feeding to less acute cases, for example to stable dogs at risk of pancreatic disease.

Low Fat Recipe 6 (R90) is a very concentrated recipe for dogs that need to regain lost weight. A possible alternative is High Calorie Recipe 5 (R60) which is slightly higher in fat at 22 grams of fat per 1000 kcal.

For dogs at risk of both pancreatic disease and calcium oxalate urolithiasis, Low Fat Recipe 1 is the best option. Alternatively, Low Oxalate Recipes 3 and 4 (R63 and R64) also have a restricted fat content.

Dogs with pancreatic or gastrointestinal disease should be fed under the supervision of a veterinarian.

Low Phosphorus /Low Protein Recipes: Nutritional Support for Dogs with Chronic Renal (Kidney) Disease

Recipes in this section are designed for dogs with chronic renal (kidney) disease. These recipes are all restricted in both phosphorus and protein. These diets do not meet AAFCO minimum requirements for adult maintenance and should only be fed to dogs with renal disease under the supervision of a veterinarian.

Dogs with kidney disease need a diet that is restricted in protein. In kidney disease, the by-products of protein metabolism are not easily cleared from the blood by the dog's kidneys. The accumulation of these metabolic by-products in the bloodstream results in a condition known as "uremia". The recipes in this section have restricted protein content and provide non-protein calories from carbohydrate and fat.

Dogs with kidney disease also have an impaired ability to excrete phosphorus from their bodies. The resulting imbalance between calcium and phosphorus leads to the overproduction of parathyroid hormone, a condition known as renal hyperparathyroidism. Parathyroid hormone is also a uremic toxin and its overproduction causes serious secondary conditions such as the calcification of soft tissue, neurological symptoms and anemia. Phosphorus restriction slows the progression of kidney disease and can significantly lengthen the life expectancy of dogs with kidney disease.

Since protein is important for the maintenance of lean muscle tissue, care should be taken not to overly restrict protein, especially during the early stages of the disease. Dogs with kidney disease should consume 2.0–3.0 grams of protein per kilogram of body weight each day[5]. In the early stages of the disease, it is best to aim for the upper end of this range (i.e. 2.5–3.0 grams), then move to the lower end as the disease progresses. Targets for phosphorus are 40–60 mg of phosphorus per kilogram of body weight per day in the early stages, moving to 25–45 mg as the disease progresses[5].

Because calorie requirements do not relate linearly to body weight (i.e. a 100 lb dog does not eat 10 times more than a 10 lb dog), a diet that delivers the appropriate protein and phosphorus for a small dog will not deliver the correct protein and phosphorus intake for a large dog. Table 21 shows the protein and phosphorus intake of dogs of different body weights being fed a diet containing 35 g of protein and 600 mg of phosphorus per 1000 kcal.

Note that this diet would be suitable for dogs weighing 11–22 lbs in the initial stages of kidney disease, or for dogs weighing 33–44 lbs in advanced stages of kidney disease. This diet contains insufficient protein to meet the minimum requirements for dogs over 55 lbs, and it contains too much protein for dogs less than 11 lbs.

[5] Buffington CA, Holloway C, Abood S. Manual of Veterinary Dietetics. St. Louis: Elsevier; 2004; 105–107.

Weight		Energy	Protein intake	Phosphorus intake
kgs	lbs	kcal/day	g/kg BW/day	mg/kg BW/day
2.5	5.5	249	3.48	59.65
5	11	418	2.93	50.16
10	22	703	2.46	42.18
15	33	953	2.22	38.11
20	44	1182	2.07	35.47
25	55	1398	1.96	33.54
30	66	1602	1.87	32.05
35	77	1799	1.80	30.84
40	88	1988	1.74	29.82

The six Renal Recipes in this book offer a range of protein and phosphorus restriction to meet the needs of dogs of different body weights at different stages of renal disease. The protein and phosphorus content of the six Renal Recipes are summarized below.

Renal Recipe	Page	Protein (g/1000 kcal)	Phosphorus (mg/1000 kcal)
R91	159	31	615
R92	160	37	709
R93	161	43	783
R94	162	48	875
R95	163	53	939
R96	164	58	1006

The appropriate recipe to feed depends on the body weight of the dog and the stage of the disease. Use Table 23 to determine which Renal Recipe is most appropriate for the dog in your care. Change recipes as clinical signs indicate disease progression.

All Renal Recipes are very high in fat. Fat is a highly concentrated source of non-protein calories. Not only do the increased calories of these recipes help to maintain the dog's lean body tissue, they also dilute the concentra-

TABLE 23

The best renal recipe (R91–R96) to feed depends on the dog's body weight and the current stage of the disease.

Dog's body weight		Stage of kidney disease		
kgs	lbs	Early	Advanced	End-stage
< 14	< 30	R93	R92	R91
15–27	31–60	R94	R93	R92
28–50	61–110	R95	R94	R93
> 50	> 110	R96	R95	R94

tion of protein and phosphorus in the recipe. Renal patients should always get the bulk of their calories from non-protein sources, and fat is palatable and digestible option. Most dogs enjoy high fat diets but care should be taken to transition slowly to these recipes to allow the dog to adjust to their higher fat content.

It is recommended that Low Phosphorus/Low Protein recipes be supplemented with potassium citrate. Dogs with kidney disease are at risk of developing metabolic acidosis. Potassium citrate is a buffer that helps to counter metabolic acidosis and it also provides supplemental potassium to offset increased urinary losses of this mineral.

These recipes do not meet the AAFCO minimum requirements for dogs. They should only be fed to dogs with chronic renal disease under the supervision of a veterinarian.

7.12

Low Sodium Recipes: For Dogs with Cardiac (Heart) Disease

The recipes in this section are designed for dogs suffering from cardiac disease. Cardiac disease is classified into four stages according to the dog's symptoms. In Class I heart disease, there are no visible signs. The disease can be detected by a veterinarian using a stethoscope, radiographs or electrocardiograms. In Class II, ordinary activity causes mild symptoms, such as shortness of breath, but the symptoms do not significantly limit the dog's activity. In Class III, symptoms begin to limit the dog's physical activity and in Class IV, the symptoms are present even when the dog is at rest.

Recommended sodium intake varies according to the stage of the disease[6]. In Class I or II of the disease, there may already be activation of the renin-angiotensin-aldosterone system, which is the body's mechanism for excreting excess sodium in urine. Severe sodium restriction at this stage is not recommended since it may further stimulate this system, leading to excessive sodium losses. However, as the disease progresses to Class III and IV, more severe sodium restriction is recommended. Sodium recommendations are shown in Table 24.

Current commercial diets for cardiac disease range from 150 to 650 mg of sodium per 1000 kcal. The AAFCO minimum for healthy dogs is 170 mg of sodium per 1000 kcal. All Low Sodium recipes in this book contain less than 400 mg of sodium/1000 kcal, and are therefore suitable for Class IV heart disease. Veterinarians can easily increase the sodium level of patients in earlier stages of the disease by adding table salt according to the directions in Table 25.

---

[6] Freeman LM. Nutritional therapy of heart disease. *26th Annual Waltham Diets/OSU Symposium for the Treatment of Small Animal Diseases (Cardiology)*. 2002;53–56.

TABLE 24

Sodium recommendations for dogs with early to advanced cardiac (heart) disease

	Recommended sodium content of dog food
AAFCO minimum	> 170 mg/1000 kcal
Class I–II	< 1200 mg/1000 kcal
Class II–III	< 900 mg/1000 kcal
Class III–IV	< 400 mg/1000 kcal

Low Sodium recipes are formulated to match current recommendations[7] for cardiac patients. They contain moderate levels of highly digestible protein, increased levels of the omega-3 fatty acids EPA and DHA, to reduce the risks of cardiac cachexia (muscle wasting) and to inhibit the production of inflammatory mediators. These recipes contain increased levels of potassium and magnesium to offset increased urinary losses with some cardiac medications (i.e. furosemide). Finally, these recipes provide moderate calorie content to promote healthy body weight. Excess weight is a major contributor to cardiac workload and it aggravates exercise intolerance.

Low Sodium recipes should be fed under the supervision of a veterinarian.

TABLE 25

Sodium content of the Low Sodium Recipes alone and with added table salt

Low Sodium Recipe #	Sodium content (mg/1000 kcal)			
	Recipe alone	Recipe plus a pinch of salt (½ gram)	Recipe plus ¼ tsp of salt (1½ grams)	Recipe plus ⅓ tsp of salt (2 grams)
R97	315	455	730	870
R98	323	450	725	860
R99	351	515	825	980
R100	341	500	820	975
R101	361	515	825	980

---

7 Freeman LM, Rush JE, Cahalane AK. Dietary patterns of dogs with cardiac disease. J. Nutr. 2002;132:1632S–1633S.

7.13

Recipe Summary Tables

Recipe	Main Ingredients	Protein (g/1000 kcal)	Fat (g/1000 kcal)	Calories (kcal/100g)
R1	Chicken, rice	75	25	139
R2	Eggs, oatmeal	56	43	90
R3	Cod, rice	80	25	124
R4	Beef, egg noodles	85	42	188
R5	Tuna, rice	74	29	132
R6	Chicken, rice, carrots	100	27	143
R7	Beef, oatmeal, blueberries	66	45	110
R8	Eggs, rice, broccoli	54	44	130
R9	Salmon, rice, beans	52	42	148
R10	Beef, potatoes, tomato sauce	78	39	147

TABLE 26

Summary of the 10 Transitioning Recipes (R1–R10)

Recipe	Main Ingredients	Protein (g/1000 kcal)	Fat (g/1000 kcal)	Calories (kcal/100g)
R11	Eggs, liver, macroni, tomato sauce	63	28	157
R12	Beef, eggs, applesauce, vegetables	88	51	142
R13	Chicken, eggs, fruits, vegetables	120	35	133
R14	Salmon, vegetables	87	60	102
R15	Cod, cottage cheese, vegetables, fruit	114	49	116
R16	Beef, spaghetti, vegetables	83	37	141
R17	Sardines, yogurt, almonds, vegetables	61	57	160
R18	Turkey, chicken liver, cheese, yogurt, vegetables	79	65	162
R19	Chicken, chicken liver, vegetables, fruit	72	51	108
R20	Liver, yogurt, fruits, vegetables	63	48	111
R21	Flatfish/sole, eggs, vegetables	90	55	117
R22	Salmon, fruits, vegetables	78	61	143
R23	Chicken, eggs, sardines, fruits, vegetables	93	59	153
R24	Tuna, cheese, almonds, vegetables, fruit	93	48	116
R25	Beef, yogurt, vegetables, fruit	90	44	112

TABLE 27

Summary of the 15 Adult Recipes (R11–R25)

TABLE 28

Summary of the
10 Puppy Recipes
(R26–R35)

Recipe	Main Ingredients	Protein (g/1000 kcal)	Fat (g/1000 kcal)	Calories (kcal/100g)
R26	Liver, yogurt, fruits, vegetables	70	37	117
R27	Chicken, sardines, eggs, yogurt, vegetables	129	43	150
R28	Chicken liver, tuna, yogurt, vegetables	93	29	121
R29	Chicken, liver, vegetables, fruit	116	30	113
R30	Liver, oatmeal, yogurt, vegetables, fruit	75	49	126
R31	Flatfish/sole, cottage cheese, yogurt, vegetables, fruit	106	40	103
R32	Liver, eggs, oatmeal, vegetables	82	56	120
R33	Liver, eggs, sardines, yogurt, vegetables	87	56	154
R34	Chicken, oatmeal, vegetables	148	20	101
R35	Liver, eggs, oatmeal, vegetables, fruit	70	51	111

TABLE 29

Summary of the
10 Senior Recipes
(R36–R45)

Recipe	Main Ingredients	Protein (g/1000 kcal)	Fat (g/1000 kcal)	Calories (kcal/100g)
R36	Chicken, rice, yogurt, carrots	56	29	123
R37	Beef, oatmeal, vegetables	57	54	110
R38	Eggs, cheese, vegetables	62	63	153
R39	Sardines, egg, potatoes, vegetables	52	46	151
R40	Flatfish/sole, rice, almonds, vegetables, fruit	57	59	168
R41	Chicken, rice, vegetables, fruit	59	24	103
R42	Beef, kidney beans, potatoes, vegetables, fruit	64	32	107
R43	Eggs, tuna, almonds, vegetables	57	64	177
R44	Flatfish/sole, yogurt, oatmeal, vegetables, fruit	66	49	117
R45	Salmon, eggs, rice, vegetables, fruit	61	56	123

Recipe	Main Ingredients	Protein	Fat	Calories
		(g/1000 kcal)	(g/1000 kcal)	(kcal/100g)
R46	Cod, eggs, vegetables	119	45	81
R47	Chicken, yogurt, vegetables, fruit	122	36	89
R48	Flatfish/sole, yogurt, vegetables, fruit	88	27	98
R49	Eggs, chicken liver, vegetables, fruit	91	58	95
R50	Tuna, egg, cottage cheese, vegetables, fruit	100	38	98
R51	Flatfish/sole, yogurt, vegetables	87	30	78
R52	Turkey, egg, chicken liver, yogurt, vegetables, fruit	117	25	81
R53	Salmon, cottage cheese, vegetables, fruit	84	40	92
R54	Chicken, yogurt, egg, vegetables	95	45	98
R55	Soybeans, egg whites, chickpeas, vegetables	89	36	94

TABLE 30

Summary of the 10 Low Calorie Recipes (R46–R55)

Recipe	Main Ingredients	Protein	Fat	Calories
		(g/1000 kcal)	(g/1000 kcal)	(kcal/100g)
R56	Chicken liver, eggs, almonds, butter	65	77	293
R57	Beef, liver, flaxseeds, almonds, butter	59	76	346
R58	Turkey, liver, oatmeal, butter	67	75	280
R59	Sardines, potato, flaxseeds, butter, carrots	53	73	270
R60	GENERAL MILLS® HoneyNut Cheerios, sardines, tuna	57	23	289

TABLE 31

Summary of the 5 High Calorie Recipes (R56–R60)

Recipe	Main Ingredients	Protein	Fat	Calories
		(g/1000 kcal)	(g/1000 kcal)	(kcal/100g)
R61	Chicken, rice, peas	84	33	151
R62	Chicken, rice, egg, peas, fruit	84	29	133
R63	Chicken, egg, potato, peas, cauliflower	111	20	105
R64	Turkey, rice, peas, bananas	64	15	107

TABLE 32

Summary of the 4 Low Oxalate Recipes (R61–R64)

TABLE 33

Summary of the
8 Vegetarian Recipes
(R65–R72)

Recipe	Main Ingredients	Protein (g/1000 kcal)	Fat (g/1000 kcal)	Calories (kcal/100g)
R65	Kidney beans, chickpeas, soybeans, vegetables	73	49	136
R66	Eggs, kidney beans, almonds, vegetables	56	56	158
R67	Eggs, kidney beans, soybeans, cheese, vegetables	72	44	134
R68	Eggs, egg noodles, kidney beans, vegetables	61	42	117
R69	Soybeans, yogurt, vegetables, fruit	62	51	125
R70	Eggs, barley, yogurt, vegetables	60	43	125
R71	Cottage cheese, flaxseeds, vegetables, fruit	62	34	108
R72	Cottage cheese, soybeans, almonds, vegetables	67	59	181

TABLE 34

Summary of the
12 Limited Antigen
Recipes (R73–R84)

Recipe	Main Ingredients	Protein (g/1000 kcal)	Fat (g/1000 kcal)	Calories (kcal/100g)
R73	Trout, barley	80	37	161
R74	Catfish, potatoes	59	52	153
R75	Salmon, oatmeal	56	58	127
R76	Tuna, potatoes	88	44	150
R77	Halibut, barley	71	25	145
R78	Pork, potatoes	91	36	149
R79	Pork, oatmeal	65	54	134
R80	Rabbit, oatmeal	98	43	132
R81	Rabbit, potatoes	95	32	144
R82	Venison, barley	81	38	169
R83	Venison, potatoes	87	34	142
R84	Goat meat, potatoes	103	23	121

Recipe	Main Ingredients	Protein	Fat	Calories
		(g/1000 kcal)	(g/1000 kcal)	(kcal/100g)
R85	Chicken, rice	73	17	128
R86	Sardines, yogurt, potato, peas	69	19	90
R87	Cod, peas, blueberries	157	15	101
R88	Halibut, vegetables, fruit	77	18	103
R89	Flatfish/sole, potatoes, vegetables, fruit	73	18	120
R90	Chicken liver, flatfish/sole, KELLOGG'S® Rice Krispies	82	19	219

Recipe	Main Ingredients	Protein	Phosphorus	Calories
		(g/1000 kcal)	(mg/1000 kcal)	(kcal/100g)
R91	Egg whites, tofu, fruits, vegetables	31	615	191
R92	Egg whites, tofu, fruits, vegetables	37	709	171
R93	Egg whites, chicken, fruits, vegetables	43	783	168
R94	Egg whites, chicken, yogurt, fruits, vegetables	48	875	171
R95	Chicken, egg whites, yogurt, fruit, vegetables	53	939	175
R96	Chicken, egg whites, yogurt, fruit, vegetables	58	1006	170

Recipe	Main Ingredients	Protein	Sodium	Calories
		(g/1000 kcal)	(mg/1000 kcal)	(kcal/100g)
R97	Salmon, egg, vegetables	53	315	140
R98	Chicken, chicken liver, vegetables, fruit	64	323	145
R99	Flatfish/sole, egg, oatmeal, vegetables	59	351	124
R100	Beef, eggs, oatmeal, vegetables, fruit	68	341	122
R101	Chicken, eggs, rice, vegetables	66	361	126

TABLE 35

Summary of the 6 Low Fat Recipes (R85–R90)

TABLE 36

Summary of the 6 Low Phosphorus/Low Protein Recipes (R91–R96)

TABLE 37

Summary of the 5 Low Sodium Recipes (R97–R101)

TABLE 38

Summary of the
ingredients used in
the recipes in this
book.

Name (In Recipes)	Inedible Portion (Discard)	Description
Alfalfa sprouts, raw		alfalfa seeds, sprouted, raw
Almonds, ground	shells	unroasted, unsalted
Apple, raw, with skin	core and stem	all varieties
Applesauce, canned		unsweetened, without added vitamin C
Bananas, raw	skin (peel)	
Barley, pearled, cooked		
Beans, green, boiled	ends, strings, trimmings	Snap, boiled and drained, without salt
Beans, green, raw	ends, strings, trimmings	Snap
Beans, kidney, canned		red, mature seeds, drained
Beef, ground, cooked		90% lean, 10% fat
Blueberries, raw	stems, green or spoiled berries	
Broccoli, raw	leaves, tough stalks, trimmings	
Brussels sprouts	outer leaves	
Butter		unsalted
Cabbage, raw	outer leaves and core	all varieties
Carrots, raw	crown, tops, scrapings	
Catfish, cooked	bones, skin	channel, farmed, filets
Cauliflower, boiled	leaf stalks, cores, trimmings	boiled and drained, without salt
Cauliflower, raw	leaf stalks, cores, trimmings	
Celery, boiled	roots and trimmings	boiled and drained, without salt
Celery, raw	roots and trimmings	
Cereal, Honey Nut Cheerios®		Ready-to-eat cereal, GENERAL MILLS®
Cereal, Rice Krispies®		Ready-to-eat cereal, KELLOGG'S®
Cheese, cheddar		mild or medium
Chicken, breast, cooked	bone, skin	broilers or fryers, breast meat only
Chickpeas, canned		mature seeds, (also called garbanzo beans), drained
Cod liver oil		
Cod, Atlantic, cooked	bones, skin	
Cornstarch		
Cottage cheese, low fat		1% milk fat
Cucumber, raw, with peel	ends, strings, trimmings	
Egg noodles, cooked		unenriched, boiled and drained, without salt
Egg, hard-boiled	shells	
Egg, white only, cooked	shells, yolks	
Flatfish/sole, cooked	bones, skin	flatfish (flounder or sole), filets
Flaxseeds, ground		
Goat meat, cooked	bone	
Grapefruit, raw	peel, seeds, core, membrane	pink or red
Halibut, cooked	bones, skin	Atlantic or Pacific

Name (In Recipes)	Inedible Portion (Discard)	Description
Honey		all varieties
Lettuce, iceberg, raw	core	crisphead or leaf
Liver, beef, cooked		
Liver, chicken, cooked		
Macaroni, enriched, cooked		boiled and drained, without salt
Oatmeal, cooked		regular or "quick & instant", unenriched, without salt
Peanut butter, smooth		without salt
Pears, raw	stem, core, seeds	all varieties
Peas, boiled	inedible peas	green, boiled and drained, without salt
Peas, thawed from frozen	inedible peas	green
Pork, ground, cooked		approximately 20% fat
Pork, loin chops, cooked	connective tissue, fat, bone	loin, center rib (chops) boneless, lean only (trim fat)
Potatoes, baked with skin	eyes	flesh and skin, without salt
Potatoes, boiled in skin	eyes	flesh and skin, without salt
Rabbit, cooked	bones	domesticated, composite cuts
Raspberries, raw	caps, stems, spoiled berries	
Rice, brown, cooked		long-grained, boiled, without salt
Safflower oil		over 70% linoleic acid
Salmon oil		or DermaPet® EicosaDerm®
Salmon, Atlantic, cooked	bones, skin	wild or farmed, filets
Salt		table salt
Sardines, Atlantic, canned		canned in water, drained solids with bone
Seaweed, spirulina, dried		
Sesame seeds, ground		
Soybean, curd cheese		
Soybeans, mature, boiled		boiled and drained, without salt
Spaghetti, cooked		unenriched, boiled and drained, without salt
Spinach, raw	large stems and roots	
Squash, winter, raw	seeds, rind and stem	all varieties
Strawberries, raw	caps and stems	
Sweet corn, boiled		kernels off cob, boiled and drained, without salt
Tofu, firm		with calcium sulfate
Tomato sauce, canned		
Tomatoes, red, raw	core, stem ends	red, ripe
Trout, rainbow, cooked	bones, skin	farmed
Tuna, white, canned		canned in water, without salt, drained solids
Turkey breast, cooked	bone, skin	fryer-roasters, meat only
Venison (deer), cooked	bone	farmed, meat only
Yogurt, plain, low fat		< 2% fat
Zucchini, raw	ends	summer squash, with skin

Calculating Feeding Guides for Individual Dogs

ENERGY NEEDS VARY WITH AGE, activity level, environmental conditions, and many other factors. As with humans, every dog is an individual with unique metabolism, temperament and energy needs. This chapter provides general energy guidelines. It is recommended that owners use these directions to calculate the calories to feed their dog.

Then, based on the response of the individual dog, daily calories may be increased or decreased to meet each individual dog's requirements. A dog that is losing weight needs more calories, whereas one that is gaining weight needs fewer calories.

8.1

Adult and Senior Dogs of Normal Body Weight

1. Determine how many kcal your dog needs to eat each day:
   - For young and mature adult dogs, refer to Appendix 1
   - For senior dogs, refer to Appendix 2
   - For dogs with diseases, refer to Appendix 4
2. Determine how many kcal are in the recipe (kcal/100g are listed below each recipe).
3. Divide the kcal your dog needs by the kcal in the food (kcal/100g) then multiply by 100. This gives you the grams to feed each day.
4. Divide 1000 grams (the amount of food produced by each recipe) by the grams to feed each day to determine how many days the recipe will last.

EXAMPLE 1

A 22 lb (10 kg) active mature adult dog being fed **Adult Recipe 3**

    1) From Appendix 1, an active mature 22 lb dog needs 731 kcal/day

    2) From page 81 (R13), Adult Recipe 3 contains 133 kcal/100g

    3) Grams to feed $\quad = \dfrac{\text{kcal needed by the dog}}{\text{kcal in the food}} \times 100$

                      $= (731/133) \times 100$

                      $= (5.50) \times 100$

                      $= 550$ grams/day

    4) Days recipe will last $= \dfrac{1000}{550}$

                                $= 1.8$ days

8.2

Puppies Being Fed a Puppy Recipe

1. Estimate the mature adult weight of the puppy.
   - (Refer to breed weight charts in Appendix 8)
2. Using the puppy's current weight and his predicted adult weight, determine how many calories to feed the puppy each day:
   - For puppies with mature adult weight up to 55 lbs (25 kg) refer to Appendix 5.
   - For puppies with mature adult weights from 55–121 lbs (25–55 kg), refer to Appendix 6.
   - For puppies with mature adult weights over 121 lbs (55 kg), refer to Appendix 7.
3. Select a Puppy Recipe (R26–R35) and determine how many kcal are in that recipe (kcal/100g are listed below each recipe).
4. Divide the kcal your puppy needs by the kcal in the food (kcal/100g) then multiply by 100. This gives you the grams to feed each day.
5. Divide 1000 grams (the amount of food produced by each recipe) by the grams to feed each day to determine how many days the recipe will last.
6. Repeat the above steps at least twice a month and adjust kcal intake accordingly, until the puppy reaches maturity.

EXAMPLE 2

A female Bulldog puppy currently weighing 11 lb (5 kg) being fed **Puppy Recipe 4**

1) From Appendix 8, a female Bulldog's predicted adult weight is 40–50 lb.

2) From Appendix 5, an 11 lb puppy with an adult weight of 44 lb needs 980 kcal/day.

3) From page 27 (R29), Puppy Recipe 4 contains 113 kcal/100g

4) Grams to feed $= \dfrac{\text{kcal needed by the puppy}}{\text{kcal in the food}} \times 100$

$= (980/113) \times 100$

$= (8.67) \times 100$

$= 867$ grams/day

5) Days recipe will last $= \dfrac{1000}{867}$

$= 1.2$ days

8.3

Adult Overweight Dogs Being Fed a Low Calorie Recipe

1. Determine how many kcal your dog needs to eat each day for weight loss:
   - For adult overweight dogs, refer to Appendix 3
2. Select a Low Calorie Recipe (R46–R55) and determine how many kcal are in the recipe (kcal/100g are listed below each recipe).
3. Divide the kcal your dog needs by the kcal in the food (kcal/100g) then multiply by 100. This gives you the grams to feed each day.
4. Divide 1000 grams (the amount of food produced by each recipe) by the grams to feed each day to determine how many days the recipe will last.
5. Feed at the above calorie intake for 10–12 weeks. The dog should lose approximately 1% of his body weight each week over this time.
6. If, at the end of 10–12 weeks, the dog still needs to lose weight, re-weigh the dog and follow steps 1–5 above at the new body weight.

EXAMPLE 3

An overweight adult dog currently weighing 44 lbs (20 kg) being fed **Low Calorie Recipe 6**

1) From Appendix 3, a 44 lb overweight dog needs 520 kcal/day

2) From page 119 (R51), Low Calorie Recipe 6 contains 78 kcal/100g

3) Grams to feed $\quad = \dfrac{\text{kcal needed by the dog}}{\text{kcal in the food}} \times 100$

$\quad\quad\quad\quad\quad\quad = (520/78) \times 100$

$\quad\quad\quad\quad\quad\quad = (6.67) \times 100$

$\quad\quad\quad\quad\quad\quad = 667$ grams/day

4) Days recipe will last $\quad = \dfrac{1000}{667}$

$\quad\quad\quad\quad\quad\quad\quad\quad = 1.5$ days

5) Feed this dog 520 kcal/day (667 grams/day) for 10–12 weeks. Re-weigh the dog. If the dog needs to lose more weight, repeat steps 1–4 above. Feed at the new calorie level for another 10–12 weeks.

Recipes

Recipe Key

INGREDIENT LIST

Recipe ingredients are listed alphabetically and all recipes make exactly one kilogram of food. Ingredient substitutions are not recommended since they will alter the nutrient balance of the recipe.

Approximate volume measurements (cups, tbsp etc) are estimates only and may vary considerably in weight depending on how the ingredients are prepared (chopping, grating, slicing etc). For this reason, it is recommended that ingredients be weighed, and the recipe be followed using gram weights rather than volume approximates.

Raw meats contain more moisture than cooked meats and meats lose both moisture and weight on cooking. Recipes list both the raw meat weight and its equivalent weight after cooking (using conversion factors published in the *Food Buying Guide for Child Nutrition Programs*, 2007 edition). Owners feeding raw meats should use the raw meat weight. Owners feeding cooked meats should start with the raw weight, cook the meat, then re-weigh to ensure it matches the recipe's cooked meat weight.

For more information about individual ingredients, refer to table 38 at the end of Chapter 7.

INSTRUCTIONS

The Instructions give one possible way of preparing the recipe. Some dogs may prefer a puree texture, while others may prefer a more chunky meal. Owners are encouraged to experiment with different ways of preparing and combining the ingredients to find what works best for their dog.

NUTRITION TABLE

The Nutrition Table reflects the nutrient content of the complete recipe when ingredients are measured in grams. Values in column 2 (per 100g dry matter) and column 3 (per 1000 kcal) can be compared to the AAFCO nutrient profiles in Appendix 9.

The bottom of this chart lists several nutrients which are not considered essential by AAFCO but which may provide health benefits to a dog. These include the omega-3 fatty acids EPA and DHA, and a partial list of antioxidants. Dogs with certain medical conditions (for example cancer, kidney disease, heart disease, and chronic inflammatory conditions such as colitis, and allergic dermatitis) may benefit from recipes with a lower omega-6 to omega-3 ratio.

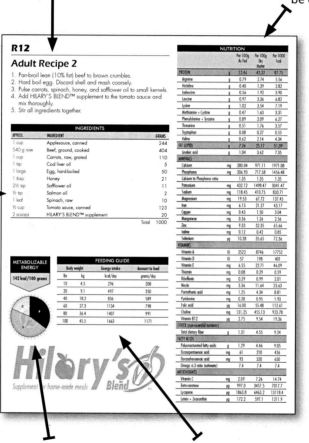

METABOLIZABLE ENERGY

The metabolizable energy reflects the calorie content of the recipe. The pie chart shows the approximate percentage of calories coming from protein (P), fat (F), and carbohydrate (C).

FEEDING GUIDES

Feeding guides are general guidelines. It is recommended that owners calculate a more precise feeding guide for their own dog using the information in the appendices and following the examples in Chapter 8.

Transitioning Recipe 1

NUTRITION				
		Per 100g As Fed	Per 100g Dry Matter	Per 1000 kcal
PROTEIN	g	10.44	32.64	74.88
Arginine	g	0.66	2.05	4.70
Histidine	g	0.32	0.98	2.25
Isoleucine	g	0.53	1.67	3.83
Leucine	g	0.80	2.49	5.71
Lysine	g	0.81	2.52	5.78
Methionine + Cystine	g	0.41	1.29	2.96
Phenylalanine + Tyrosine	g	0.79	2.48	5.69
Threonine	g	0.43	1.35	3.10
Tryptophan	g	0.12	0.39	0.89
Valine	g	0.53	1.67	3.83
FAT (LIPID)	g	3.51	10.98	25.19
Linoleic acid	g	1.43	4.45	10.21
MINERALS				
Calcium	mg	275.01	859.52	1971.74
Phosphorus	mg	208.36	651.22	1493.90
Calcium to Phosphorus ratio		1.32	1.32	1.32
Potassium	mg	250.96	784.36	1799.32
Sodium	mg	27.62	86.33	198.04
Magnesium	mg	41.66	130.21	298.70
Iron	mg	5.18	16.20	37.16
Copper	mg	0.45	1.39	3.19
Manganese	mg	0.92	2.88	6.61
Zinc	mg	7.16	22.36	51.29
Iodine	mg	0.12	0.38	0.87
Selenium	µg	14.40	45.01	103.25
VITAMINS				
Vitamin A	IU	506	1580	3625
Vitamin D	IU	57	178	409
Vitamin E	mg	6.10	19.05	43.70
Thiamin	mg	0.13	0.42	0.96
Riboflavin	mg	0.21	0.65	1.49
Niacin	mg	5.20	16.25	37.28
Pantothenic acid	mg	1.26	3.95	9.06
Pyridoxine	mg	0.33	1.02	2.34
Folic acid	µg	16.00	50.01	114.72
Choline	mg	86.27	269.61	618.49
Vitamin B12	µg	1.70	5.30	12.16
OTHER (non-essential nutrients)				
Total dietary fiber	g	1.73	5.39	12.36
FATTY ACIDS				
Polyunsaturated fatty acids	g	1.59	4.98	11.42
Eicosapentaenoic acid	mg	37	120	275
Docosahexaenoic acid	mg	60	190	436
Omega 6:3 ratio (estimate)		15.4	15.4	15.4
ANTIOXIDANTS				
Vitamin C	mg	0	0	0
Beta-carotene	µg	0	0	0
Lycopene	µg	0	0	0
Lutein + Zeaxanthin	µg	0	0	0

1. Gently simmer chicken until tender. Dice finely.
2. Cook rice according to the package directions to yield 3½ cups of cooked rice.
3. Stir the cod liver oil and safflower oil into the rice.
4. Sprinkle HILARY'S BLEND™ supplement over the rice and blend in.
5. Stir in the chicken.

INGREDIENTS		
APPROX.	INGREDIENT	GRAMS
540 g raw	Chicken breast, cooked	280
1 tsp	Cod liver oil	5
3½ cups	Rice, brown, cooked	681
3 tsp	Safflower oil	14
2 scoops	HILARY'S BLEND™ supplement	20
	Total	1000

FEEDING GUIDE			
Body weight		Energy intake	Amount to feed
lbs	kg	kcal/day	grams/day
10	4.5	296	213
20	9.1	497	358
40	18.2	836	602
60	27.3	1134	816
80	36.4	1407	1012
100	45.5	1663	1196

METABOLIZABLE ENERGY

139 kcal/100 grams

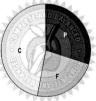

Hilary's Blend™

Supplement for home-made meals

Transitioning Recipe 2

1. Hard boil eggs. Discard shell and mash eggs coarsely.
2. Prepare the oatmeal according to the package directions to yield 3⅛ cups of cooked oatmeal.
3. Stir the cod liver oil into the oatmeal.
4. Sprinkle HILARY'S BLEND™ supplement over the oatmeal and blend in.
5. Stir in the mashed eggs.

INGREDIENTS		
APPROX.	INGREDIENT	GRAMS
1 tsp	Cod liver oil	5
5 large	Eggs, hard boiled	250
3⅛ cups	Oatmeal, cooked	730
1½ scoops	HILARY'S BLEND™ supplement	15
	Total	1000

METABOLIZABLE ENERGY

90 kcal/100 grams

FEEDING GUIDE			
Body weight		Energy intake	Amount to feed
lbs	kg	kcal/day	grams/day
10	4.5	296	329
20	9.1	497	553
40	18.2	836	929
60	27.3	1134	1260
80	36.4	1407	1563
100	45.5	1663	1848

NUTRITION		Per 100g As Fed	Per 100g Dry Matter	Per 1000 kcal
PROTEIN	g	5.04	26.47	56.13
Arginine	g	0.32	1.69	3.58
Histidine	g	0.12	0.63	1.34
Isoleucine	g	0.25	1.31	2.78
Leucine	g	0.41	2.16	4.58
Lysine	g	0.30	1.60	3.39
Methionine + Cystine	g	0.25	1.32	2.80
Phenylalanine + Tyrosine	g	0.46	2.41	5.11
Threonine	g	0.22	1.13	2.40
Tryptophan	g	0.07	0.34	0.72
Valine	g	0.30	1.55	3.29
FAT (LIPID)	g	3.88	20.38	43.22
Linoleic acid	g	0.56	2.96	6.28
MINERALS				
Calcium	mg	216.34	1135.43	2407.77
Phosphorus	mg	164.48	863.25	1830.59
Calcium to Phosphorus ratio		1.32	1.32	1.32
Potassium	mg	184.88	970.32	2057.64
Sodium	mg	34.50	181.08	383.99
Magnesium	mg	22.47	117.94	250.10
Iron	mg	4.25	22.30	47.29
Copper	mg	0.32	1.66	3.52
Manganese	mg	0.66	3.46	7.34
Zinc	mg	5.46	28.63	60.71
Iodine	mg	0.09	0.47	1.00
Selenium	µg	13.61	71.45	151.52
VITAMINS				
Vitamin A	IU	647	3393	7195
Vitamin D	IU	55	290	615
Vitamin E	mg	4.83	25.35	53.76
Thiamin	mg	0.13	0.70	1.48
Riboflavin	mg	0.26	1.38	2.93
Niacin	mg	0.35	1.84	3.90
Pantothenic acid	mg	1.10	5.75	12.19
Pyridoxine	mg	0.09	0.47	1.00
Folic acid	µg	12.00	62.98	133.55
Choline	mg	121.73	638.87	1354.77
Vitamin B12	µg	1.48	7.75	16.43
OTHER (non-essential nutrients)				
Total dietary fiber	g	1.62	8.48	17.98
FATTY ACIDS				
Polyunsaturated fatty acids	g	0.74	3.90	8.27
Eicosapentaenoic acid	mg	36	190	403
Docosahexaenoic acid	mg	64	340	721
Omega 6:3 ratio (estimate)		6.4	6.4	6.4
ANTIOXIDANTS				
Vitamin C	mg	0	0	0
Beta-carotene	µg	2.8	14.4	30.6
Lycopene	µg	0	0	0
Lutein + Zeaxanthin	µg	219.7	1152.8	2444.6

Hilary's Blend™

Supplement for home-made meals

Transitioning Recipe 3

NUTRITION		Per 100g As Fed	Per 100g Dry Matter	Per 1000 kcal
PROTEIN	g	10.00	34.57	80.41
Arginine	g	0.62	2.15	5.00
Histidine	g	0.29	1.00	2.33
Isoleucine	g	0.46	1.57	3.65
Leucine	g	0.82	2.82	6.56
Lysine	g	0.84	2.90	6.75
Methionine + Cystine	g	0.39	1.37	3.19
Phenylalanine + Tyrosine	g	0.75	2.60	6.05
Threonine	g	0.43	1.48	3.44
Tryptophan	g	0.12	0.40	0.93
Valine	g	0.53	1.82	4.23
FAT (LIPID)	g	3.16	10.91	25.38
Linoleic acid	g	1.53	5.29	12.30
MINERALS				
Calcium	mg	275.06	950.44	2210.79
Phosphorus	mg	187.89	649.24	1510.18
Calcium to Phosphorus ratio		1.46	1.46	1.46
Potassium	mg	265.92	918.87	2137.35
Sodium	mg	34.94	120.74	280.85
Magnesium	mg	50.52	174.56	406.04
Iron	mg	4.83	16.68	38.80
Copper	mg	0.43	1.49	3.47
Manganese	mg	0.74	2.55	5.93
Zinc	mg	6.98	24.13	56.13
Iodine	mg	0.12	0.41	0.95
Selenium	µg	19.97	69.01	160.52
VITAMINS				
Vitamin A	IU	517	1788	4159
Vitamin D	IU	57	197	458
Vitamin E	mg	6.32	21.83	50.78
Thiamin	mg	0.14	0.47	1.09
Riboflavin	mg	0.20	0.70	1.63
Niacin	mg	2.15	7.42	17.26
Pantothenic acid	mg	1.03	3.57	8.30
Pyridoxine	mg	0.25	0.86	2.00
Folic acid	µg	16.00	55.29	128.61
Choline	mg	116.52	402.62	936.52
Vitamin B12	µg	1.99	6.88	16.00
OTHER (non-essential nutrients)				
Total dietary fiber	g	1.41	4.88	11.35
FATTY ACIDS				
Polyunsaturated fatty acids	g	1.75	6.06	14.10
Eicosapentaenoic acid	mg	36	120	279
Docosahexaenoic acid	mg	112	390	907
Omega 6:3 ratio (estimate)		10.8	10.8	10.8
ANTIOXIDANTS				
Vitamin C	mg	0.37	1.29	3.00
Beta-carotene	µg	0	0	0
Lycopene	µg	0	0	0
Lutein + Zeaxanthin	µg	0	0	0

1. Poach the cod until it flakes easily.
2. Prepare rice according to the package directions to yield 3 cups of cooked rice.
3. Stir the cod liver oil and safflower oil into the rice.
4. Sprinkle HILARY'S BLEND™ supplement over the rice and blend in.
5. Stir in flaked fish.

INGREDIENTS		
APPROX.	INGREDIENT	GRAMS
530 g raw	Cod, Atlantic, cooked	372
1 tsp	Cod liver oil	5
3 cups	Rice, brown, cooked	585
4 tsp	Safflower oil	18
2 scoops	HILARY'S BLEND™ supplement	20
	Total	1000

FEEDING GUIDE			
Body weight		Energy intake	Amount to feed
lbs	kg	kcal/day	grams/day
10	4.5	296	238
20	9.1	497	401
40	18.2	836	675
60	27.3	1134	914
80	36.4	1407	1134
100	45.5	1663	1341

METABOLIZABLE ENERGY

124 kcal/100 grams

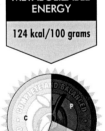

Supplement for home-made meals

R4

Transitioning Recipe 4

1. Pan-broil lean (10% fat) beef to brown crumbles. Cool.
2. Prepare the egg noodles according to the package to yield 3 cups of cooked noodles. Drain and cool.
3. Mix the cod liver oil and safflower oil into the beef crumbles.
4. Sprinkle HILARY'S BLEND™ supplement over the beef mixture and blend in.
5. Stir in the noodles.

INGREDIENTS

APPROX.	INGREDIENT	GRAMS
650 g raw	Beef, ground, cooked	485
1 tsp	Cod liver oil	5
3 cups	Egg noodles, cooked	480
1 tsp	Safflower oil	5
2½ scoops	HILARY'S BLEND™ supplement	15
	Total	1000

METABOLIZABLE ENERGY

188 kcal/100 grams

FEEDING GUIDE

Body weight		Energy intake	Amount to feed
lbs	kg	kcal/day	grams/day
10	4.5	296	157
20	9.1	497	265
40	18.2	836	445
60	27.3	1134	603
80	36.4	1407	748
100	45.5	1663	885

NUTRITION

		Per 100g As Fed	Per 100g Dry Matter	Per 1000 kcal
PROTEIN	g	15.98	40.93	85.12
Arginine	g	0.98	2.50	5.20
Histidine	g	0.51	1.31	2.72
Isoleucine	g	0.70	1.79	3.72
Leucine	g	1.25	3.20	6.66
Lysine	g	1.21	3.10	6.45
Methionine + Cystine	g	0.59	1.52	3.16
Phenylalanine + Tyrosine	g	1.12	2.88	5.99
Threonine	g	0.61	1.55	3.22
Tryptophan	g	0.10	0.25	0.52
Valine	g	0.78	2.00	4.16
FAT (LIPID)	g	7.83	20.06	41.72
Linoleic acid	g	0.79	2.01	4.18
MINERALS				
Calcium	mg	343.52	879.90	1829.96
Phosphorus	mg	267.73	685.77	1426.22
Calcium to Phosphorus ratio		1.28	1.28	1.28
Potassium	mg	415.75	1064.90	2214.71
Sodium	mg	49.22	126.06	262.17
Magnesium	mg	27.26	69.83	145.23
Iron	mg	7.54	19.31	40.16
Copper	mg	0.55	1.41	2.93
Manganese	mg	0.53	1.36	2.83
Zinc	mg	11.69	29.94	62.27
Iodine	mg	0.15	0.38	0.79
Selenium	µg	21.80	55.85	116.15
VITAMINS				
Vitamin A	IU	510	1307	2717
Vitamin D	IU	59	150	313
Vitamin E	mg	7.80	19.97	41.53
Thiamin	mg	0.10	0.24	0.50
Riboflavin	mg	0.30	0.78	1.62
Niacin	mg	3.89	9.97	20.73
Pantothenic acid	mg	1.52	3.89	8.09
Pyridoxine	mg	0.31	0.78	1.62
Folic acid	µg	20.00	51.23	106.54
Choline	mg	144.38	369.81	769.11
Vitamin B12	µg	3.36	8.60	17.89
OTHER (non-essential nutrients)				
Total dietary fiber	g	1.20	3.08	6.41
FATTY ACIDS				
Polyunsaturated fatty acids	g	0.96	2.46	5.12
Eicosapentaenoic acid	mg	34	90	187
Docosahexaenoic acid	mg	55	140	291
Omega 6:3 ratio (estimate)		9.8	9.8	9.8
ANTIOXIDANTS				
Vitamin C	mg	0	0	0
Beta-carotene	µg	0.5	1.2	2.6
Lycopene	µg	0	0	0
Lutein + Zeaxanthin	µg	18.2	46.7	97.2

Hilary's Blend™
Supplement for home-made meals

NUTRITION		Per 100g As Fed	Per 100g Dry Matter	Per 1000 kcal
PROTEIN	g	9.70	32.30	73.50
Arginine	g	0.61	2.02	4.60
Histidine	g	0.28	0.93	2.12
Isoleucine	g	0.44	1.47	3.35
Leucine	g	0.79	2.63	5.98
Lysine	g	0.81	2.69	6.12
Methionine + Cystine	g	0.38	1.27	2.89
Phenylalanine + Tyrosine	g	0.73	2.44	5.55
Threonine	g	0.41	1.38	3.14
Tryptophan	g	0.11	0.37	0.84
Valine	g	0.51	1.70	3.87
FAT (LIPID)	g	3.88	12.93	29.42
Linoleic acid	g	1.55	5.18	11.79
MINERALS				
Calcium	mg	340.90	1135.43	2583.69
Phosphorus	mg	235.11	783.10	1781.96
Calcium to Phosphorus ratio		1.45	1.45	1.45
Potassium	mg	295.17	983.14	2237.15
Sodium	mg	23.99	79.90	181.81
Magnesium	mg	49.67	165.44	376.46
Iron	mg	6.09	20.28	46.15
Copper	mg	0.52	1.75	3.98
Manganese	mg	0.81	2.69	6.12
Zinc	mg	8.55	28.47	64.78
Iodine	mg	0.15	0.50	1.14
Selenium	µg	28.87	96.17	218.84
VITAMINS				
Vitamin A	IU	507	1687	3839
Vitamin D	IU	59	196	445
Vitamin E	mg	7.52	25.04	56.98
Thiamin	mg	0.12	0.40	0.91
Riboflavin	mg	0.24	0.79	1.80
Niacin	mg	3.32	11.07	25.19
Pantothenic acid	mg	1.22	4.05	9.22
Pyridoxine	mg	0.24	0.79	1.80
Folic acid	µg	20.00	66.61	151.57
Choline	mg	105.59	351.70	800.30
Vitamin B12	µg	2.40	8.00	18.20
OTHER (non-essential nutrients)				
Total dietary fiber	g	1.54	5.14	11.70
FATTY ACIDS				
Polyunsaturated fatty acids	g	2.03	6.77	15.41
Eicosapentaenoic acid	mg	115	380	865
Docosahexaenoic acid	mg	271	900	2048
Omega 6:3 ratio (estimate)		4.3	4.3	4.3
ANTIOXIDANTS				
Vitamin C	mg	0	0	0
Beta-carotene	µg	0	0	0
Lycopene	µg	0	0	0
Lutein + Zeaxanthin	µg	0	0	0

Transitioning Recipe 5

1. Prepare rice according to the package to yield 3⅛ cups of cooked rice. Cool.
2. Stir in the cod liver oil and safflower oil.
3. Sprinkle HILARY'S BLEND™ supplement over the rice and blend in.
4. Stir in the tuna.

INGREDIENTS		
APPROX.	INGREDIENT	GRAMS
1 tsp	Cod liver oil	5
3⅛ cups	Rice, brown, cooked	608
4 tsp	Safflower oil	18
	Tuna, canned in water, drained	344
2½ scoops	HILARY'S BLEND™ supplement	25
	Total	1000

FEEDING GUIDE			
Body weight		Energy intake	Amount to feed
lbs	kg	kcal/day	grams/day
10	4.5	296	224
20	9.1	497	377
40	18.2	836	634
60	27.3	1134	859
80	36.4	1407	1066
100	45.5	1663	1260

METABOLIZABLE ENERGY

132 kcal/100 grams

Hilary's Blend™
Supplement for home-made meals

Transitioning Recipe 6

1. Gently simmer chicken until tender. Dice finely.
2. Prepare rice according to the package to yield 2½ cups of cooked rice. Cool.
3. Stir the cod liver oil and safflower oil into the rice.
4. Sprinkle HILARY'S BLEND™ supplement over the rice and blend in.
5. Stir in the grated carrots and diced chicken.

INGREDIENTS		
APPROX.	INGREDIENT	GRAMS
½ cup	Carrots, raw, grated	55
810 g raw	Chicken breast, cooked	420
1 tsp	Cod liver oil	5
2½ cups	Rice, brown, cooked	486
3 tsp	Safflower oil	14
2 scoops	HILARY'S BLEND™ supplement	20
	Total	1000

METABOLIZABLE ENERGY

143 kcal/100 grams

FEEDING GUIDE			
Body weight		Energy intake	Amount to feed
lbs	kg	kcal/day	grams/day
10	4.5	296	207
20	9.1	497	348
40	18.2	836	585
60	27.3	1134	793
80	36.4	1407	984
100	45.5	1663	1163

Hilary's Blend™
Supplement for home-made meals

NUTRITION		Per 100g As Fed	Per 100g Dry Matter	Per 1000 kcal
PROTEIN	g	14.33	44.39	100.11
Arginine	g	0.89	2.74	6.18
Histidine	g	0.44	1.36	3.07
Isoleucine	g	0.75	2.31	5.21
Leucine	g	1.09	3.37	7.60
Lysine	g	1.16	3.59	8.10
Methionine + Cystine	g	0.58	1.79	4.04
Phenylalanine + Tyrosine	g	1.07	3.33	7.51
Threonine	g	0.61	1.88	4.24
Tryptophan	g	0.17	0.52	1.17
Valine	g	0.72	2.24	5.05
FAT (LIPID)	g	3.85	11.92	26.88
Linoleic acid	g	1.45	4.50	10.15
MINERALS				
Calcium	mg	276.98	857.71	1934.35
Phosphorus	mg	226.02	699.93	1578.52
Calcium to Phosphorus ratio		1.23	1.23	1.23
Potassium	mg	296.02	916.68	2067.34
Sodium	mg	41.00	126.97	286.35
Magnesium	mg	37.01	114.60	258.45
Iron	mg	5.26	16.30	36.76
Copper	mg	0.44	1.35	3.04
Manganese	mg	0.76	2.34	5.28
Zinc	mg	7.19	22.25	50.18
Iodine	mg	0.12	0.37	0.83
Selenium	µg	16.36	50.66	114.25
VITAMINS				
Vitamin A	IU	1433	4438	10008
Vitamin D	IU	57	177	398
Vitamin E	mg	6.16	19.09	43.05
Thiamin	mg	0.13	0.40	0.90
Riboflavin	mg	0.22	0.69	1.56
Niacin	mg	6.88	21.29	48.01
Pantothenic acid	mg	1.36	4.21	9.49
Pyridoxine	mg	0.39	1.21	2.73
Folic acid	µg	16.00	49.55	111.75
Choline	mg	84.96	263.08	593.31
Vitamin B12	µg	1.74	5.40	12.18
OTHER (non-essential nutrients)				
Total dietary fiber	g	1.53	4.73	10.67
FATTY ACIDS				
Polyunsaturated fatty acids	g	1.64	5.09	11.48
Eicosapentaenoic acid	mg	39	120	271
Docosahexaenoic acid	mg	63	200	451
Omega 6:3 ratio (estimate)		15.1	15.1	15.1
ANTIOXIDANTS				
Vitamin C	mg	0.33	1.00	2.26
Beta-carotene	µg	456	1411	3182
Lycopene	µg	0	0	0
Lutein + Zeaxanthin	µg	14	44	98

Transitioning Recipe 7

NUTRITION				
		Per 100g As Fed	Per 100g Dry Matter	Per 1000 kcal
PROTEIN	g	7.29	32.05	66.47
Arginine	g	0.48	2.10	4.36
Histidine	g	0.22	0.98	2.03
Isoleucine	g	0.31	1.38	2.86
Leucine	g	0.56	2.47	5.12
Lysine	g	0.53	2.31	4.79
Methionine + Cystine	g	0.28	1.21	2.51
Phenylalanine + Tyrosine	g	0.54	2.37	4.91
Threonine	g	0.28	1.21	2.51
Tryptophan	g	0.06	0.24	0.50
Valine	g	0.37	1.62	3.36
FAT (LIPID)	g	4.91	21.61	44.82
Linoleic acid	g	1.37	6.02	12.48
MINERALS				
Calcium	mg	207.10	910.92	1889.09
Phosphorus	mg	167.74	737.80	1530.07
Calcium to Phosphorus ratio		1.23	1.23	1.23
Potassium	mg	239.78	1054.67	2187.20
Sodium	mg	20.08	88.31	183.14
Magnesium	mg	24.88	109.41	226.90
Iron	mg	4.54	19.96	41.39
Copper	mg	0.33	1.47	3.05
Manganese	mg	0.66	2.92	6.06
Zinc	mg	6.49	28.55	59.21
Iodine	mg	0.09	0.40	0.83
Selenium	µg	9.74	42.84	88.84
VITAMINS				
Vitamin A	IU	504	2217	4597
Vitamin D	IU	55	243	504
Vitamin E	mg	4.70	20.66	42.85
Thiamin	mg	0.12	0.55	1.14
Riboflavin	mg	0.17	0.76	1.58
Niacin	mg	1.66	7.28	15.10
Pantothenic acid	mg	0.90	3.97	8.23
Pyridoxine	mg	0.14	0.63	1.31
Folic acid	µg	12.00	52.78	109.46
Choline	mg	83.02	365.18	757.32
Vitamin B12	µg	1.72	7.54	15.64
OTHER (non-essential nutrients)				
Total dietary fiber	g	1.75	7.68	15.93
FATTY ACIDS				
Polyunsaturated fatty acids	g	1.52	6.67	13.83
Eicosapentaenoic acid	mg	34	150	311
Docosahexaenoic acid	mg	55	240	498
Omega 6:3 ratio (estimate)		16.0	16.0	16.0
ANTIOXIDANTS				
Vitamin C	mg	0.7	3.2	6.6
Beta-carotene	µg	2.4	10.4	21.6
Lycopene	µg	0	0	0
Lutein + Zeaxanthin	µg	132.3	581.8	1206.6

1. Pan-broil lean (10% fat) beef to brown crumbles. Cool.
2. Prepare oatmeal according to the package directions to yield 3 cups of cooked oatmeal. Cool.
3. Mix the cod liver oil and safflower oil into the oatmeal.
4. Sprinkle HILARY'S BLEND™ supplement over the oatmeal and blend in.
5. Stir in the beef crumbles and blueberries.

INGREDIENTS		
APPROX.	INGREDIENT	GRAMS
250 g raw	Beef, ground, cooked	190
1 cup	Blueberries, raw	74
1 tsp	Cod liver oil	5
3 cups	Oatmeal, cooked	702
3 tsp	Safflower oil	14
1½ scoops	HILARY'S BLEND™ supplement	15
	Total	1000

FEEDING GUIDE			
Body weight		Energy intake	Amount to feed
lbs	kg	kcal/day	grams/day
10	4.5	296	269
20	9.1	497	452
40	18.2	836	760
60	27.3	1134	1031
80	36.4	1407	1279
100	45.5	1663	1512

METABOLIZABLE ENERGY

110 kcal/100 grams

Hilary's Blend™

Supplement for home-made meals

R8

Transitioning Recipe 8

1. Hard boil eggs. Discard shells and mash coarsely.
2. Prepare rice according to the package to yield 2½ cups of cooked rice. Cool.
3. Stir the cod liver oil into the rice.
4. Sprinkle HILARY'S BLEND™ supplement over the rice and blend in.
5. Stir in the chopped broccoli and egg.

INGREDIENTS

APPROX.	INGREDIENT	GRAMS
½ cup	Broccoli, raw, chopped	46
1 tsp	Cod liver oil	5
9 large	Eggs, hard-boiled	450
2½ cups	Rice, brown, cooked	479
2 scoops	HILARY'S BLEND™ supplement	20
	Total	1000

METABOLIZABLE ENERGY

130 kcal/100 grams

FEEDING GUIDE

Body weight		Energy intake	Amount to feed
lbs	kg	kcal/day	grams/day
10	4.5	296	227
20	9.1	497	383
40	18.2	836	643
60	27.3	1134	872
80	36.4	1407	1082
100	45.5	1663	1279

Hilary's Blend™
Supplement for home-made meals

NUTRITION

		Per 100g As Fed	Per 100g Dry Matter	Per 1000 kcal
PROTEIN	g	7.03	25.76	54.13
Arginine	g	0.44	1.62	3.40
Histidine	g	0.17	0.62	1.30
Isoleucine	g	0.37	1.34	2.82
Leucine	g	0.59	2.17	4.56
Lysine	g	0.46	1.69	3.55
Methionine + Cystine	g	0.35	1.30	2.73
Phenylalanine + Tyrosine	g	0.65	2.39	5.02
Threonine	g	0.32	1.18	2.48
Tryptophan	g	0.09	0.32	0.67
Valine	g	0.42	1.55	3.26
FAT (LIPID)	g	5.72	20.98	44.08
Linoleic acid	g	0.69	2.52	5.30
MINERALS				
Calcium	mg	293.45	1075.98	2260.94
Phosphorus	mg	208.19	763.36	1604.03
Calcium to Phosphorus ratio		1.41	1.41	1.41
Potassium	mg	241.83	886.71	1863.23
Sodium	mg	63.41	232.50	488.55
Magnesium	mg	29.33	107.55	225.99
Iron	mg	5.38	19.71	41.42
Copper	mg	0.42	1.54	3.24
Manganese	mg	0.76	2.77	5.82
Zinc	mg	7.24	26.54	55.77
Iodine	mg	0.12	0.44	0.92
Selenium	µg	18.67	68.45	143.83
VITAMINS				
Vitamin A	IU	792	2905	6105
Vitamin D	IU	57	209	439
Vitamin E	mg	6.51	23.88	50.18
Thiamin	mg	0.13	0.47	0.99
Riboflavin	mg	0.41	1.50	3.15
Niacin	mg	1.11	4.07	8.55
Pantothenic acid	mg	1.59	5.84	12.27
Pyridoxine	mg	0.19	0.70	1.47
Folic acid	µg	16.00	58.67	123.28
Choline	mg	186.65	684.38	1438.08
Vitamin B12	µg	2.10	7.70	16.18
OTHER (non-essential nutrients)				
Total dietary fiber	g	1.48	5.43	11.41
FATTY ACIDS				
Polyunsaturated fatty acids	g	0.91	3.32	6.98
Eicosapentaenoic acid	mg	37	130	273
Docosahexaenoic acid	mg	72	260	546
Omega 6:3 ratio (estimate)		7.3	7.3	7.3
ANTIOXIDANTS				
Vitamin C	mg	4.10	15.04	31.60
Beta-carotene	µg	21.6	79.0	166.1
Lycopene	µg	0	0	0
Lutein + Zeaxanthin	µg	223.4	819.1	1721.1

Transitioning Recipe 9

1. Poach the salmon until it flakes easily.
2. Prepare the rice according to the package to yield 3¼ cups of cooked rice. Cool.
3. Stir the cod liver oil and safflower oil into the rice.
4. Sprinkle HILARY'S BLEND™ supplement over the rice and blend in.
5. Stir in the chopped beans and salmon.

NUTRITION		Per 100g As Fed	Per 100g Dry Matter	Per 1000 kcal
PROTEIN	g	7.68	24.54	51.95
Arginine	g	0.48	1.55	3.28
Histidine	g	0.22	0.70	1.48
Isoleucine	g	0.35	1.11	2.35
Leucine	g	0.63	2.00	4.23
Lysine	g	0.61	1.96	4.15
Methionine + Cystine	g	0.30	0.95	2.01
Phenylalanine + Tyrosine	g	0.58	1.86	3.94
Threonine	g	0.33	1.04	2.20
Tryptophan	g	0.09	0.28	0.59
Valine	g	0.41	1.30	2.75
FAT (LIPID)	g	6.21	19.84	42.00
Linoleic acid	g	1.72	5.51	11.67
MINERALS				
Calcium	mg	276.40	883.31	1870.03
Phosphorus	mg	210.42	672.44	1423.61
Calcium to Phosphorus ratio		1.31	1.31	1.31
Potassium	mg	292.01	933.19	1975.63
Sodium	mg	42.25	135.03	285.87
Magnesium	mg	46.40	148.30	313.96
Iron	mg	4.82	15.39	32.58
Copper	mg	0.44	1.41	2.99
Manganese	mg	0.79	2.52	5.34
Zinc	mg	6.93	22.14	46.87
Iodine	mg	0.12	0.38	0.80
Selenium	µg	17.63	56.33	119.25
VITAMINS				
Vitamin A	IU	551	1762	3731
Vitamin D	IU	57	182	386
Vitamin E	mg	6.04	19.31	40.88
Thiamin	mg	0.21	0.65	1.38
Riboflavin	mg	0.22	0.70	1.48
Niacin	mg	3.49	11.16	23.63
Pantothenic acid	mg	1.38	4.42	9.36
Pyridoxine	mg	0.33	1.05	2.22
Folic acid	µg	16.00	51.13	108.25
Choline	mg	86.67	276.96	586.34
Vitamin B12	µg	2.35	7.52	15.92
OTHER (non-essential nutrients)				
Total dietary fiber	g	1.69	5.39	11.41
FATTY ACIDS				
Polyunsaturated fatty acids	g	2.85	9.12	19.31
Eicosapentaenoic acid	mg	220	700	1482
Docosahexaenoic acid	mg	447	1430	3027
Omega 6:3 ratio (estimate)		3.3	3.3	3.3
ANTIOXIDANTS				
Vitamin C	mg	1.89	6.05	12.81
Beta-carotene	µg	20.8	66.6	141.0
Lycopene	µg	0	0	0
Lutein + Zeaxanthin	µg	35.2	112.5	238.1

INGREDIENTS		
APPROX.	INGREDIENT	GRAMS
½ cup	Beans, green, raw, chopped	55
1 tsp	Cod liver oil	5
3¼ cups	Rice, brown, cooked	633
4 tsp	Safflower oil	18
385 g raw	Salmon, cooked	269
1 pinch	Salt	<1
2 scoops	HILARY'S BLEND™ supplement	20
	Total	1000

FEEDING GUIDE				
Body weight		Energy intake	Amount to feed	
lbs	kg	kcal/day	grams/day	
10	4.5	296	200	
20	9.1	497	336	
40	18.2	836	565	
60	27.3	1134	766	
80	36.4	1407	951	
100	45.5	1663	1124	

METABOLIZABLE ENERGY

148 kcal/100 grams

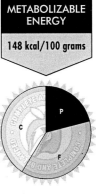

Supplement for home-made meals

Transitioning Recipe 10

1. Prick potatoes with a fork, then microwave until soft.
2. Add the tomato sauce to the potatoes and mash.
3. Pan-broil lean (10% fat) beef to brown crumbles. Cool.
4. Mix the cod liver oil and safflower oil into the cooled beef crumbles.
5. Sprinkle HILARY'S BLEND™ supplement over the beef crumbles and mix thoroughly.
6. Stir the mashed potatoes into the beef crumbles.

INGREDIENTS		
APPROX.	INGREDIENT	GRAMS
470 g raw	Beef, ground, cooked	350
1 tsp	Cod liver oil	5
4 small	Potatoes, baked in skin	555
2 tsp	Safflower oil	9
¼ cup	Tomato sauce, canned	61
2 scoops	HILARY'S BLEND™ supplement	20
	Total	1000

METABOLIZABLE ENERGY

147 kcal/100 grams

FEEDING GUIDE		
Body weight	Energy intake	Amount to feed
lbs / kg	kcal/day	grams/day
10 / 4.5	296	201
20 / 9.1	497	338
40 / 18.2	836	569
60 / 27.3	1134	771
80 / 36.4	1407	957
100 / 45.5	1663	1131

Hilary's Bleñd™

Supplement for home-made meals

NUTRITION		Per 100g As Fed	Per 100g Dry Matter	Per 1000 kcal
PROTEIN	g	11.43	35.32	77.81
Arginine	g	0.70	2.17	4.78
Histidine	g	0.36	1.11	2.45
Isoleucine	g	0.50	1.53	3.37
Leucine	g	0.86	2.66	5.86
Lysine	g	0.91	2.82	6.21
Methionine + Cystine	g	0.40	1.25	2.75
Phenylalanine + Tyrosine	g	0.81	2.52	5.55
Threonine	g	0.44	1.37	3.02
Tryptophan	g	0.08	0.24	0.53
Valine	g	0.57	1.76	3.88
FAT (LIPID)	g	5.70	17.61	38.80
Linoleic acid	g	0.82	2.53	5.57
MINERALS				
Calcium	mg	278.72	861.52	1898.04
Phosphorus	mg	215.94	667.46	1470.50
Calcium to Phosphorus ratio		1.29	1.29	1.29
Potassium	mg	618.67	1912.29	4213.02
Sodium	mg	71.66	221.50	487.99
Magnesium	mg	29.24	90.37	199.10
Iron	mg	6.35	19.61	43.20
Copper	mg	0.47	1.45	3.19
Manganese	mg	0.43	1.34	2.95
Zinc	mg	9.05	27.98	61.64
Iodine	mg	0.12	0.37	0.82
Selenium	µg	7.69	23.77	52.37
VITAMINS				
Vitamin A	IU	527	1628	3587
Vitamin D	IU	57	176	388
Vitamin E	mg	6.26	19.36	42.65
Thiamin	mg	0.10	0.31	0.68
Riboflavin	mg	0.26	0.80	1.76
Niacin	mg	3.54	10.95	24.12
Pantothenic acid	mg	1.29	3.99	8.79
Pyridoxine	mg	0.39	1.20	2.64
Folic acid	µg	16.00	49.46	108.97
Choline	mg	112.63	348.14	767.00
Vitamin B12	µg	2.55	7.88	17.36
OTHER (non-essential nutrients)				
Total dietary fiber	g	1.81	5.60	12.34
FATTY ACIDS				
Polyunsaturated fatty acids	g	0.97	3.00	6.61
Eicosapentaenoic acid	mg	34	110	242
Docosahexaenoic acid	mg	55	170	375
Omega 6:3 ratio (estimate)		9.7	9.7	9.7
ANTIOXIDANTS				
Vitamin C	mg	5.8	17.8	39.2
Beta-carotene	µg	16.1	49.7	109.5
Lycopene	µg	924.3	2856.9	6294.2
Lutein + Zeaxanthin	µg	16.7	51.5	113.4

Adult Recipe 1

NUTRITION		Per 100g As Fed	Per 100g Dry Matter	Per 1000 kcal
PROTEIN	g	9.82	27.68	62.62
Arginine	g	0.51	1.43	3.23
Histidine	g	0.25	0.72	1.63
Isoleucine	g	0.45	1.27	2.87
Leucine	g	0.83	2.33	5.27
Lysine	g	0.56	1.59	3.60
Methionine + Cystine	g	0.41	1.17	2.65
Phenylalanine + Tyrosine	g	0.83	2.34	5.29
Threonine	g	0.40	1.14	2.58
Tryptophan	g	0.13	0.36	0.81
Valine	g	0.54	1.52	3.44
FAT (LIPID)	g	4.36	12.28	27.78
Linoleic acid	g	0.84	2.37	5.36
MINERALS				
Calcium	mg	279.61	788.45	1783.58
Phosphorus	mg	229.16	646.19	1461.77
Calcium to Phosphorus ratio		1.22	1.22	1.22
Potassium	mg	272.64	768.80	1739.13
Sodium	mg	72.57	204.63	462.90
Magnesium	mg	19.61	55.29	125.07
Iron	mg	6.55	18.46	41.76
Copper	mg	2.62	7.38	16.69
Manganese	mg	0.55	1.54	3.48
Zinc	mg	7.74	21.82	49.36
Iodine	mg	0.12	0.34	0.77
Selenium	µg	25.85	72.89	164.89
VITAMINS				
Vitamin A	IU	4552	12835	29034
Vitamin D	IU	57	161	364
Vitamin E	mg	6.40	18.03	40.79
Thiamin	mg	0.24	0.68	1.54
Riboflavin	mg	0.86	2.41	5.45
Niacin	mg	3.96	11.16	25.25
Pantothenic acid	mg	2.18	6.16	13.93
Pyridoxine	mg	0.27	0.77	1.74
Folic acid	µg	16.00	45.12	102.07
Choline	mg	191.97	541.33	1224.56
Vitamin B12	µg	14.29	40.30	91.16
OTHER (non-essential nutrients)				
Total dietary fiber	g	1.60	4.51	10.20
FATTY ACIDS				
Polyunsaturated fatty acids	g	1.04	2.94	6.65
Eicosapentaenoic acid	mg	35	100	226
Docosahexaenoic acid	mg	62	180	407
Omega 6:3 ratio (estimate)		9.7	9.7	9.7
ANTIOXIDANTS				
Vitamin C	mg	0.53	1.50	3.39
Beta-carotene	µg	42.2	119.1	269.5
Lycopene	µg	924.3	2606.3	5895.8
Lutein + Zeaxanthin	µg	74.5	210.1	475.3

1. Boil liver in water until cooked through. Dice finely.
2. Prepare macaroni according to package directions to yield 4 cups of cooked macaroni.
3. Hard boil eggs. Discard shell and mash coarsely.
4. Add cod liver oil, safflower oil, and HILARY'S BLEND™ supplement to the tomato sauce and mix thoroughly.
5. Stir all ingredients together.

INGREDIENTS		
APPROX.	**INGREDIENT**	**GRAMS**
1 tsp	Cod liver oil	5
4 large	Eggs, hard-boiled	200
215 g raw	Liver, beef, cooked	150
4 cups	Macaroni, elbow, boiled	560
1 tsp	Safflower oil	5
¼ cup	Tomato sauce, canned	60
2 scoops	HILARY'S BLEND™ supplement	20
	Total	1000

FEEDING GUIDE			
Body weight		Energy intake	Amount to feed
lbs	kg	kcal/day	grams/day
10	4.5	296	188
20	9.1	497	317
40	18.2	836	533
60	27.3	1134	722
80	36.4	1407	896
100	45.5	1663	1059

METABOLIZABLE ENERGY

157 kcal/100 grams

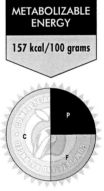

Supplement for home-made meals

Adult Recipe 2

1. Pan-broil lean (10% fat) beef to brown crumbles.
2. Hard boil egg. Discard shell and mash coarsely.
3. Pulse carrots, spinach, honey, and safflower oil to small kernels.
4. Add HILARY'S BLEND™ supplement to the tomato sauce and mix thoroughly.
5. Stir all ingredients together.

INGREDIENTS

APPROX.	INGREDIENT	GRAMS
1 cup	Applesauce, canned	244
540 g raw	Beef, ground, cooked	404
1 cup	Carrots, raw, grated	110
1 tsp	Cod liver oil	5
1 large	Egg, hard-boiled	50
1 tbsp	Honey	21
2½ tsp	Safflower oil	11
½ tsp	Salmon oil	2
1 leaf	Spinach, raw	10
½ cup	Tomato sauce, canned	123
2 scoops	HILARY'S BLEND™ supplement	20
	Total	1000

METABOLIZABLE ENERGY

142 kcal/100 grams

FEEDING GUIDE

Body weight		Energy intake	Amount to feed
lbs	kg	kcal/day	grams/day
10	4.5	296	208
20	9.1	497	350
40	18.2	836	589
60	27.3	1134	798
80	36.4	1407	991
100	45.5	1663	1171

NUTRITION

		Per 100g As Fed	Per 100g Dry Matter	Per 1000 kcal
PROTEIN	g	12.46	43.22	87.72
Arginine	g	0.79	2.74	5.56
Histidine	g	0.40	1.39	2.82
Isoleucine	g	0.56	1.92	3.90
Leucine	g	0.97	3.36	6.82
Lysine	g	1.02	3.54	7.19
Methionine + Cystine	g	0.47	1.63	3.31
Phenylalanine + Tyrosine	g	0.89	3.09	6.27
Threonine	g	0.51	1.76	3.57
Tryptophan	g	0.08	0.27	0.55
Valine	g	0.62	2.14	4.34
FAT (LIPID)	g	7.26	25.17	51.09
Linoleic acid	g	1.04	3.62	7.35
MINERALS				
Calcium	mg	280.04	971.11	1971.08
Phosphorus	mg	206.93	717.58	1456.48
Calcium to Phosphorus ratio		1.35	1.35	1.35
Potassium	mg	432.12	1498.47	3041.47
Sodium	mg	118.45	410.75	833.71
Magnesium	mg	19.53	67.72	137.45
Iron	mg	6.13	21.27	43.17
Copper	mg	0.43	1.50	3.04
Manganese	mg	0.36	1.26	2.56
Zinc	mg	9.33	32.35	65.66
Iodine	mg	0.12	0.42	0.85
Selenium	µg	10.28	35.65	72.36
VITAMINS				
Vitamin A	IU	2522	8746	17752
Vitamin D	IU	57	198	401
Vitamin E	mg	6.55	22.71	46.09
Thiamin	mg	0.08	0.29	0.59
Riboflavin	mg	0.29	0.99	2.01
Niacin	mg	3.36	11.64	23.63
Pantothenic acid	mg	1.25	4.34	8.81
Pyridoxine	mg	0.28	0.95	1.93
Folic acid	µg	16.00	55.48	112.61
Choline	mg	131.25	455.13	923.78
Vitamin B12	µg	2.75	9.54	19.36
OTHER (non-essential nutrients)				
Total dietary fiber	g	1.31	4.55	9.24
FATTY ACIDS				
Polyunsaturated fatty acids	g	1.29	4.46	9.05
Eicosapentaenoic acid	mg	61	210	426
Docosahexaenoic acid	mg	93	320	650
Omega 6:3 ratio (estimate)		7.4	7.4	7.4
ANTIOXIDANTS				
Vitamin C	mg	2.09	7.26	14.74
Beta-carotene	µg	997.0	3457.5	7017.7
Lycopene	µg	1863.8	6463.2	13118.4
Lutein + Zeaxanthin	µg	172.2	597.1	1211.9

Hilary's Blend™

Supplement for home-made meals

Adult Recipe 3

NUTRITION		Per 100g As Fed	Per 100g Dry Matter	Per 1000 kcal
PROTEIN	g	16.03	54.17	120.12
Arginine	g	0.96	3.25	7.21
Histidine	g	0.49	1.64	3.64
Isoleucine	g	0.85	2.86	6.34
Leucine	g	1.23	4.14	9.18
Lysine	g	1.33	4.49	9.96
Methionine + Cystine	g	0.67	2.25	4.99
Phenylalanine + Tyrosine	g	1.21	4.09	9.07
Threonine	g	0.69	2.34	5.19
Tryptophan	g	0.19	0.63	1.40
Valine	g	0.82	2.76	6.12
FAT (LIPID)	g	4.71	15.92	35.30
Linoleic acid	g	1.49	5.02	11.13
MINERALS				
Calcium	mg	279.89	945.71	2097.15
Phosphorus	mg	223.03	753.59	1671.12
Calcium to Phosphorus ratio		1.25	1.25	1.25
Potassium	mg	346.64	1171.27	2597.34
Sodium	mg	70.85	239.41	530.90
Magnesium	mg	22.78	76.96	170.66
Iron	mg	5.34	18.04	40.00
Copper	mg	0.41	1.38	3.06
Manganese	mg	0.37	1.25	2.77
Zinc	mg	7.11	24.03	53.29
Iodine	mg	0.12	0.41	0.91
Selenium	µg	15.81	53.41	118.44
VITAMINS				
Vitamin A	IU	1509	5100	11310
Vitamin D	IU	57	193	427
Vitamin E	mg	6.37	21.52	47.72
Thiamin	mg	0.11	0.37	0.82
Riboflavin	mg	0.29	0.96	2.13
Niacin	mg	6.92	23.38	51.85
Pantothenic acid	mg	1.44	4.86	10.78
Pyridoxine	mg	0.38	1.30	2.88
Folic acid	µg	16.00	54.06	119.88
Choline	mg	107.79	364.20	807.63
Vitamin B12	µg	1.87	6.31	13.99
OTHER (non-essential nutrients)				
Total dietary fiber	g	1.52	5.15	11.42
FATTY ACIDS				
Polyunsaturated fatty acids	g	1.71	5.76	12.77
Eicosapentaenoic acid	mg	40	130	288
Docosahexaenoic acid	mg	68	230	510
Omega 6:3 ratio (estimate)		14.8	14.8	14.8
ANTIOXIDANTS				
Vitamin C	mg	2.11	7.12	15.79
Beta-carotene	µg	466.8	1577.4	3498.0
Lycopene	µg	469.8	1587.3	3519.9
Lutein + Zeaxanthin	µg	67.1	226.9	503.1

1. Gently simmer chicken until tender. Dice finely.
2. Hard boil eggs. Discard shells and mash coarsely.
3. Boil sweet corn until tender.
4. Pulse blueberries, carrots, pears, cooked sweet corn, cod liver oil, and safflower oil to small kernels.
5. Add HILARY'S BLEND™ supplement to the tomato sauce and mix thoroughly.
6. Stir all ingredients together.

INGREDIENTS		
APPROX.	INGREDIENT	GRAMS
½ cup	Blueberries, raw	74
½ cup	Carrots, raw, grated	55
875 g raw	Chicken breast, cooked	456
1 tsp	Cod liver oil	5
2 large	Eggs, hard-boiled	100
½ cup	Pears, raw, chopped	81
3 tsp	Safflower oil	14
1 cup	Sweet corn, boiled	164
⅛ cup	Tomato sauce, canned	31
2 scoops	HILARY'S BLEND™ supplement	20
	Total	1000

FEEDING GUIDE			
Body weight		Energy intake	Amount to feed
lbs	kg	kcal/day	grams/day
10	4.5	296	222
20	9.1	497	374
40	18.2	836	629
60	27.3	1134	852
80	36.4	1407	1058
100	45.5	1663	1250

METABOLIZABLE ENERGY

133 kcal/100 grams

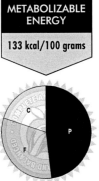

Hilary's
Supplement for home-made meals *Blend* ™

Adult Recipe 4

1. Poach salmon until it flakes easily.
2. Pulse broccoli, cucumber, spinach, zucchini, safflower oil and cod liver oil to small kernels.
3. Add HILARY'S BLEND™ supplement to the tomato sauce and mix thoroughly.
4. Stir all ingredients together.

INGREDIENTS		
APPROX.	INGREDIENT	GRAMS
2 cups	Broccoli, raw, chopped	182
½ tsp	Cod liver oil	2
1½ cups	Cucumber, raw with peel, sliced	156
3 tsp	Safflower oil	14
510 g raw	Salmon, Atlantic, cooked	356
4 leaves	Spinach, raw	40
½ cup	Tomato sauce, canned	122
1 cup	Zucchini, raw, sliced	113
1½ scoops	HILARY'S BLEND™ supplement	15
	Total	1000

METABOLIZABLE ENERGY

102 kcal/100 grams

FEEDING GUIDE			
Body weight		Energy intake	Amount to feed
lbs	kg	kcal/day	grams/day
10	4.5	296	290
20	9.1	497	488
40	18.2	836	820
60	27.3	1134	1112
80	36.4	1407	1379
100	45.5	1663	1630

Hilary's Blend™
Supplement for home-made meals

NUTRITION		Per 100g As Fed	Per 100g Dry Matter	Per 1000 kcal
PROTEIN	g	8.90	43.67	86.94
Arginine	g	0.53	2.59	5.16
Histidine	g	0.25	1.24	2.47
Isoleucine	g	0.39	1.94	3.86
Leucine	g	0.69	3.38	6.73
Lysine	g	0.77	3.79	7.54
Methionine + Cystine	g	0.34	1.67	3.32
Phenylalanine + Tyrosine	g	0.64	3.15	6.27
Threonine	g	0.38	1.85	3.68
Tryptophan	g	0.10	0.50	1.00
Valine	g	0.45	2.20	4.38
FAT (LIPID)	g	6.14	30.14	60.00
Linoleic acid	g	1.30	6.40	12.74
MINERALS				
Calcium	mg	221.63	1088.26	2166.47
Phosphorus	mg	180.89	888.23	1768.26
Calcium to Phosphorus ratio		1.23	1.23	1.23
Potassium	mg	421.96	2071.90	4124.66
Sodium	mg	99.02	486.23	967.97
Magnesium	mg	26.02	127.74	254.30
Iron	mg	4.02	19.76	39.34
Copper	mg	0.33	1.62	3.23
Manganese	mg	0.35	1.72	3.42
Zinc	mg	5.17	25.39	50.55
Iodine	mg	0.09	0.44	0.88
Selenium	µg	15.33	75.26	149.82
VITAMINS				
Vitamin A	IU	788	3868	7700
Vitamin D	IU	25	124	247
Vitamin E	mg	4.92	24.13	48.04
Thiamin	mg	0.19	0.91	1.81
Riboflavin	mg	0.23	1.11	2.21
Niacin	mg	3.44	16.88	33.60
Pantothenic acid	mg	1.29	6.33	12.60
Pyridoxine	mg	0.36	1.76	3.50
Folic acid	µg	12.00	58.92	117.30
Choline	mg	66.62	327.12	651.22
Vitamin B12	µg	2.20	10.79	21.48
OTHER (non-essential nutrients)				
Total dietary fiber	g	1.32	6.49	12.92
FATTY ACIDS				
Polyunsaturated fatty acids	g	2.70	13.26	26.40
Eicosapentaenoic acid	mg	259	1270	2528
Docosahexaenoic acid	mg	541	2650	5276
Omega 6:3 ratio (estimate)		2.4	2.4	2.4
ANTIOXIDANTS				
Vitamin C	mg	21.89	107.47	213.95
Beta-carotene	µg	336.8	1653.9	3292.4
Lycopene	µg	1848.5	9076.8	18069.7
Lutein + Zeaxanthin	µg	987.0	4846.3	9647.8

Adult Recipe 5

NUTRITION		Per 100g As Fed	Per 100g Dry Matter	Per 1000 kcal
PROTEIN	g	13.29	56.22	114.34
Arginine	g	0.74	3.11	6.33
Histidine	g	0.40	1.69	3.44
Isoleucine	g	0.65	2.76	5.61
Leucine	g	1.15	4.86	9.88
Lysine	g	1.16	4.91	9.99
Methionine + Cystine	g	0.52	2.21	4.49
Phenylalanine + Tyrosine	g	1.08	4.58	9.31
Threonine	g	0.58	2.47	5.02
Tryptophan	g	0.15	0.62	1.26
Valine	g	0.72	3.04	6.18
FAT (LIPID)	g	5.74	24.28	49.38
Linoleic acid	g	2.73	11.56	23.51
MINERALS				
Calcium	mg	229.53	971.22	1975.27
Phosphorus	mg	172.57	730.19	1485.06
Calcium to Phosphorus ratio		1.33	1.33	1.33
Potassium	mg	288.67	1221.45	2484.19
Sodium	mg	161.24	682.25	1387.56
Magnesium	mg	24.90	105.37	214.30
Iron	mg	3.83	16.22	32.99
Copper	mg	0.31	1.31	2.66
Manganese	mg	0.30	1.25	2.54
Zinc	mg	5.27	22.28	45.31
Iodine	mg	0.09	0.38	0.77
Selenium	µg	17.96	75.98	154.53
VITAMINS				
Vitamin A	IU	1065	4504	9161
Vitamin D	IU	55	234	475
Vitamin E	mg	4.94	20.90	42.51
Thiamin	mg	0.09	0.38	0.77
Riboflavin	mg	0.22	0.93	1.89
Niacin	mg	1.41	5.98	12.16
Pantothenic acid	mg	0.83	3.49	7.10
Pyridoxine	mg	0.20	0.86	1.75
Folic acid	µg	12.00	50.78	103.28
Choline	mg	96.22	407.11	827.98
Vitamin B12	µg	1.81	7.65	15.56
OTHER (non-essential nutrients)				
Total dietary fiber	g	0.92	3.90	7.93
FATTY ACIDS				
Polyunsaturated fatty acids	g	3.32	14.05	28.57
Eicosapentaenoic acid	mg	153	650	1322
Docosahexaenoic acid	mg	280	1190	2420
Omega 6:3 ratio (estimate)		6.7	6.7	6.7
ANTIOXIDANTS				
Vitamin C	mg	13.89	58.77	119.53
Beta-carotene	µg	269.2	1139.0	2316.6
Lycopene	µg	0.03	0.12	0.24
Lutein + Zeaxanthin	µg	137.0	579.8	1179.2

1. Poach cod until it flakes easily.
2. Pulse alfalfa, broccoli, strawberries, cod liver oil, safflower oil, and salmon oil to small kernels.
3. Add HILARY'S BLEND™ supplement to the cottage cheese and mix thoroughly.
4. Stir all ingredients together.

INGREDIENTS		
APPROX.	INGREDIENT	GRAMS
1 cup	Alfalfa sprouts, raw	33
1 cup	Broccoli, raw, chopped	91
¼ cup	Carrots, raw, grated	28
1 tsp	Cod liver oil	5
570 g raw	Cod, Atlantic, cooked	398
1 ⅓ cup	Cottage cheese, low fat	301
8 tsp	Safflower oil	36
2 tsp	Salmon oil	9
½ cup	Strawberries, raw, sliced	84
1 ½ scoops	HILARY'S BLEND™ supplement	15
	Total	1000

FEEDING GUIDE			
Body weight		Energy intake	Amount to feed
lbs	kg	kcal/day	grams/day
10	4.5	296	255
20	9.1	497	429
40	18.2	836	721
60	27.3	1134	977
80	36.4	1407	1213
100	45.5	1663	1434

METABOLIZABLE ENERGY

116 kcal/100 grams

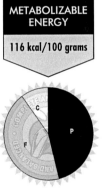

Supplement for home-made meals

Adult Recipe 6

1. Thaw frozen peas overnight in the refrigerator.
2. Pan-broil lean (10% fat) beef to brown crumbles.
3. Prepare spaghetti according to the package to yield 2 cups of cooked spaghetti.
4. Pulse broccoli, peas, spinach, tomatoes, cod liver oil and safflower oil to small kernels.
5. Add HILARY'S BLEND™ supplement to the tomato sauce and mix thoroughly.
6. Stir all ingredients together.

INGREDIENTS

APPROX.	INGREDIENT	GRAMS
425 g raw	Beef, ground, cooked	320
1 cup	Broccoli, raw, chopped	91
1 tsp	Cod liver oil	5
½ cup	Peas, thawed from frozen	72
1 tsp	Safflower oil	5
2 cups	Spaghetti, cooked	280
1 leaf	Spinach, raw	10
½ cup	Tomatoes, cherry, raw	75
½ cup	Tomato sauce, canned	122
2 scoops	HILARY'S BLEND™ supplement	20
	Total	1000

METABOLIZABLE ENERGY

141 kcal/100 grams

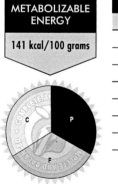

FEEDING GUIDE

Body weight		Energy intake	Amount to feed
lbs	kg	kcal/day	grams/day
10	4.5	296	210
20	9.1	497	353
40	18.2	836	593
60	27.3	1134	804
80	36.4	1407	998
100	45.5	1663	1179

Supplement for home-made meals

NUTRITION

		Per 100g As Fed	Per 100g Dry Matter	Per 1000 kcal
PROTEIN	g	11.63	37.62	82.50
Arginine	g	0.70	2.25	4.93
Histidine	g	0.35	1.15	2.52
Isoleucine	g	0.49	1.59	3.49
Leucine	g	0.88	2.83	6.21
Lysine	g	0.84	2.71	5.94
Methionine + Cystine	g	0.40	1.29	2.83
Phenylalanine + Tyrosine	g	0.81	2.62	5.75
Threonine	g	0.45	1.44	3.16
Tryptophan	g	0.08	0.27	0.59
Valine	g	0.55	1.79	3.93
FAT (LIPID)	g	5.22	16.87	36.99
Linoleic acid	g	0.59	1.91	4.19
MINERALS				
Calcium	mg	280.48	907.12	1989.21
Phosphorus	mg	203.48	658.09	1443.12
Calcium to Phosphorus ratio		1.38	1.38	1.38
Potassium	mg	410.94	1329.03	2914.41
Sodium	mg	100.27	324.29	711.13
Magnesium	mg	24.80	80.22	175.91
Iron	mg	6.29	20.35	44.63
Copper	mg	0.46	1.49	3.27
Manganese	mg	0.47	1.53	3.36
Zinc	mg	8.95	28.93	63.44
Iodine	mg	0.12	0.39	0.86
Selenium	µg	14.60	47.22	103.55
VITAMINS				
Vitamin A	IU	810	2621	5748
Vitamin D	IU	57	184	404
Vitamin E	mg	6.47	20.93	45.90
Thiamin	mg	0.10	0.32	0.70
Riboflavin	mg	0.26	0.84	1.84
Niacin	mg	2.99	9.67	21.21
Pantothenic acid	mg	1.16	3.74	8.20
Pyridoxine	mg	0.26	0.84	1.84
Folic acid	µg	16.00	51.75	113.48
Choline	mg	112.69	364.46	799.22
Vitamin B12	µg	2.47	7.98	17.50
OTHER (non-essential nutrients)				
Total dietary fiber	g	1.90	6.15	13.49
FATTY ACIDS				
Polyunsaturated fatty acids	g	0.75	2.42	5.31
Eicosapentaenoic acid	mg	34	110	241
Docosahexaenoic acid	mg	55	180	395
Omega 6:3 ratio (estimate)		7.4	7.4	7.4
ANTIOXIDANTS				
Vitamin C	mg	13.09	42.32	92.80
Beta-carotene	µg	180.6	584.1	1280.9
Lycopene	µg	2041.5	6602.5	14478.6
Lutein + Zeaxanthin	µg	437.2	1414.0	3100.8

Adult Recipe 7

NUTRITION		Per 100g As Fed	Per 100g Dry Matter	Per 1000 kcal
PROTEIN	g	9.77	29.12	61.04
Arginine	g	0.65	1.94	4.07
Histidine	g	0.28	0.83	1.74
Isoleucine	g	0.43	1.29	2.70
Leucine	g	0.77	2.28	4.78
Lysine	g	0.77	2.28	4.78
Methionine + Cystine	g	0.36	1.05	2.20
Phenylalanine + Tyrosine	g	0.73	2.17	4.55
Threonine	g	0.42	1.24	2.60
Tryptophan	g	0.11	0.31	0.65
Valine	g	0.50	1.49	3.12
FAT (LIPID)	g	9.05	26.98	56.56
Linoleic acid	g	3.43	10.22	21.42
MINERALS				
Calcium	mg	358.28	1067.92	2238.64
Phosphorus	mg	271.58	809.49	1696.90
Calcium to Phosphorus ratio		1.32	1.32	1.32
Potassium	mg	457.06	1362.34	2855.82
Sodium	mg	203.91	607.77	1274.04
Magnesium	mg	41.86	124.77	261.55
Iron	mg	4.95	14.75	30.92
Copper	mg	0.43	1.28	2.68
Manganese	mg	0.53	1.58	3.31
Zinc	mg	5.66	16.87	35.36
Iodine	mg	0.09	0.27	0.57
Selenium	µg	15.51	46.23	96.91
VITAMINS				
Vitamin A	IU	1717	5117	10726
Vitamin D	IU	80	239	502
Vitamin E	mg	7.25	21.60	45.28
Thiamin	mg	0.11	0.33	0.69
Riboflavin	mg	0.31	0.94	1.97
Niacin	mg	2.28	6.80	14.25
Pantothenic acid	mg	0.98	2.92	6.12
Pyridoxine	mg	0.18	0.53	1.11
Folic acid	µg	12.00	35.77	74.98
Choline	mg	94.61	282.00	591.15
Vitamin B12	µg	3.74	11.14	23.35
OTHER (non-essential nutrients)				
Total dietary fiber	g	2.36	7.03	14.74
FATTY ACIDS				
Polyunsaturated fatty acids	g	3.90	11.61	24.34
Eicosapentaenoic acid	mg	131	390	818
Docosahexaenoic acid	mg	140	420	880
Omega 6:3 ratio (estimate)		13.4	13.4	13.4
ANTIOXIDANTS				
Vitamin C	mg	15.53	46.30	97.06
Beta-carotene	µg	860.1	2563.7	5374.1
Lycopene	µg	1242.5	3703.6	7763.7
Lutein + Zeaxanthin	µg	267.2	796.3	1669.2

1. Pulse Brussels sprouts, honey, squash, and safflower oil to small kernels.
2. Add HILARY'S BLEND™ supplement to the tomato sauce and mix thoroughly.
3. Mash sardines.
4. Stir all ingredients together.

INGREDIENTS		
APPROX.	INGREDIENT	GRAMS
¾ cup	Almonds, ground	71
8	Brussels sprouts, raw	152
¾ cup	Carrots, raw, grated	82
3 tbsp	Honey	63
5 tsp	Safflower oil	21
	Sardines, canned in water, drained	276
1 cup	Squash, raw, cubed	116
⅓ cup	Tomato sauce, canned	82
½ cup	Yogurt, plain, low fat	122
1 ½ scoops	HILARY'S BLEND™ supplement	15
	Total	1000

FEEDING GUIDE			
Body weight		Energy intake	Amount to feed
lbs	kg	kcal/day	grams/day
10	4.5	296	185
20	9.1	497	311
40	18.2	836	523
60	27.3	1134	709
80	36.4	1407	879
100	45.5	1663	1039

METABOLIZABLE ENERGY

160 kcal/100 grams

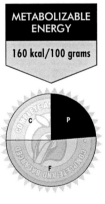

Supplement for home-made meals

Adult Recipe 8

1. Poach turkey until tender. Dice finely.
2. Simmer chicken liver until tender. Dice finely.
3. Pulse broccoli, cabbage, cheese, raspberries, cod liver oil, safflower oil, and salmon oil to small kernels.
4. Add HILARY'S BLEND™ supplement to the tomato sauce and mix thoroughly.
5. Stir all ingredients together.

INGREDIENTS

APPROX.	INGREDIENT	GRAMS
1 cup	Broccoli, raw, chopped	91
1 cup	Cabbage, raw, shredded	70
¾ cup	Carrots, raw, grated	83
¾ cup	Cheese, cheddar, shredded	85
1 tsp	Cod liver oil	5
220 g raw	Liver, chicken, cooked	136
⅔ cup	Raspberries, raw	82
11 tsp	Safflower oil	50
2 tsp	Salmon oil	9
⅓ cup	Tomato sauce, canned	82
370 g raw	Turkey breast, cooked	210
⅓ cup	Yogurt, plain, low fat	82
1½ scoops	HILARY'S BLEND™ supplement	15
	Total	1000

METABOLIZABLE ENERGY

162 kcal/100 grams

FEEDING GUIDE

Body weight		Energy intake	Amount to feed
lbs	kg	kcal/day	grams/day
10	4.5	296	183
20	9.1	497	307
40	18.2	836	516
60	27.3	1134	700
80	36.4	1407	868
100	45.5	1663	1027

NUTRITION

		Per 100g As Fed	Per 100g Dry Matter	Per 1000 kcal
PROTEIN	g	12.82	42.68	78.92
Arginine	g	0.78	2.58	4.77
Histidine	g	0.39	1.30	2.40
Isoleucine	g	0.66	2.19	4.05
Leucine	g	1.07	3.55	6.56
Lysine	g	1.09	3.64	6.73
Methionine + Cystine	g	0.48	1.61	2.98
Phenylalanine + Tyrosine	g	1.08	3.60	6.66
Threonine	g	0.54	1.81	3.35
Tryptophan	g	0.14	0.47	0.87
Valine	g	0.73	2.42	4.47
FAT (LIPID)	g	10.51	35.01	64.74
Linoleic acid	g	3.96	13.20	24.41
MINERALS				
Calcium	mg	291.24	969.91	1793.44
Phosphorus	mg	238.69	794.90	1469.83
Calcium to Phosphorus ratio		1.22	1.22	1.22
Potassium	mg	343.85	1145.11	2117.40
Sodium	mg	135.59	451.56	834.97
Magnesium	mg	22.58	75.20	139.05
Iron	mg	5.69	18.94	35.02
Copper	mg	0.39	1.28	2.37
Manganese	mg	0.39	1.29	2.39
Zinc	mg	6.20	20.65	38.18
Iodine	mg	0.09	0.30	0.55
Selenium	µg	19.69	65.57	121.24
VITAMINS				
Vitamin A	IU	3892	12962	23967
Vitamin D	IU	56	187	347
Vitamin E	mg	4.98	16.59	30.68
Thiamin	mg	0.11	0.37	0.68
Riboflavin	mg	0.50	1.65	3.05
Niacin	mg	3.62	12.05	22.28
Pantothenic acid	mg	1.86	6.18	11.43
Pyridoxine	mg	0.32	1.08	2.00
Folic acid	µg	12.00	39.96	73.89
Choline	mg	124.23	413.72	765.00
Vitamin B12	µg	3.69	12.29	22.73
OTHER (non-essential nutrients)				
Total dietary fiber	g	1.68	5.58	10.32
FATTY ACIDS				
Polyunsaturated fatty acids	g	4.56	15.18	28.07
Eicosapentaenoic acid	mg	152	510	943
Docosahexaenoic acid	mg	227	760	1405
Omega 6:3 ratio (estimate)		11.0	11.0	11.0
ANTIOXIDANTS				
Vitamin C	mg	17.75	59.12	109.32
Beta-carotene	µg	752.9	2507.3	4636.2
Lycopene	µg	1245.4	4147.6	7669.2
Lutein + Zeaxanthin	µg	173.5	577.7	1068.2

Hilary's Blend™
Supplement for home-made meals

Adult Recipe 9

NUTRITION

		Per 100g As Fed	Per 100g Dry Matter	Per 1000 kcal
PROTEIN	**g**	**7.77**	**33.95**	**72.00**
Arginine	g	0.49	2.13	4.52
Histidine	g	0.22	0.98	2.08
Isoleucine	g	0.38	1.65	3.50
Leucine	g	0.58	2.52	5.34
Lysine	g	0.60	2.62	5.56
Methionine + Cystine	g	0.30	1.29	2.74
Phenylalanine + Tyrosine	g	0.57	2.49	5.28
Threonine	g	0.34	1.50	3.18
Tryptophan	g	0.09	0.37	0.78
Valine	g	0.39	1.71	3.63
FAT (LIPID)	**g**	**5.47**	**23.88**	**50.64**
Linoleic acid	g	2.23	9.76	20.70
MINERALS				
Calcium	mg	221.01	965.11	2046.81
Phosphorus	mg	163.47	713.83	1513.89
Calcium to Phosphorus ratio		1.35	1.35	1.35
Potassium	mg	368.41	1608.79	3411.92
Sodium	mg	100.20	437.53	927.91
Magnesium	mg	22.26	97.20	206.14
Iron	mg	5.09	22.24	47.17
Copper	mg	0.38	1.65	3.50
Manganese	mg	0.42	1.81	3.84
Zinc	mg	5.58	24.39	51.73
Iodine	mg	0.09	0.39	0.83
Selenium	µg	10.54	46.02	97.60
VITAMINS				
Vitamin A	IU	4402	19221	40764
Vitamin D	IU	25	110	234
Vitamin E	mg	5.06	22.07	46.81
Thiamin	mg	0.14	0.62	1.31
Riboflavin	mg	0.34	1.49	3.16
Niacin	mg	3.68	16.09	34.12
Pantothenic acid	mg	1.35	5.88	12.47
Pyridoxine	mg	0.28	1.23	2.61
Folic acid	µg	12.00	52.40	111.13
Choline	mg	87.03	380.02	805.95
Vitamin B12	µg	2.51	10.97	23.27
OTHER (non-essential nutrients)				
Total dietary fiber	g	2.60	11.37	24.11
FATTY ACIDS				
Polyunsaturated fatty acids	g	2.91	12.70	26.93
Eicosapentaenoic acid	mg	198	860	1824
Docosahexaenoic acid	mg	280	1220	2587
Omega 6:3 ratio (estimate)		5.1	5.1	5.1
ANTIOXIDANTS				
Vitamin C	mg	21.43	93.56	198.42
Beta-carotene	µg	1621.1	7078.9	15012.9
Lycopene	µg	1850.3	8079.8	17135.7
Lutein + Zeaxanthin	µg	807.9	3528.1	7482.4

1. Thaw frozen peas overnight in the refrigerator.
2. Poach chicken and chicken liver until tender. Dice finely.
3. Pulse apple, Brussels sprouts, cabbage, peas, spinach, cod liver oil, safflower oil, and salmon oil to small kernels.
4. Add HILARY'S BLEND™ supplement to the tomato sauce and mix thoroughly.
5. Stir all ingredients together.

INGREDIENTS

APPROX.	INGREDIENT	GRAMS
1 cup	Apple, raw with skin, sliced	110
5	Brussels sprouts, raw	95
1 cup	Cabbage, raw, shredded	70
1½ cups	Carrots, raw, grated	165
270 g raw	Chicken breast, cooked	140
½ tsp	Cod liver oil	2
120 g raw	Liver, chicken, cooked	75
1 cup	Peas, thawed from frozen	145
6 tsp	Safflower oil	27
3 tsp	Salmon oil	14
2 leaves	Spinach, raw	20
½ cup	Tomato sauce, canned	122
1½ scoops	HILARY'S BLEND™ supplement	15
	Total	1000

FEEDING GUIDE

Body weight		Energy intake	Amount to feed
lbs	kg	kcal/day	grams/day
10	4.5	296	274
20	9.1	497	461
40	18.2	836	775
60	27.3	1134	1050
80	36.4	1407	1303
100	45.5	1663	1540

METABOLIZABLE ENERGY

108 kcal/100 grams

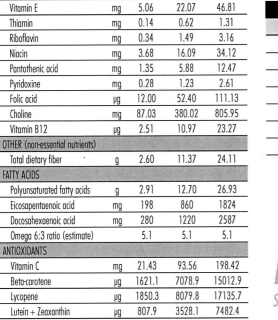

Supplement for home-made meals

Adult Recipe 10

1. Thaw frozen peas overnight in the refrigerator.
2. Poach beef liver to crumbles.
3. Pulse alfalfa sprouts, apple, broccoli, cucumber, honey, peas, spinach, cod liver oil, safflower oil and salmon oil until small kernels.
4. Sprinkle HILARY'S BLEND™ supplement over the yogurt and mix thoroughly.
5. Stir all ingredients together.

INGREDIENTS		
APPROX.	INGREDIENT	GRAMS
1 cup	Alfalfa sprouts, raw	33
1 ½ cups	Apple, raw with skin, sliced	165
1 ½ cups	Broccoli, raw, chopped	137
1 tsp	Cod liver oil	5
1 ½ cups	Cucumber, raw with skin, sliced	156
1 tbsp	Honey	21
270 g raw	Liver, beef, cooked	190
1 cup	Peas, thawed from frozen	145
6 tsp	Safflower oil	27
2 tsp	Salmon oil	9
1 leaf	Spinach, raw	10
⅓ cup	Yogurt, plain, low fat	82
2 scoops	HILARY'S BLEND™ supplement	20
	Total	1000

METABOLIZABLE ENERGY

111 kcal/100 grams

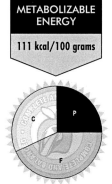

FEEDING GUIDE			
Body weight		Energy intake	Amount to feed
lbs	kg	kcal/day	grams/day
10	4.5	296	266
20	9.1	497	448
40	18.2	836	754
60	27.3	1134	1021
80	36.4	1407	1267
100	45.5	1663	1498

Supplement for home-made meals

NUTRITION				
		Per 100g As Fed	Per 100g Dry Matter	Per 1000 kcal
PROTEIN	g	6.95	28.69	62.88
Arginine	g	0.41	1.70	3.73
Histidine	g	0.19	0.78	1.71
Isoleucine	g	0.31	1.27	2.78
Leucine	g	0.59	2.43	5.33
Lysine	g	0.51	2.09	4.58
Methionine + Cystine	g	0.27	1.10	2.41
Phenylalanine + Tyrosine	g	0.58	2.40	5.26
Threonine	g	0.28	1.15	2.52
Tryptophan	g	0.08	0.32	0.70
Valine	g	0.40	1.67	3.66
FAT (LIPID)	g	5.30	21.86	47.91
Linoleic acid	g	2.15	8.87	19.00
MINERALS				
Calcium	mg	295.87	1220.87	2675.82
Phosphorus	mg	225.10	928.87	2035.83
Calcium to Phosphorus ratio		1.31	1.31	1.31
Potassium	mg	364.42	1503.73	3295.77
Sodium	mg	30.86	127.35	279.12
Magnesium	mg	21.08	86.99	190.66
Iron	mg	6.23	25.70	56.33
Copper	mg	3.19	13.14	28.80
Manganese	mg	0.49	2.03	4.45
Zinc	mg	7.83	32.30	70.79
Iodine	mg	0.12	0.50	1.10
Selenium	µg	7.20	29.71	65.12
VITAMINS				
Vitamin A	IU	5781	23856	52287
Vitamin D	IU	57	235	516
Vitamin E	mg	6.27	25.88	56.72
Thiamin	mg	0.14	0.59	1.29
Riboflavin	mg	0.88	3.63	7.96
Niacin	mg	4.10	16.90	37.04
Pantothenic acid	mg	2.33	9.62	21.08
Pyridoxine	mg	0.32	1.34	2.94
Folic acid	µg	16.00	66.02	144.70
Choline	mg	165.24	681.84	1494.41
Vitamin B12	µg	17.44	71.97	157.74
OTHER (non-essential nutrients)				
Total dietary fiber	g	2.16	8.91	19.53
FATTY ACIDS				
Polyunsaturated fatty acids	g	2.67	11.01	24.00
Eicosapentaenoic acid	mg	152	630	1376
Docosahexaenoic acid	mg	219	900	1983
Omega 6:3 ratio (estimate)		6.2	6.2	6.2
ANTIOXIDANTS				
Vitamin C	mg	19.98	82.43	180.66
Beta-carotene	µg	219.7	906.8	1987.4
Lycopene	µg	0	0	0
Lutein + Zeaxanthin	µg	681.7	2813.1	6165.6

Adult Recipe 11

NUTRITION		Per 100g As Fed	Per 100g Dry Matter	Per 1000 kcal
PROTEIN	g	10.51	43.18	89.85
Arginine	g	0.66	2.73	5.68
Histidine	g	0.30	1.22	2.54
Isoleucine	g	0.47	1.94	4.04
Leucine	g	0.83	3.41	7.10
Lysine	g	0.88	3.62	7.53
Methionine + Cystine	g	0.42	1.73	3.60
Phenylalanine + Tyrosine	g	0.79	3.25	6.76
Threonine	g	0.47	1.93	4.02
Tryptophan	g	0.12	0.49	1.02
Valine	g	0.53	2.17	4.52
FAT (LIPID)	g	6.48	26.61	55.37
Linoleic acid	g	2.28	9.36	19.48
MINERALS				
Calcium	mg	290.20	1192.24	2480.78
Phosphorus	mg	225.63	926.94	1928.75
Calcium to Phosphorus ratio		1.29	1.29	1.29
Potassium	mg	448.01	1840.55	3829.77
Sodium	mg	132.41	543.97	1131.88
Magnesium	mg	37.65	154.66	321.81
Iron	mg	5.18	21.30	44.32
Copper	mg	0.42	1.74	3.62
Manganese	mg	0.44	1.79	3.72
Zinc	mg	6.92	28.45	59.20
Iodine	mg	0.12	0.49	1.02
Selenium	µg	22.24	91.36	190.10
VITAMINS				
Vitamin A	IU	4035	16577	34493
Vitamin D	IU	57	234	487
Vitamin E	mg	6.96	28.58	59.47
Thiamin	mg	0.11	0.45	0.94
Riboflavin	mg	0.27	1.09	2.27
Niacin	mg	1.94	7.96	16.56
Pantothenic acid	mg	1.19	4.88	10.15
Pyridoxine	mg	0.22	0.91	1.89
Folic acid	µg	16.00	65.73	136.77
Choline	mg	126.69	520.47	1082.98
Vitamin B12	µg	2.53	10.41	21.66
OTHER (non-essential nutrients)				
Total dietary fiber	g	1.93	7.94	16.52
FATTY ACIDS				
Polyunsaturated fatty acids	g	2.98	12.23	25.45
Eicosapentaenoic acid	mg	237	970	2018
Docosahexaenoic acid	mg	311	1280	2663
Omega 6:3 ratio (estimate)		4.4	4.4	4.4
ANTIOXIDANTS				
Vitamin C	mg	4.31	17.69	36.81
Beta-carotene	µg	1743.5	7162.6	14903.8
Lycopene	µg	1863.9	7657.4	15933.2
Lutein + Zeaxanthin	µg	280.7	1153.0	2399.2

1. Poach sole until it flakes easily.
2. Hard boil the egg. Discard shell and mash coarsely.
3. Pulse beans, celery, peanut butter, spinach, cod liver oil, safflower oil and salmon oil to small kernels.
4. Add HILARY'S BLEND™ supplement to the tomato sauce and mix thoroughly.
5. Stir all ingredients together.

INGREDIENTS		
APPROX.	**INGREDIENT**	**GRAMS**
1 cup	Beans, green, raw, chopped	110
1¾ cups	Carrots, raw, grated	193
¾ cup	Celery, raw, chopped	75
1 tsp	Cod liver oil	5
1 large	Egg, hard-boiled	50
500 g raw	Flatfish/sole, cooked	350
2 tbsp	Peanut butter, smooth, unsalted	32
5 tsp	Safflower oil	23
2 tsp	Salmon oil	9
1 leaf	Spinach, raw	10
½ cup	Tomato sauce, canned	123
2 scoops	HILARY'S BLEND™ supplement	20
	Total	1000

FEEDING GUIDE			
Body weight		Energy intake	Amount to feed
lbs	kg	kcal/day	grams/day
10	4.5	296	253
20	9.1	497	425
40	18.2	836	715
60	27.3	1134	969
80	36.4	1407	1202
100	45.5	1663	1421

METABOLIZABLE ENERGY

117 kcal/100 grams

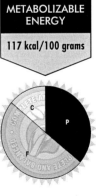

Supplement for home-made meals

Adult Recipe 12

1. Poach salmon until it flakes easily.
2. Pulse bananas, beans, blueberries, carrots, zucchini, cod liver oil, and safflower oil to small kernels.
3. Add HILARY'S BLEND™ supplement to the tomato sauce and mix thoroughly.
4. Stir all ingredients together.

INGREDIENTS

APPROX.	INGREDIENT	GRAMS
½ cup	Bananas, raw, sliced	75
1 cup	Beans, green, raw, chopped	110
¼ cup	Blueberries, raw	37
1 cup	Carrots, raw, grated	110
1 tsp	Cod liver oil	5
5 tsp	Safflower oil	23
675 g raw	Salmon, Atlantic, cooked	474
¼ cup	Tomato sauce, canned	61
¾ cup	Zucchini, raw, sliced	85
2 scoops	HILARY'S BLEND™ supplement	20
	Total	1000

METABOLIZABLE ENERGY

143 kcal/100 grams

FEEDING GUIDE

Body weight		Energy intake	Amount to feed
lbs	kg	kcal/day	grams/day
10	4.5	296	207
20	9.1	497	348
40	18.2	836	585
60	27.3	1134	793
80	36.4	1407	984
100	45.5	1663	1163

NUTRITION

		Per 100g As Fed	Per 100g Dry Matter	Per 1000 kcal
PROTEIN	g	11.07	40.54	77.52
Arginine	g	0.66	2.40	4.59
Histidine	g	0.33	1.20	2.29
Isoleucine	g	0.51	1.86	3.56
Leucine	g	0.89	3.26	6.23
Lysine	g	1.00	3.65	6.98
Methionine + Cystine	g	0.44	1.62	3.10
Phenylalanine + Tyrosine	g	0.81	2.95	5.64
Threonine	g	0.50	1.82	3.48
Tryptophan	g	0.12	0.45	0.86
Valine	g	0.57	2.08	3.98
FAT (LIPID)	g	8.76	32.07	61.32
Linoleic acid	g	2.07	7.56	14.46
MINERALS				
Calcium	mg	281.48	1030.76	1970.94
Phosphorus	mg	222.39	814.38	1557.19
Calcium to Phosphorus ratio		1.27	1.27	1.27
Potassium	mg	462.37	1693.18	3237.56
Sodium	mg	73.79	270.20	516.65
Magnesium	mg	26.23	96.05	183.66
Iron	mg	5.04	18.44	35.26
Copper	mg	0.42	1.53	2.93
Manganese	mg	0.40	1.47	2.81
Zinc	mg	6.76	24.74	47.31
Iodine	mg	0.12	0.44	0.84
Selenium	µg	19.81	72.54	138.71
VITAMINS				
Vitamin A	IU	2494	9132	17462
Vitamin D	IU	57	209	399
Vitamin E	mg	6.24	22.86	43.71
Thiamin	mg	0.24	0.86	1.64
Riboflavin	mg	0.27	0.97	1.85
Niacin	mg	4.49	16.44	31.44
Pantothenic acid	mg	1.58	5.79	11.07
Pyridoxine	mg	0.44	1.63	3.12
Folic acid	µg	16.00	58.59	112.03
Choline	mg	85.02	311.34	595.32
Vitamin B12	µg	2.93	10.72	20.50
OTHER (non-essential nutrients)				
Total dietary fiber	g	1.65	6.05	11.57
FATTY ACIDS				
Polyunsaturated fatty acids	g	3.97	14.53	27.78
Eicosapentaenoic acid	mg	362	1320	2524
Docosahexaenoic acid	mg	745	2730	5220
Omega 6:3 ratio (estimate)		2.6	2.6	2.6
ANTIOXIDANTS				
Vitamin C	mg	7.08	25.92	49.56
Beta-carotene	µg	979.1	3585.6	6856.0
Lycopene	µg	924.4	3385.1	6472.7
Lutein + Zeaxanthin	µg	283.8	1039.3	1987.2

Hilary's Blend™
Supplement for home-made meals

Adult Recipe 13

NUTRITION		Per 100g As Fed	Per 100g Dry Matter	Per 1000 kcal
PROTEIN	g	14.21	47.68	92.80
Arginine	g	0.83	2.80	5.45
Histidine	g	0.43	1.43	2.78
Isoleucine	g	0.73	2.45	4.77
Leucine	g	1.13	3.79	7.38
Lysine	g	1.15	3.86	7.51
Methionine + Cystine	g	0.56	1.87	3.64
Phenylalanine + Tyrosine	g	1.14	3.84	7.47
Threonine	g	0.59	1.99	3.87
Tryptophan	g	0.16	0.55	1.07
Valine	g	0.75	2.53	4.92
FAT (LIPID)	g	8.97	30.10	58.58
Linoleic acid	g	1.79	6.02	11.72
MINERALS				
Calcium	mg	326.51	1095.30	2131.80
Phosphorus	mg	256.61	860.82	1675.43
Calcium to Phosphorus ratio		1.27	1.27	1.27
Potassium	mg	366.05	1227.94	2389.96
Sodium	mg	182.83	613.32	1193.72
Magnesium	mg	28.50	95.62	186.11
Iron	mg	4.40	14.75	28.71
Copper	mg	0.34	1.15	2.24
Manganese	mg	0.37	1.24	2.41
Zinc	mg	5.78	19.39	37.74
Iodine	mg	0.09	0.30	0.58
Selenium	µg	16.01	53.71	104.54
VITAMINS				
Vitamin A	IU	2161	7250	14111
Vitamin D	IU	32	109	211
Vitamin E	mg	5.40	18.11	35.25
Thiamin	mg	0.09	0.30	0.58
Riboflavin	mg	0.29	0.98	1.91
Niacin	mg	4.53	15.19	29.56
Pantothenic acid	mg	1.19	3.98	7.75
Pyridoxine	mg	0.28	0.93	1.81
Folic acid	µg	12.00	40.26	78.36
Choline	mg	97.93	328.53	639.42
Vitamin B12	µg	2.35	7.88	15.34
OTHER (non-essential nutrients)				
Total dietary fiber	g	1.30	4.36	8.49
FATTY ACIDS				
Polyunsaturated fatty acids	g	2.25	7.54	14.68
Eicosapentaenoic acid	mg	113	380	740
Docosahexaenoic acid	mg	148	500	973
Omega 6:3 ratio (estimate)		7.6	7.6	7.6
ANTIOXIDANTS				
Vitamin C	mg	7.41	24.87	48.40
Beta-carotene	µg	1009.9	3387.7	6593.6
Lycopene	µg	924.4	3100.9	6035.4
Lutein + Zeaxanthin	µg	323.2	1084.1	2109.9

1. Poach chicken until tender. Dice finely.
2. Hard boil eggs. Discard shells and mash coarsely.
3. Mash sardines.
4. Pulse celery, cheese, peanut butter, spinach, strawberries, zucchini, safflower oil, and salmon oil to small kernels.
5. Mix HILARY'S BLEND™ supplement into the tomato sauce.
6. Stir all ingredients together.

INGREDIENTS		
APPROX.	INGREDIENT	GRAMS
1 cup	Carrots, raw, grated	110
½ cup	Celery, raw, chopped	51
¾ cup	Cheese, cheddar, shredded	85
430 g raw	Chicken breast, cooked	225
2 large	Eggs, hard-boiled	100
2 tbsp	Peanut butter, smooth, unsalted	32
2 tsp	Safflower oil	9
1 tsp	Salmon oil	5
	Sardines, canned in water, drained	96
1 leaf	Spinach, raw	10
½ cup	Strawberries, raw, sliced	83
¼ cup	Tomato sauce, canned	61
¼ cup	Yogurt, plain, low fat	61
½ cup	Zucchini, raw, sliced	57
1 ½ scoops	HILARY'S BLEND™ supplement	15
	Total	1000

FEEDING GUIDE			
Body weight		Energy intake	Amount to feed
lbs	kg	kcal/day	grams/day
10	4.5	296	193
20	9.1	497	325
40	18.2	836	547
60	27.3	1134	741
80	36.4	1407	919
100	45.5	1663	1087

METABOLIZABLE ENERGY

153 kcal/100 grams

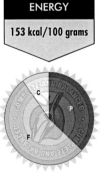

Supplement for home-made meals

Adult Recipe 14

1. Thaw frozen peas overnight in the refrigerator.
2. Pulse almonds, apple, broccoli, carrots, celery, cheese, peas, spinach, cod liver oil, and safflower oil to small kernels.
3. Add HILARY'S BLEND™ supplement to the tomato sauce and mix thoroughly.
4. Stir all ingredients together.

INGREDIENTS

APPROX.	INGREDIENT	GRAMS
¼ cup	Almonds, ground	24
½ cup	Apple, raw with skin, sliced	55
1¼ cup	Broccoli, raw, chopped	114
1 cup	Carrots, raw, grated	110
½ cup	Celery, raw, sliced	51
¼ cup	Cheese, cheddar, shredded	28
1 tsp	Cod liver oil	5
1 cup	Peas, thawed from frozen	145
4 tsp	Safflower oil	18
3 leaves	Spinach, raw	30
¼ cup	Tomato sauce, canned	61
	Tuna, canned in water, drained	344
1½ scoops	HILARY'S BLEND™ supplement	15
	Total	1000

METABOLIZABLE ENERGY

116 kcal/100 grams

FEEDING GUIDE

Body weight		Energy intake	Amount to feed
lbs	kg	kcal/day	grams/day
10	4.5	296	255
20	9.1	497	429
40	18.2	836	721
60	27.3	1134	977
80	36.4	1407	1213
100	45.5	1663	1434

Hilary's Blend™

Supplement for home-made meals

NUTRITION

		Per 100g As Fed	Per 100g Dry Matter	Per 1000 kcal
PROTEIN	g	10.76	44.49	92.66
Arginine	g	0.67	2.79	5.81
Histidine	g	0.31	1.28	2.67
Isoleucine	g	0.49	2.02	4.21
Leucine	g	0.85	3.50	7.29
Lysine	g	0.90	3.73	7.77
Methionine + Cystine	g	0.40	1.65	3.44
Phenylalanine + Tyrosine	g	0.79	3.29	6.85
Threonine	g	0.47	1.92	4.00
Tryptophan	g	0.12	0.49	1.02
Valine	g	0.55	2.27	4.73
FAT (LIPID)	g	5.60	23.17	48.26
Linoleic acid	g	1.72	7.11	14.81
MINERALS				
Calcium	mg	248.09	1025.98	2136.84
Phosphorus	mg	198.52	821.00	1709.92
Calcium to Phosphorus ratio		1.25	1.25	1.25
Potassium	mg	376.37	1556.52	3241.80
Sodium	mg	87.78	363.03	756.09
Magnesium	mg	34.44	142.45	296.68
Iron	mg	4.39	18.14	37.78
Copper	mg	0.36	1.49	3.10
Manganese	mg	0.43	1.79	3.73
Zinc	mg	5.45	22.54	46.94
Iodine	mg	0.09	0.37	0.77
Selenium	µg	23.68	97.92	203.94
VITAMINS				
Vitamin A	IU	2894	11970	24929
Vitamin D	IU	56	230	479
Vitamin E	mg	5.49	22.70	47.28
Thiamin	mg	0.10	0.43	0.90
Riboflavin	mg	0.23	0.95	1.98
Niacin	mg	2.91	12.01	25.01
Pantothenic acid	mg	0.79	3.28	6.83
Pyridoxine	mg	0.20	0.84	1.75
Folic acid	µg	12.00	49.63	103.37
Choline	mg	65.91	272.59	567.73
Vitamin B12	µg	1.63	6.72	14.00
OTHER (non-essential nutrients)				
Total dietary fiber	g	2.38	9.85	20.51
FATTY ACIDS				
Polyunsaturated fatty acids	g	2.21	9.15	19.06
Eicosapentaenoic acid	mg	115	470	979
Docosahexaenoic acid	mg	271	1120	2333
Omega 6:3 ratio (estimate)		4.8	4.8	4.8
ANTIOXIDANTS				
Vitamin C	mg	18.30	75.68	157.62
Beta-carotene	µg	1216.8	5032.2	10480.7
Lycopene	µg	924.4	3822.9	7962.0
Lutein + Zeaxanthin	µg	929.3	3843.0	8004.0

Adult Recipe 15

NUTRITION		Per 100g As Fed	Per 100g Dry Matter	Per 1000 kcal
PROTEIN	g	10.12	41.93	90.18
Arginine	g	0.62	2.58	5.55
Histidine	g	0.30	1.25	2.69
Isoleucine	g	0.44	1.84	3.96
Leucine	g	0.78	3.25	6.99
Lysine	g	0.80	3.33	7.16
Methionine + Cystine	g	0.35	1.45	3.12
Phenylalanine + Tyrosine	g	0.74	3.04	6.54
Threonine	g	0.40	1.65	3.55
Tryptophan	g	0.06	0.25	0.54
Valine	g	0.53	2.20	4.73
FAT (LIPID)	g	4.96	20.57	44.24
Linoleic acid	g	0.81	3.36	7.23
MINERALS				
Calcium	mg	263.77	1093.00	2350.84
Phosphorus	mg	200.34	830.17	1785.54
Calcium to Phosphorus ratio		1.32	1.32	1.32
Potassium	mg	411.32	1704.39	3665.83
Sodium	mg	52.11	215.92	464.40
Magnesium	mg	27.68	114.69	246.68
Iron	mg	4.78	19.80	42.59
Copper	mg	0.35	1.46	3.14
Manganese	mg	0.40	1.66	3.57
Zinc	mg	7.12	29.50	63.45
Iodine	mg	0.09	0.37	0.80
Selenium	µg	6.92	28.68	61.69
VITAMINS				
Vitamin A	IU	1668	6911	14864
Vitamin D	IU	55	229	492
Vitamin E	mg	4.85	20.11	43.25
Thiamin	mg	0.13	0.54	1.16
Riboflavin	mg	0.27	1.14	2.45
Niacin	mg	2.59	10.73	23.08
Pantothenic acid	mg	1.07	4.42	9.51
Pyridoxine	mg	0.24	0.99	2.13
Folic acid	µg	12.00	49.73	106.96
Choline	mg	89.80	372.11	800.34
Vitamin B12	µg	2.02	8.35	17.96
OTHER (non-essential nutrients)				
Total dietary fiber	g	2.12	8.77	18.86
FATTY ACIDS				
Polyunsaturated fatty acids	g	0.97	4.00	8.60
Eicosapentaenoic acid	mg	34	140	301
Docosahexaenoic acid	mg	55	230	495
Omega 6:3 ratio (estimate)		9.9	9.9	9.9
ANTIOXIDANTS				
Vitamin C	mg	25.39	105.22	226.31
Beta-carotene	µg	622.6	2579.9	5548.9
Lycopene	µg	0.04	0.15	0.32
Lutein + Zeaxanthin	µg	1106.6	4585.3	9862.2

1. Thaw frozen peas overnight in the refrigerator.
2. Pan-broil lean (10% fat) beef to brown crumbles. Cool.
3. Pulse broccoli, carrots, peas, spinach, strawberries, cod liver oil, and safflower oil to small kernels.
4. Add HILARY'S BLEND™ supplement to the yogurt and mix thoroughly.
5. Stir all ingredients together.

INGREDIENTS		
APPROX.	INGREDIENT	GRAMS
330 g raw	Beef, ground, cooked	250
1½ cups	Broccoli, raw, chopped	137
⅓ cup	Carrots, raw, grated	37
1 tsp	Cod liver oil	5
1½ cups	Peas, thawed from frozen	217
2 tsp	Safflower oil	9
3 leaves	Spinach, raw	30
⅓ cup	Strawberries, raw, sliced	55
1 cup	Yogurt, plain, low fat	245
1½ scoops	HILARY'S BLEND™ supplement	15
	Total	1000

FEEDING GUIDE			
Body weight		Energy intake	Amount to feed
lbs	kg	kcal/day	grams/day
10	4.5	296	264
20	9.1	497	444
40	18.2	836	747
60	27.3	1134	1012
80	36.4	1407	1256
100	45.5	1663	1485

METABOLIZABLE ENERGY

112 kcal/100 grams

Supplement for home-made meals

R26

Puppy Recipe 1

1. Thaw frozen peas overnight in the refrigerator.
2. Poach beef liver until cooked. Dice finely.
3. Boil potato until soft. Mash coarsely.
4. Pulse blueberries, peas, cod liver oil, safflower oil, and salmon oil.
5. Add HILARY'S BLEND™ supplement to the yogurt and mix thoroughly.
6. Stir ingredients together.

INGREDIENTS		
APPROX.	INGREDIENT	GRAMS
1¼ cups	Blueberries, raw	185
½ tsp	Cod liver oil	2
320 g raw	Liver, beef, cooked	221
1¼ cups	Peas, thawed from frozen	180
1 medium	Potato, boiled in skin	173
4 tsp	Safflower oil	18
2 tsp	Salmon oil	9
½ tsp	Salt	3
¾ cup	Yogurt, plain, low fat	184
2½ scoops	HILARY'S BLEND™ supplement	25
	Total	1000

METABOLIZABLE ENERGY

117 kcal/100 grams

FEEDING GUIDE

See section 8.2 for instructions on how to calculate feeding guides for your puppy.

Hilary's Blend
Supplement for home-made meals

NUTRITION				
		Per 100g As Fed	Per 100g Dry Matter	Per 1000 kcal
PROTEIN	g	8.26	30.03	70.45
Arginine	g	0.48	1.74	4.08
Histidine	g	0.23	0.83	1.95
Isoleucine	g	0.38	1.37	3.21
Leucine	g	0.72	2.62	6.15
Lysine	g	0.62	2.25	5.28
Methionine + Cystine	g	0.33	1.20	2.82
Phenylalanine + Tyrosine	g	0.72	2.63	6.17
Threonine	g	0.34	1.22	2.86
Tryptophan	g	0.09	0.33	0.77
Valine	g	0.50	1.82	4.27
FAT (LIPID)	g	4.37	15.88	37.26
Linoleic acid	g	1.50	5.43	12.74
MINERALS				
Calcium	mg	371.55	1350.40	3168.09
Phosphorus	mg	272.95	992.07	2327.44
Calcium to Phosphorus ratio		1.36	1.36	1.36
Potassium	mg	431.88	1569.71	3682.60
Sodium	mg	152.32	553.62	1298.82
Magnesium	mg	24.17	87.86	206.12
Iron	mg	7.51	27.28	64.00
Copper	mg	3.75	13.64	32.00
Manganese	mg	0.62	2.23	5.23
Zinc	mg	9.68	35.19	82.56
Iodine	mg	0.15	0.55	1.29
Selenium	µg	8.25	29.99	70.36
VITAMINS				
Vitamin A	IU	6123	22255	52210
Vitamin D	IU	29	104	245
Vitamin E	mg	7.74	28.12	65.97
Thiamin	mg	0.18	0.66	1.55
Riboflavin	mg	1.03	3.75	8.80
Niacin	mg	4.99	18.12	42.51
Pantothenic acid	mg	2.78	10.09	23.67
Pyridoxine	mg	0.40	1.46	3.43
Folic acid	µg	20.00	72.69	170.53
Choline	mg	196.33	713.57	1674.06
Vitamin B12	µg	20.48	74.42	174.59
OTHER (non-essential nutrients)				
Total dietary fiber	g	2.30	8.35	19.59
FATTY ACIDS				
Polyunsaturated fatty acids	g	1.96	7.12	16.70
Eicosapentaenoic acid	mg	131	480	1126
Docosahexaenoic acid	mg	186	680	1595
Omega 6:3 ratio (estimate)		5.2	5.2	5.2
ANTIOXIDANTS				
Vitamin C	mg	11.55	41.96	98.44
Beta-carotene	µg	127.3	462.7	1085.5
Lycopene	µg	0	0	0
Lutein + Zeaxanthin	µg	462.2	1680.0	3941.3

Puppy Recipe 2

NUTRITION				
		Per 100g As Fed	Per 100g Dry Matter	Per 1000 kcal
PROTEIN	g	19.29	59.73	128.77
Arginine	g	1.17	3.63	7.83
Histidine	g	0.58	1.78	3.84
Isoleucine	g	0.97	3.01	6.49
Leucine	g	1.51	4.68	10.09
Lysine	g	1.64	5.07	10.93
Methionine + Cystine	g	0.79	2.45	5.28
Phenylalanine + Tyrosine	g	1.46	4.53	9.77
Threonine	g	0.84	2.59	5.58
Tryptophan	g	0.22	0.67	1.44
Valine	g	1.00	3.09	6.66
FAT (LIPID)	g	6.46	20.00	43.12
Linoleic acid	g	1.48	4.58	9.87
MINERALS				
Calcium	g	464.17	1437.28	3098.52
Phosphorus	g	358.63	1110.46	2393.96
Calcium to Phosphorus ratio		1.29	1.29	1.29
Potassium	g	471.69	1460.54	3148.67
Sodium	g	178.66	553.21	1192.62
Magnesium	g	36.28	112.33	242.16
Iron	mg	7.08	21.93	47.28
Copper	mg	0.55	1.70	3.66
Manganese	mg	0.49	1.53	3.30
Zinc	mg	9.05	28.01	60.38
Iodine	mg	0.15	0.46	0.99
Selenium	µg	25.85	80.04	172.55
VITAMINS				
Vitamin A	IU	1505	4659	10043
Vitamin D	IU	74	229	494
Vitamin E	mg	8.88	27.50	59.29
Thiamin	mg	0.13	0.40	0.86
Riboflavin	mg	0.41	1.27	2.74
Niacin	mg	6.66	20.61	44.43
Pantothenic acid	mg	1.75	5.40	11.64
Pyridoxine	mg	0.37	1.15	2.48
Folic acid	µg	20.00	61.93	133.51
Choline	mg	147.31	456.13	983.34
Vitamin B12	µg	4.44	13.76	29.66
OTHER (non-essential nutrients)				
Total dietary fiber	g	1.21	3.76	8.11
FATTY ACIDS				
Polyunsaturated fatty acids	g	1.96	6.05	13.04
Eicosapentaenoic acid	mg	118	360	776
Docosahexaenoic acid	mg	133	410	884
Omega 6:3 ratio (estimate)		6.8	6.8	6.8
ANTIOXIDANTS				
Vitamin C	mg	1.56	4.82	10.39
Beta-carotene	µg	695.6	2153.9	4643.5
Lycopene	µg	0.1	0.3	0.6
Lutein + Zeaxanthin	µg	177.7	550.2	1186.2

1. Poach chicken until tender. Dice finely.
2. Hard boil eggs. Discard shells and mash coarsely.
3. Mash sardines.
4. Pulse almonds, carrots, and zucchini to small kernels.
5. Add HILARY'S BLEND™ supplement to the yogurt and mix thoroughly.
6. Stir all ingredients together.

INGREDIENTS		
APPROX.	INGREDIENT	GRAMS
¼ cup	Almonds, ground	24
¾ cup	Carrots, raw, grated	83
670 g raw	Chicken breast, cooked	349
2 large	Eggs, hard-boiled	100
	Sardines, canned in water, drained	240
½ cup	Yogurt, plain, low fat	122
½ cup	Zucchini, raw, sliced	57
2½ scoops	HILARY'S BLEND™ supplement	25
	Total	1000

FEEDING GUIDE

See section 8.2 for instructions on how to calculate feeding guides for your puppy.

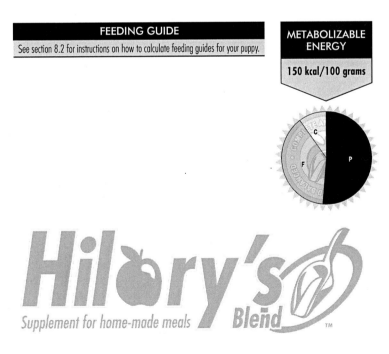

METABOLIZABLE ENERGY

150 kcal/100 grams

Hilary's
Supplement for home-made meals
Blend™

Puppy Recipe 3

1. Prick potato with a fork, then microwave until soft. Mash.
2. Boil sweet corn until tender.
3. Poach chicken liver until cooked. Dice finely. Mix with tuna.
4. Pulse cooked sweet corn, peanut butter, mashed potato and cod liver oil.
5. Add HILARY'S BLEND™ supplement to yogurt and mix thoroughly.
6. Stir all ingredients together.

INGREDIENTS

APPROX.	INGREDIENT	GRAMS
½ tsp	Cod liver oil	2
330 g raw	Liver, chicken, cooked	202
1½ tbsp	Peanut butter, smooth, unsalted	24
1 med./large	Potato, baked in skin	260
½ tsp	Salt	3
1½ cups	Sweet corn, boiled	246
	Tuna, canned in water, drained	172
¼ cup	Yogurt, plain, low fat	61
3 scoops	HILARY'S BLEND™ supplement	30
	Total	1000

NUTRITION

		Per 100g As Fed	Per 100g Dry Matter	Per 1000 kcal
PROTEIN	g	11.25	37.33	93.34
Arginine	g	0.69	2.30	5.75
Histidine	g	0.32	1.05	2.63
Isoleucine	g	0.51	1.70	4.25
Leucine	g	0.93	3.10	7.75
Lysine	g	0.88	2.91	7.28
Methionine + Cystine	g	0.43	1.44	3.60
Phenylalanine + Tyrosine	g	0.91	3.03	7.58
Threonine	g	0.46	1.54	3.85
Tryptophan	g	0.12	0.40	1.00
Valine	g	0.62	2.05	5.13
FAT (LIPID)	g	3.47	11.51	28.78
Linoleic acid	g	0.55	1.82	4.55
MINERALS				
Calcium	mg	417.78	1385.78	3465.06
Phosphorus	mg	300.73	997.53	2494.26
Calcium to Phosphorus ratio		1.39	1.39	1.39
Potassium	mg	524.03	1738.20	4346.26
Sodium	mg	154.28	511.74	1279.57
Magnesium	mg	32.32	107.21	268.07
Iron	mg	9.84	32.65	81.64
Copper	mg	0.70	2.33	5.83
Manganese	mg	0.65	2.16	5.40
Zinc	mg	10.87	36.06	90.17
Iodine	mg	0.18	0.60	1.50
Selenium	µg	28.56	94.73	236.87
VITAMINS				
Vitamin A	IU	2902	9626	24069
Vitamin D	IU	31	101	253
Vitamin E	mg	9.41	31.22	78.06
Thiamin	mg	0.17	0.58	1.45
Riboflavin	mg	0.70	2.32	5.80
Niacin	mg	4.72	15.67	39.18
Pantothenic acid	mg	2.77	9.19	22.98
Pyridoxine	mg	0.41	1.35	3.38
Folic acid	µg	24.00	79.61	199.06
Choline	mg	185.56	615.51	1539.04
Vitamin B12	µg	6.04	20.03	50.08
OTHER (non-essential nutrients)				
Total dietary fiber	g	2.06	6.82	17.05
FATTY ACIDS				
Polyunsaturated fatty acids	g	0.90	2.98	7.45
Eicosapentaenoic acid	mg	54	180	450
Docosahexaenoic acid	mg	130	430	1075
Omega 6:3 ratio (estimate)		3.9	3.9	3.9
ANTIOXIDANTS				
Vitamin C	mg	8.94	29.66	74.16
Beta-carotene	µg	7.9	26.1	65.2
Lycopene	µg	4.2	14.1	35.2
Lutein + Zeaxanthin	µg	36.9	122.3	305.8

METABOLIZABLE ENERGY

121 kcal/100 grams

FEEDING GUIDE

See section 8.2 for instructions on how to calculate feeding guides for your puppy.

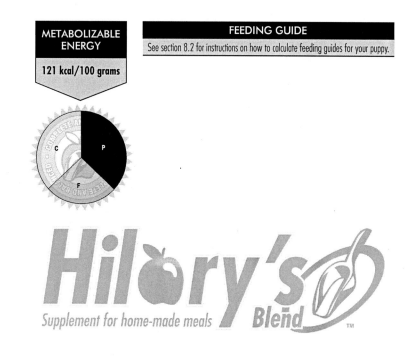

Hilary's Blend™
Supplement for home-made meals

Puppy Recipe 4

NUTRITION		Per 100g As Fed	Per 100g Dry Matter	Per 1000 kcal
PROTEIN	g	13.06	48.24	115.67
Arginine	g	0.79	2.93	7.03
Histidine	g	0.39	1.42	3.40
Isoleucine	g	0.64	2.35	5.63
Leucine	g	1.02	3.76	9.02
Lysine	g	1.03	3.80	9.11
Methionine + Cystine	g	0.52	1.91	4.58
Phenylalanine + Tyrosine	g	1.01	3.75	8.99
Threonine	g	0.54	1.99	4.77
Tryptophan	g	0.15	0.56	1.34
Valine	g	0.68	2.50	5.99
FAT (LIPID)	g	3.36	12.40	29.73
Linoleic acid	g	0.94	3.47	8.32
MINERALS				
Calcium	mg	342.91	1266.81	3037.62
Phosphorus	mg	267.43	987.94	2368.93
Calcium to Phosphorus ratio		1.28	1.28	1.28
Potassium	mg	425.81	1573.06	3771.96
Sodium	mg	131.77	486.80	1167.27
Magnesium	mg	26.20	96.78	232.06
Iron	mg	7.47	27.61	66.20
Copper	mg	2.75	10.15	24.34
Manganese	mg	0.59	2.20	5.28
Zinc	mg	9.40	34.74	83.30
Iodine	mg	0.15	0.55	1.32
Selenium	µg	12.15	44.89	107.64
VITAMINS				
Vitamin A	IU	4392	16225	38905
Vitamin D	IU	29	106	255
Vitamin E	mg	8.03	29.66	71.12
Thiamin	mg	0.17	0.62	1.49
Riboflavin	mg	0.79	2.93	7.03
Niacin	mg	7.08	26.14	62.68
Pantothenic acid	mg	2.34	8.63	20.69
Pyridoxine	mg	0.44	1.62	3.88
Folic acid	µg	20.00	73.88	177.15
Choline	mg	166.50	615.08	1474.87
Vitamin B12	µg	14.72	54.38	130.40
OTHER (non-essential nutrients)				
Total dietary fiber	g	2.33	8.60	20.62
FATTY ACIDS				
Polyunsaturated fatty acids	g	1.28	4.71	11.29
Eicosapentaenoic acid	mg	81	300	719
Docosahexaenoic acid	mg	118	440	1055
Omega 6:3 ratio (estimate)		5.4	5.4	5.4
ANTIOXIDANTS				
Vitamin C	mg	10.91	40.30	96.63
Beta-carotene	µg	158.7	586.3	1405.8
Lycopene	µg	2788.0	10299.4	24696.5
Lutein + Zeaxanthin	µg	492.9	1820.8	4365.9

1. Thaw frozen peas overnight in the refrigerator.
2. Poach chicken and liver until tender. Dice finely.
3. Pulse blueberries, peas, cod liver oil, safflower oil and salmon oil.
4. Add HILARY'S BLEND™ supplement to the tomato sauce and mix thoroughly.
5. Stir all ingredients together.

INGREDIENTS		
APPROX.	INGREDIENT	GRAMS
1¼ cups	Blueberries, raw	185
470 g raw	Chicken breast, cooked	245
½ tsp	Cod liver oil	2
215 g raw	Liver, beef, cooked	152
1⅓ cups	Peas, thawed from frozen	193
2 tsp	Safflower oil	9
1 tsp	Salmon oil	5
¾ cup	Tomato sauce, canned	184
2½ scoops	HILARY'S BLEND™ supplement	25
	Total	1000

FEEDING GUIDE

See section 8.2 for instructions on how to calculate feeding guides for your puppy.

METABOLIZABLE ENERGY

113 kcal/100 grams

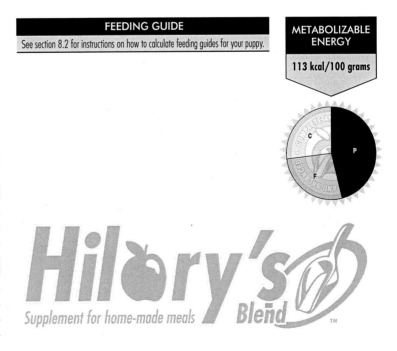

Hilary's Blend™
Supplement for home-made meals

Puppy Recipe 5

1. Thaw frozen peas overnight in the refrigerator.
2. Simmer liver until tender. Dice finely.
3. Prepare oatmeal according to package directions to yield ½ cup of cooked oatmeal.
4. Pulse almonds, apple, peas, cod liver oil and salmon oil to small kernels.
5. Add HILARY'S BLEND™ supplement to the tomato sauce and mix thoroughly.
6. Stir all ingredients together.

INGREDIENTS

APPROX.	INGREDIENT	GRAMS
¾ cup	Almonds, ground	71
1 cup	Apple, raw with skin, sliced	110
½ tsp	Cod liver oil	2
385 g raw	Liver, chicken, cooked	239
½ cup	Oatmeal, cooked	117
1 cup	Peas, thawed from frozen	145
1 tsp	Salmon oil	5
1 pinch	Salt	<1
½ cup	Tomato sauce, canned	123
⅔ cup	Yogurt, plain, low fat	163
2½ scoops	HILARY'S BLEND™ supplement	25
	Total	1000

METABOLIZABLE ENERGY

126 kcal/100 grams

FEEDING GUIDE

See section 8.2 for instructions on how to calculate feeding guides for your puppy.

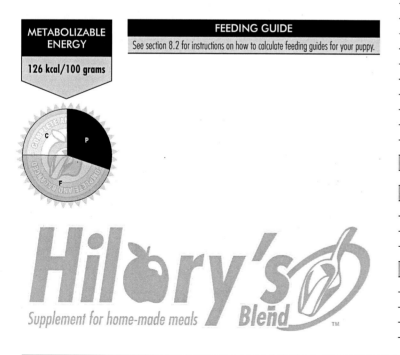

Hilary's Blend™
Supplement for home-made meals

NUTRITION		Per 100g As Fed	Per 100g Dry Matter	Per 1000 kcal
PROTEIN	g	9.49	34.17	75.26
Arginine	g	0.66	2.36	5.20
Histidine	g	0.26	0.94	2.07
Isoleucine	g	0.41	1.49	3.28
Leucine	g	0.78	2.79	6.14
Lysine	g	0.63	2.28	5.02
Methionine + Cystine	g	0.34	1.21	2.67
Phenylalanine + Tyrosine	g	0.79	2.86	6.30
Threonine	g	0.37	1.34	2.95
Tryptophan	g	0.09	0.33	0.73
Valine	g	0.52	1.87	4.12
FAT (LIPID)	g	6.23	22.44	49.42
Linoleic acid	g	1.12	4.03	8.88
MINERALS				
Calcium	g	388.02	1397.00	3076.89
Phosphorus	g	293.59	1057.02	2328.08
Calcium to Phosphorus ratio		1.32	1.32	1.32
Potassium	g	432.97	1558.82	3433.30
Sodium	g	114.89	413.26	911.55
Magnesium	g	43.21	155.57	342.64
Iron	mg	9.25	33.29	73.32
Copper	mg	0.69	2.50	5.51
Manganese	mg	0.79	2.83	6.23
Zinc	mg	9.64	34.70	76.43
Iodine	mg	0.15	0.54	1.19
Selenium	µg	21.66	78.00	171.79
VITAMINS				
Vitamin A	IU	3554	12795	28180
Vitamin D	IU	29	104	228
Vitamin E	mg	9.79	35.24	77.62
Thiamin	mg	0.21	0.75	1.65
Riboflavin	mg	0.82	2.94	6.48
Niacin	mg	3.75	13.49	29.71
Pantothenic acid	mg	2.77	9.97	21.96
Pyridoxine	mg	0.32	1.14	2.51
Folic acid	µg	20.00	72.01	158.60
Choline	mg	176.92	636.95	1402.88
Vitamin B12	µg	6.12	22.03	48.52
OTHER (non-essential nutrients)				
Total dietary fiber	g	2.88	10.36	22.82
FATTY ACIDS				
Polyunsaturated fatty acids	g	1.51	5.42	11.94
Eicosapentaenoic acid	mg	79	280	617
Docosahexaenoic acid	mg	113	410	903
Omega 6:3 ratio (estimate)		6.8	6.8	6.8
ANTIOXIDANTS				
Vitamin C	mg	13.97	50.28	110.74
Beta-carotene	µg	101.0	363.7	801.1
Lycopene	µg	1868.7	6728.0	14818.3
Lutein + Zeaxanthin	µg	403.3	1452.1	3198.2

Puppy Recipe 6

NUTRITION		Per 100g As Fed	Per 100g Dry Matter	Per 1000 kcal
PROTEIN	g	10.90	46.80	105.78
Arginine	g	0.61	2.62	5.92
Histidine	g	0.31	1.35	3.05
Isoleucine	g	0.52	2.24	5.06
Leucine	g	0.92	3.94	8.91
Lysine	g	0.93	4.00	9.04
Methionine + Cystine	g	0.41	1.78	4.02
Phenylalanine + Tyrosine	g	0.88	3.78	8.54
Threonine	g	0.47	2.00	4.52
Tryptophan	g	0.12	0.49	1.11
Valine	g	0.60	2.57	5.81
FAT (LIPID)	g	4.17	17.90	40.46
Linoleic acid	g	1.70	7.29	16.48
MINERALS				
Calcium	mg	318.17	1365.77	3087.11
Phosphorus	mg	239.16	1026.59	2320.45
Calcium to Phosphorus ratio		1.33	1.33	1.33
Potassium	mg	386.60	1659.50	3751.05
Sodium	mg	149.16	640.28	1447.25
Magnesium	mg	32.07	137.67	311.18
Iron	mg	5.09	21.85	49.39
Copper	mg	0.42	1.79	4.05
Manganese	mg	0.40	1.74	3.93
Zinc	mg	7.07	30.34	68.58
Iodine	mg	0.12	0.52	1.18
Selenium	µg	18.93	81.24	183.63
VITAMINS				
Vitamin A	IU	718	3083	6969
Vitamin D	IU	57	245	553
Vitamin E	mg	6.39	27.43	62.00
Thiamin	mg	0.13	0.55	1.24
Riboflavin	mg	0.29	1.25	2.83
Niacin	mg	1.41	6.05	13.68
Pantothenic acid	mg	1.17	5.01	11.32
Pyridoxine	mg	0.20	0.84	1.90
Folic acid	µg	16.00	68.68	155.24
Choline	mg	107.77	462.59	1045.61
Vitamin B12	µg	2.50	10.75	24.30
OTHER (non-essential nutrients)				
Total dietary fiber	g	1.66	7.11	16.07
FATTY ACIDS				
Polyunsaturated fatty acids	g	2.19	9.40	21.25
Eicosapentaenoic acid	mg	168	720	1627
Docosahexaenoic acid	mg	218	940	2125
Omega 6:3 ratio (estimate)		4.7	4.7	4.7
ANTIOXIDANTS				
Vitamin C	mg	14.83	63.67	143.92
Beta-carotene	µg	112.4	482.5	1090.6
Lycopene	µg	924.3	3967.5	8967.9
Lutein + Zeaxanthin	µg	489.8	2102.5	4752.3

1. Thaw frozen peas overnight in the refrigerator.
2. Poach fish until it flakes easily.
3. Pulse blueberries, broccoli, peas, cod liver oil, safflower oil and salmon oil to small kernels.
4. Add HILARY'S BLEND™ supplement to the tomato sauce and mix thoroughly.
5. Stir all ingredients together.

INGREDIENTS		
APPROX.	INGREDIENT	GRAMS
¼ cup	Blueberries, raw	37
1 cup	Broccoli, raw, chopped	91
1 tsp	Cod liver oil	5
¾ cup	Cottage cheese, low fat	170
400 g raw	Flatfish/sole, cooked	281
1 cup	Peas, thawed from frozen	145
5 tsp	Safflower oil	22
1 tsp	Salmon oil	5
¼ cup	Tomato sauce, canned	61
⅔ cup	Yogurt, plain, low fat	163
2 scoops	HILARY'S BLEND™ supplement	20
	Total	1000

FEEDING GUIDE

See section 8.2 for instructions on how to calculate feeding guides for your puppy.

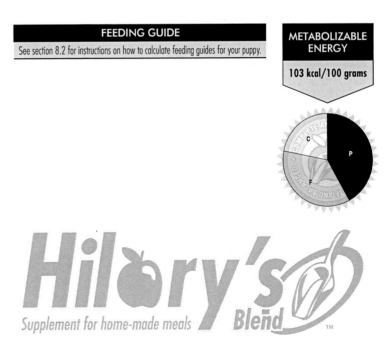

METABOLIZABLE ENERGY

103 kcal/100 grams

Hilary's Blend™

Supplement for home-made meals

Puppy Recipe 7

1. Simmer liver until cooked. Dice finely.
2. Hard boil eggs. Discard shell and mash coarsely.
3. Prepare oatmeal according to the package directions to yield 1 cup of cooked oatmeal.
4. Pulse alfalfa sprouts, broccoli, cod liver oil, safflower oil and salmon oil to small kernels.
5. Add HILARY'S BLEND™ supplement to the tomato sauce and mix thoroughly.
6. Stir all ingredients together.

INGREDIENTS		
APPROX.	INGREDIENT	GRAMS
1½ cups	Alfalfa sprouts, raw	51
2 cups	Broccoli, raw, chopped	182
½ tsp	Cod liver oil	2
2 large	Eggs, hard-boiled	100
470 g raw	Liver, chicken, cooked	292
1 cup	Oatmeal, cooked	234
4 tsp	Safflower oil	18
3 tsp	Salmon oil	14
1 pinch	Salt	<1
⅓ cup	Tomato sauce, canned	82
2½ scoops	HILARY'S BLEND™ supplement	25
	Total	1000

METABOLIZABLE ENERGY

120 kcal/100 grams

FEEDING GUIDE

See section 8.2 for instructions on how to calculate feeding guides for your puppy.

NUTRITION				
		Per 100g As Fed	Per 100g Dry Matter	Per 1000 kcal
PROTEIN	g	9.83	40.00	82.16
Arginine	g	0.61	2.46	5.05
Histidine	g	0.27	1.08	2.22
Isoleucine	g	0.45	1.84	3.78
Leucine	g	0.82	3.32	6.82
Lysine	g	0.70	2.85	5.85
Methionine + Cystine	g	0.40	1.62	3.33
Phenylalanine + Tyrosine	g	0.82	3.33	6.84
Threonine	g	0.41	1.65	3.39
Tryptophan	g	0.10	0.42	0.86
Valine	g	0.55	2.25	4.62
FAT (LIPID)	g	6.71	27.31	56.10
Linoleic acid	g	1.80	7.32	15.04
MINERALS				
Calcium	mg	351.34	1429.16	2935.64
Phosphorus	mg	280.96	1142.88	2347.60
Calcium to Phosphorus ratio		1.25	1.25	1.25
Potassium	mg	378.68	1540.40	3164.14
Sodium	mg	102.92	418.33	860.81
Magnesium	mg	25.75	104.75	215.17
Iron	mg	9.70	39.44	81.01
Copper	mg	0.64	2.60	5.34
Manganese	mg	0.68	2.75	5.65
Zinc	mg	9.58	38.96	80.03
Iodine	mg	0.15	0.61	1.25
Selenium	µg	29.54	120.16	246.82
VITAMINS				
Vitamin A	IU	4300	17492	35931
Vitamin D	IU	29	117	240
Vitamin E	mg	8.13	33.05	67.89
Thiamin	mg	0.20	0.80	1.64
Riboflavin	mg	0.87	3.54	7.27
Niacin	mg	3.88	15.79	32.43
Pantothenic acid	mg	3.27	13.29	27.30
Pyridoxine	mg	0.35	1.44	2.96
Folic acid	µg	20.00	81.36	167.12
Choline	mg	212.64	864.96	1776.72
Vitamin B12	µg	7.03	28.60	58.75
OTHER (non-essential nutrients)				
Total dietary fiber	g	1.72	6.98	14.34
FATTY ACIDS				
Polyunsaturated fatty acids	g	2.59	10.55	21.67
Eicosapentaenoic acid	mg	197	800	1643
Docosahexaenoic acid	mg	281	1140	2342
Omega 6:3 ratio (estimate)		4.4	4.4	4.4
ANTIOXIDANTS				
Vitamin C	mg	25.37	103.21	212.00
Beta-carotene	µg	97.1	395.1	811.6
Lycopene	µg	1248.6	5079.0	10432.9
Lutein + Zeaxanthin	µg	357.0	1452.2	2983.0

Hilary's Blend™

Supplement for home-made meals

Puppy Recipe 8

NUTRITION		Per 100g As Fed	Per 100g Dry Matter	Per 1000 kcal
PROTEIN	g	13.30	40.59	86.58
Arginine	g	0.88	2.69	5.74
Histidine	g	0.37	1.12	2.39
Isoleucine	g	0.60	1.84	3.92
Leucine	g	1.11	3.37	7.19
Lysine	g	0.96	2.92	6.23
Methionine + Cystine	g	0.52	1.57	3.35
Phenylalanine + Tyrosine	g	1.11	3.39	7.23
Threonine	g	0.54	1.65	3.52
Tryptophan	g	0.14	0.42	0.90
Valine	g	0.73	2.24	4.78
FAT (LIPID)	g	8.60	26.24	55.97
Linoleic acid	g	1.56	4.76	10.15
MINERALS				
Calcium	mg	483.09	1474.63	3145.61
Phosphorus	mg	371.55	1134.15	2419.31
Calcium to Phosphorus ratio		1.30	1.30	1.30
Potassium	mg	505.83	1544.03	3293.65
Sodium	mg	215.31	657.23	1401.97
Magnesium	mg	43.07	131.46	280.42
Iron	mg	11.04	33.69	71.87
Copper	mg	0.78	2.38	5.08
Manganese	mg	0.80	2.44	5.20
Zinc	mg	11.46	34.97	74.60
Iodine	mg	0.18	0.55	1.17
Selenium	µg	31.88	97.30	207.56
VITAMINS				
Vitamin A	IU	4293	13104	27952
Vitamin D	IU	33	102	217
Vitamin E	mg	11.17	34.10	72.74
Thiamin	mg	0.21	0.63	1.34
Riboflavin	mg	0.98	3.00	6.40
Niacin	mg	4.80	14.66	31.27
Pantothenic acid	mg	3.50	10.67	22.76
Pyridoxine	mg	0.40	1.23	2.62
Folic acid	µg	24.00	73.26	156.27
Choline	mg	241.29	736.53	1571.13
Vitamin B12	µg	8.08	24.67	52.62
OTHER (non-essential nutrients)				
Total dietary fiber	g	2.21	6.75	14.40
FATTY ACIDS				
Polyunsaturated fatty acids	g	2.24	6.84	14.59
Eicosapentaenoic acid	mg	157	480	1024
Docosahexaenoic acid	mg	211	640	1365
Omega 6:3 ratio (estimate)		5.1	5.1	5.1
ANTIOXIDANTS				
Vitamin C	mg	21.60	65.94	140.66
Beta-carotene	µg	283.9	866.5	1848.4
Lycopene	µg	5.9	18.1	38.6
Lutein + Zeaxanthin	µg	743.6	2269.9	4842.1

1. Poach chicken liver until cooked. Dice finely.
2. Hard boil eggs. Discard shells and mash coarsely.
3. Mash sardines. Blend with eggs and liver.
4. Boil sweet corn until cooked.
5. Pulse almonds, broccoli, peanut butter, spinach, cooked sweet corn and salmon oil to small kernels.
6. Add HILARY'S BLEND™ supplement to the yogurt and mix thoroughly.
7. Stir all ingredients together.

INGREDIENTS		
APPROX.	**INGREDIENT**	**GRAMS**
½ cup	Almonds, ground	48
1½ cups	Broccoli, raw, chopped	136
2 large	Eggs, hard-boiled	100
460 g raw	Liver, chicken, cooked	282
1½ tbsp	Peanut butter, smooth, unsalted	23
2 tsp	Salmon oil	9
½ tsp	Salt	3
	Sardines, canned in water, drained	84
4 leaves	Spinach, raw	40
¾ cup	Sweet corn, boiled	123
½ cup	Yogurt, plain, low fat	122
3 scoops	HILARY'S BLEND™ supplement	30
	Total	1000

FEEDING GUIDE

See section 8.2 for instructions on how to calculate feeding guides for your puppy.

METABOLIZABLE ENERGY

154 kcal/100 grams

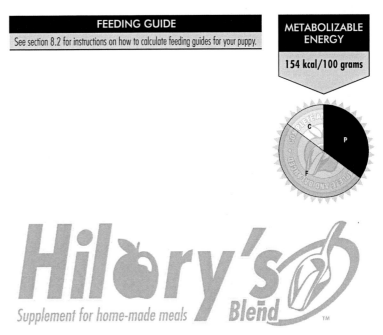

Hilary's
Supplement for home-made meals *Blend* ™

Puppy Recipe 9

1. Thaw peas overnight in the refrigerator.
2. Poach chicken until tender. Dice finely.
3. Prepare oatmeal according to package instructions to yield ½ cup of cooked oatmeal.
4. Add HILARY'S BLEND™ supplement and the cod liver oil to the tomato sauce and mix thoroughly.
5. Stir all ingredients together.

INGREDIENTS

APPROX.	INGREDIENT	GRAMS
2½ cups	Broccoli, raw, chopped	227
810 g raw	Chicken breast, cooked	420
½ tsp	Cod liver oil	2
½ cup	Oatmeal, cooked	117
1 cup	Peas, thawed from frozen	148
1 pinch	Salt	<1
¼ cup	Tomato sauce, canned	61
2½ scoops	HILARY'S BLEND™ supplement	25
	Total	1000

NUTRITION

		Per 100g As Fed	Per 100g Dry Matter	Per 1000 kcal
PROTEIN	g	14.86	58.98	147.61
Arginine	g	0.92	3.64	9.11
Histidine	g	0.44	1.76	4.40
Isoleucine	g	0.75	2.97	7.43
Leucine	g	1.08	4.29	10.74
Lysine	g	1.20	4.76	11.91
Methionine + Cystine	g	0.57	2.28	5.71
Phenylalanine + Tyrosine	g	1.07	4.26	10.66
Threonine	g	0.61	2.43	6.08
Tryptophan	g	0.17	0.68	1.70
Valine	g	0.73	2.89	7.23
FAT (LIPID)	g	1.97	7.82	19.57
Linoleic acid	g	0.32	1.28	3.20
MINERALS				
Calcium	mg	352.40	1399.01	3501.38
Phosphorus	mg	247.20	981.40	2456.20
Calcium to Phosphorus ratio		1.43	1.43	1.43
Potassium	mg	429.61	1705.53	4268.52
Sodium	mg	91.24	361.84	907.12
Magnesium	mg	30.94	122.83	307.41
Iron	mg	6.72	26.67	66.75
Copper	mg	0.53	2.08	5.21
Manganese	mg	0.57	2.24	5.61
Zinc	mg	8.82	35.03	87.67
Iodine	mg	0.15	0.60	1.50
Selenium	µg	13.39	53.14	133.00
VITAMINS				
Vitamin A	IU	484	1923	4812
Vitamin D	IU	29	114	286
Vitamin E	mg	7.91	31.39	78.56
Thiamin	mg	0.16	0.63	1.58
Riboflavin	mg	0.30	1.19	2.98
Niacin	mg	6.69	26.55	66.45
Pantothenic acid	mg	1.57	6.25	15.64
Pyridoxine	mg	0.40	1.59	3.98
Folic acid	µg	20.00	79.40	198.72
Choline	mg	105.72	419.69	1050.38
Vitamin B12	µg	2.14	8.51	21.30
OTHER (non-essential nutrients)				
Total dietary fiber	g	2.26	8.97	22.45
FATTY ACIDS				
Polyunsaturated fatty acids	g	0.45	1.80	4.50
Eicosapentaenoic acid	mg	18	70	175
Docosahexaenoic acid	mg	30	120	300
Omega 6:3 ratio (estimate)		8.5	8.5	8.5
ANTIOXIDANTS				
Vitamin C	mg	26.60	105.58	264.24
Beta-carotene	µg	161.1	639.8	1601.1
Lycopene	µg	924.3	3669.3	9183.5
Lutein + Zeaxanthin	µg	706.1	2803.4	7016.1

METABOLIZABLE ENERGY

101 kcal/100 grams

FEEDING GUIDE

See section 8.2 for instructions on how to calculate feeding guides for your puppy.

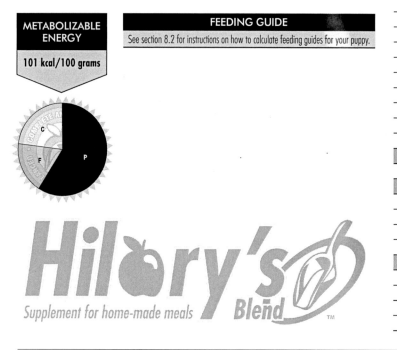

Hilary's Blend™
Supplement for home-made meals

Puppy Recipe 10

NUTRITION		Per 100g As Fed	Per 100g Dry Matter	Per 1000 kcal
PROTEIN	g	7.76	31.51	70.06
Arginine	g	0.52	2.11	4.69
Histidine	g	0.21	0.87	1.93
Isoleucine	g	0.35	1.40	3.11
Leucine	g	0.65	2.64	5.87
Lysine	g	0.51	2.05	4.56
Methionine + Cystine	g	0.32	1.30	2.89
Phenylalanine + Tyrosine	g	0.68	2.76	6.14
Threonine	g	0.31	1.26	2.80
Tryptophan	g	0.09	0.37	0.82
Valine	g	0.44	1.77	3.94
FAT (LIPID)	g	5.66	22.99	51.12
Linoleic acid	g	0.88	3.57	7.94
MINERALS				
Calcium	mg	364.37	1480.54	3291.84
Phosphorus	mg	262.79	1067.78	2374.11
Calcium to Phosphorus ratio		1.39	1.39	1.39
Potassium	mg	396.12	1609.56	3578.71
Sodium	mg	167.60	681.00	1514.14
Magnesium	mg	34.62	140.69	312.81
Iron	mg	7.38	29.98	66.66
Copper	mg	2.83	11.49	25.55
Manganese	mg	0.79	3.22	7.16
Zinc	mg	9.37	38.09	84.69
Iodine	mg	0.15	0.61	1.36
Selenium	µg	10.66	43.31	96.30
VITAMINS				
Vitamin A	IU	4451	18086	40212
Vitamin D	IU	29	117	260
Vitamin E	mg	9.15	37.19	82.69
Thiamin	mg	0.15	0.61	1.36
Riboflavin	mg	0.88	3.59	7.98
Niacin	mg	3.55	14.43	32.08
Pantothenic acid	mg	2.41	9.78	21.74
Pyridoxine	mg	0.31	1.27	2.82
Folic acid	µg	20.00	81.27	180.70
Choline	mg	196.88	799.99	1778.70
Vitamin B12	µg	15.18	61.68	137.14
OTHER (non-essential nutrients)				
Total dietary fiber	g	2.36	9.58	21.30
FATTY ACIDS				
Polyunsaturated fatty acids	g	1.35	5.49	12.21
Eicosapentaenoic acid	mg	132	530	1178
Docosahexaenoic acid	mg	190	770	1712
Omega 6:3 ratio (estimate)		3.2	3.2	3.2
ANTIOXIDANTS				
Vitamin C	mg	15.98	64.94	144.39
Beta-carotene	µg	85.4	346.8	771.1
Lycopene	µg	454.6	1847.0	4106.7
Lutein + Zeaxanthin	µg	453.3	1842.1	4095.7

1. Poach liver until cooked. Dice finely.
2. Hard boil eggs. Discard shells and mash coarsely.
3. Prepare oatmeal according to package directions to yield 1 cup of cooked oatmeal.
4. Pulse almonds, blueberries, broccoli, strawberries, zucchini, cod liver oil and salmon oil to small kernels.
5. Add HILARY'S BLEND™ supplement to the tomato sauce.
6. Stir all ingredients together.

INGREDIENTS		
APPROX.	INGREDIENT	GRAMS
½ cup	Almonds, ground	48
½ cup	Blueberries, raw	74
1 cup	Broccoli, raw, chopped	91
½ tsp	Cod liver oil	2
2 large	Eggs, hard-boiled	100
230 g raw	Liver, beef, cooked	157
1 cup	Oatmeal, cooked	234
2 tsp	Salmon oil	9
½ tsp	Salt	3
½ cup	Strawberries, raw, sliced	83
⅛ cup	Tomato sauce, canned	30
⅛ cup	Yogurt, plain, low fat	31
1 cup	Zucchini, raw, sliced	113
2½ scoops	HILARY'S BLEND™ supplement	25
	Total	1000

FEEDING GUIDE

See section 8.2 for instructions on how to calculate feeding guides for your puppy.

METABOLIZABLE ENERGY

111 kcal/100 grams

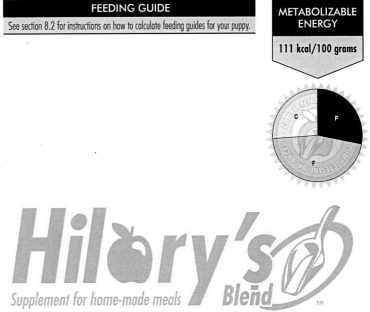

Hilary's Blend
Supplement for home-made meals

Senior Recipe 1

1. Poach chicken until tender. Dice finely.
2. Prepare rice according to package instructions to yield 3 cups of cooked rice.
3. Add cod liver oil, safflower oil and salmon oil to rice and mix thoroughly.
4. Add HILARY'S BLEND™ supplement to the yogurt and mix thoroughly.
5. Stir all ingredients together.

INGREDIENTS

APPROX.	INGREDIENT	GRAMS
½ cup	Carrots, raw, grated	55
270 g raw	Chicken breast, cooked	140
1 tsp	Cod liver oil	5
3 cups	Rice, brown, cooked	585
3 tsp	Safflower oil	13
1 tsp	Salmon oil	5
¾ cup	Yogurt, plain, low fat	182
1½ scoops	HILARY'S BLEND™ supplement	15
	Total	1000

METABOLIZABLE ENERGY

123 kcal/100 grams

FEEDING GUIDE

Body weight		Energy intake	Amount to feed
lbs	kg	kcal/day	grams/day
10	4.5	265	215
20	9.1	445	362
40	18.2	748	608
60	27.3	1014	825
80	36.4	1259	1023
100	45.5	1488	1210

Hilary's Blend™
Supplement for home-made meals

NUTRITION

		Per 100g As Fed	Per 100g Dry Matter	Per 1000 kcal
PROTEIN	g	6.86	24.69	55.83
Arginine	g	0.41	1.48	3.35
Histidine	g	0.20	0.72	1.63
Isoleucine	g	0.35	1.26	2.85
Leucine	g	0.55	1.99	4.50
Lysine	g	0.52	1.86	4.21
Methionine + Cystine	g	0.27	0.97	2.19
Phenylalanine + Tyrosine	g	0.56	2.01	4.54
Threonine	g	0.29	1.04	2.35
Tryptophan	g	0.08	0.27	0.61
Valine	g	0.39	1.39	3.14
FAT (LIPID)	g	3.62	13.04	29.48
Linoleic acid	g	1.26	4.53	10.24
MINERALS				
Calcium	mg	241.07	867.75	1962.04
Phosphorus	mg	174.61	628.51	1421.10
Calcium to Phosphorus ratio		1.38	1.38	1.38
Potassium	mg	233.68	841.16	1901.92
Sodium	mg	32.59	117.32	265.27
Magnesium	mg	35.42	127.50	288.29
Iron	mg	3.88	13.95	31.54
Copper	mg	0.34	1.23	2.78
Manganese	mg	0.77	2.76	6.24
Zinc	mg	5.52	19.86	44.90
Iodine	mg	0.09	0.32	0.72
Selenium	µg	10.20	36.73	83.05
VITAMINS				
Vitamin A	IU	1437	5171	11693
Vitamin D	IU	55	199	450
Vitamin E	mg	4.60	16.55	37.42
Thiamin	mg	0.11	0.41	0.93
Riboflavin	mg	0.19	0.69	1.56
Niacin	mg	3.13	11.26	25.46
Pantothenic acid	mg	1.02	3.69	8.34
Pyridoxine	mg	0.23	0.83	1.88
Folic acid	µg	12.00	43.19	97.66
Choline	mg	68.63	247.05	558.60
Vitamin B12	µg	1.35	4.86	10.99
OTHER (non-essential nutrients)				
Total dietary fiber	g	1.58	5.69	12.87
FATTY ACIDS				
Polyunsaturated fatty acids	g	1.60	5.74	12.98
Eicosapentaenoic acid	mg	101	360	814
Docosahexaenoic acid	mg	149	540	1221
Omega 6:3 ratio (estimate)		5.4	5.4	5.4
ANTIOXIDANTS				
Vitamin C	mg	0.47	1.69	3.82
Beta-carotene	µg	455.7	1640.2	3708.7
Lycopene	µg	0.1	0.2	0.5
Lutein + Zeaxanthin	µg	14.1	50.7	114.6

Senior Recipe 2

NUTRITION		Per 100g As Fed	Per 100g Dry Matter	Per 1000 kcal
PROTEIN	g	6.34	29.20	57.44
Arginine	g	0.42	1.91	3.76
Histidine	g	0.19	0.88	1.73
Isoleucine	g	0.27	1.26	2.48
Leucine	g	0.49	2.24	4.41
Lysine	g	0.45	2.08	4.09
Methionine + Cystine	g	0.24	1.10	2.16
Phenylalanine + Tyrosine	g	0.47	2.16	4.25
Threonine	g	0.24	1.10	2.16
Tryptophan	g	0.06	0.28	0.54
Valine	g	0.32	1.47	2.89
FAT (LIPID)	g	5.98	27.56	54.21
Linoleic acid	g	2.02	9.30	18.29
MINERALS				
Calcium	mg	209.74	966.87	1901.90
Phosphorus	mg	158.64	731.31	1438.54
Calcium to Phosphorus ratio		1.32	1.32	1.32
Potassium	mg	247.57	1141.25	2244.92
Sodium	mg	18.94	87.30	171.73
Magnesium	mg	26.17	120.62	237.27
Iron	mg	4.47	20.61	40.54
Copper	mg	0.33	1.53	3.01
Manganese	mg	0.63	2.91	5.72
Zinc	mg	6.27	28.92	56.89
Iodine	mg	0.09	0.41	0.81
Selenium	µg	8.65	39.86	78.41
VITAMINS				
Vitamin A	IU	401	1849	3638
Vitamin D	IU	25	116	229
Vitamin E	mg	4.68	21.57	42.43
Thiamin	mg	0.12	0.55	1.08
Riboflavin	mg	0.17	0.79	1.55
Niacin	mg	1.43	6.60	12.98
Pantothenic acid	mg	0.89	4.11	8.08
Pyridoxine	mg	0.14	0.62	1.22
Folic acid	µg	12.00	55.32	108.82
Choline	mg	80.08	369.15	726.14
Vitamin B12	µg	1.63	7.52	14.79
OTHER (non-essential nutrients)				
Total dietary fiber	g	1.58	7.26	14.28
FATTY ACIDS				
Polyunsaturated fatty acids	g	2.44	11.27	22.17
Eicosapentaenoic acid	mg	131	600	1180
Docosahexaenoic acid	mg	186	860	1692
Omega 6:3 ratio (estimate)		6.7	6.7	6.7
ANTIOXIDANTS				
Vitamin C	mg	0.93	4.27	8.40
Beta-carotene	µg	118.4	545.7	1073.4
Lycopene	µg	0	0	0
Lutein + Zeaxanthin	µg	362.5	1671.1	3287.2

1. Pan-broil lean (10% fat) beef to brown crumbles. Cool.
2. Prepare oatmeal according to package instructions to yield 2¾ cups of cooked oatmeal.
3. Pulse cucumber, spinach, cod liver oil, safflower oil, and salmon oil to small pieces.
4. Add HILARY'S BLEND™ supplement to the cooled beef crumbles and mix thoroughly.
5. Stir all ingredients together.

INGREDIENTS		
APPROX.	INGREDIENT	GRAMS
210 g raw	Beef, ground, cooked	159
½ tsp	Cod liver oil	2
1¼ cups	Cucumber, raw, sliced	130
2¾ cups	Oatmeal, cooked	642
5 tsp	Safflower oil	23
2 tsp	Salmon oil	9
2 leaves	Spinach, raw	20
1½ scoops	HILARY'S BLEND™ supplement	15
	Total	1000

FEEDING GUIDE			
Body weight		Energy intake	Amount to feed
lbs	kg	kcal/day	grams/day
10	4.5	265	241
20	9.1	445	405
40	18.2	748	680
60	27.3	1014	922
80	36.4	1259	1144
100	45.5	1488	1353

METABOLIZABLE ENERGY

110 kcal/100 grams

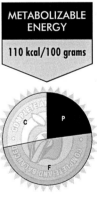

Supplement for home-made meals

Hilory's Blend ™

Senior Recipe 3

1. Thaw frozen peas overnight in the refrigerator.
2. Hard boil eggs. Discard shells and mash coarsely.
3. Boil sweet corn until tender.
4. Pulse cheese, peas, spinach, sweet corn, cod liver oil, safflower oil, and salmon oil to small kernels.
5. Sprinkle HILARY'S BLEND™ supplement over the eggs and mix thoroughly.
6. Stir all ingredients together.

INGREDIENTS

APPROX.	INGREDIENT	GRAMS
½ cup	Cheese, cheddar, shredded	55
1 tsp	Cod liver oil	5
10 large	Eggs, hard-boiled	500
1¾ cups	Peas, thawed from frozen	254
3 tsp	Safflower oil	14
1 tsp	Salmon oil	5
3 leaves	Spinach	30
¾ cups	Sweet corn, boiled	122
1½ scoops	HILARY'S BLEND™ supplement	15
	Total	1000

METABOLIZABLE ENERGY

153 kcal/100 grams

FEEDING GUIDE

Body weight		Energy intake	Amount to feed
lbs	kg	kcal/day	grams/day
10	4.5	265	173
20	9.1	445	291
40	18.2	748	489
60	27.3	1014	663
80	36.4	1259	823
100	45.5	1488	973

NUTRITION

		Per 100g As Fed	Per 100g Dry Matter	Per 1000 kcal
PROTEIN	g	9.46	33.17	61.94
Arginine	g	0.56	1.96	3.66
Histidine	g	0.24	0.82	1.53
Isoleucine	g	0.50	1.75	3.27
Leucine	g	0.79	2.77	5.17
Lysine	g	0.67	2.36	4.41
Methionine + Cystine	g	0.43	1.51	2.82
Phenylalanine + Tyrosine	g	0.85	2.97	5.55
Threonine	g	0.42	1.48	2.76
Tryptophan	g	0.11	0.38	0.71
Valine	g	0.56	1.97	3.68
FAT (LIPID)	g	9.69	34.00	63.49
Linoleic acid	g	1.75	6.12	11.43
MINERALS				
Calcium	mg	272.46	955.58	1784.46
Phosphorus	mg	216.02	757.61	1414.77
Calcium to Phosphorus ratio		1.26	1.26	1.26
Potassium	mg	277.54	973.39	1817.72
Sodium	mg	103.03	361.34	674.77
Magnesium	mg	22.81	79.98	149.36
Iron	mg	4.58	16.08	30.03
Copper	mg	0.33	1.17	2.18
Manganese	mg	0.39	1.35	2.52
Zinc	mg	5.91	20.73	38.71
Iodine	mg	0.09	0.32	0.60
Selenium	µg	16.74	58.70	109.62
VITAMINS				
Vitamin A	IU	1324	4644	8672
Vitamin D	IU	56	196	366
Vitamin E	mg	5.13	18.00	33.61
Thiamin	mg	0.15	0.53	0.99
Riboflavin	mg	0.45	1.56	2.91
Niacin	mg	0.99	3.46	6.46
Pantothenic acid	mg	1.37	4.81	8.98
Pyridoxine	mg	0.17	0.61	1.14
Folic acid	µg	12.00	42.09	78.60
Choline	mg	176.24	618.11	1154.27
Vitamin B12	µg	1.80	6.32	11.80
OTHER (non-essential nutrients)				
Total dietary fiber	g	2.03	7.12	13.30
FATTY ACIDS				
Polyunsaturated fatty acids	g	2.20	7.70	14.38
Eicosapentaenoic acid	mg	102	360	672
Docosahexaenoic acid	mg	165	580	1083
Omega 6:3 ratio (estimate)		7.2	7.2	7.2
ANTIOXIDANTS				
Vitamin C	mg	11.38	39.92	74.55
Beta-carotene	µg	293.1	1028.0	1919.8
Lycopene	µg	0	0	0
Lutein + Zeaxanthin	µg	1177.7	4130.4	7713.2

Hilary's Blend™

Supplement for home-made meals

Senior Recipe 4

NUTRITION				
		Per 100g As Fed	Per 100g Dry Matter	Per 1000 kcal
PROTEIN	g	7.80	23.56	51.66
Arginine	g	0.51	1.53	3.35
Histidine	g	0.21	0.63	1.38
Isoleucine	g	0.33	1.00	2.19
Leucine	g	0.58	1.76	3.86
Lysine	g	0.58	1.75	3.84
Methionine + Cystine	g	0.28	0.85	1.86
Phenylalanine + Tyrosine	g	0.60	1.81	3.97
Threonine	g	0.31	0.94	2.06
Tryptophan	g	0.09	0.28	0.61
Valine	g	0.39	1.18	2.59
FAT (LIPID)	g	6.92	20.91	45.85
Linoleic acid	g	2.37	7.16	15.70
MINERALS				
Calcium	mg	281.90	851.86	1867.70
Phosphorus	mg	222.69	672.94	1475.42
Calcium to Phosphorus ratio		1.27	1.27	1.27
Potassium	mg	564.93	1707.14	3742.91
Sodium	mg	110.00	332.40	728.79
Magnesium	mg	36.44	110.13	241.46
Iron	mg	4.77	14.41	31.59
Copper	mg	0.40	1.22	2.67
Manganese	mg	0.47	1.41	3.09
Zinc	mg	5.49	16.58	36.35
Iodine	mg	0.09	0.27	0.59
Selenium	µg	11.60	35.05	76.85
VITAMINS				
Vitamin A	IU	984	2973	6518
Vitamin D	IU	54	164	359
Vitamin E	mg	5.42	16.37	35.89
Thiamin	mg	0.10	0.30	0.66
Riboflavin	mg	0.23	0.69	1.51
Niacin	mg	2.72	8.23	18.04
Pantothenic acid	mg	1.09	3.28	7.19
Pyridoxine	mg	0.32	0.96	2.10
Folic acid	µg	12.00	36.26	79.50
Choline	mg	90.81	274.41	601.64
Vitamin B12	µg	2.87	8.66	18.99
OTHER (non-essential nutrients)				
Total dietary fiber	g	2.24	6.77	14.84
FATTY ACIDS				
Polyunsaturated fatty acids	g	2.88	8.70	19.07
Eicosapentaenoic acid	mg	151	450	987
Docosahexaenoic acid	mg	185	560	1228
Omega 6:3 ratio (estimate)		7.6	7.6	7.6
ANTIOXIDANTS				
Vitamin C	mg	6.34	19.17	42.03
Beta-carotene	µg	461.5	1394.7	3057.8
Lycopene	µg	0.1	0.2	0.4
Lutein + Zeaxanthin	µg	50.2	151.6	332.3

1. Prick potatoes with a fork, then microwave until soft. Mash coarsely.
2. Hard boil egg. Discard shell and mash coarsely.
3. Pulse bananas, carrots, peanut butter, safflower oil, and salmon oil to small kernels.
4. Mash sardines.
5. Sprinkle HILARY'S BLEND™ supplement over the sardines and mix thoroughly.
6. Stir all ingredients together.

INGREDIENTS		
APPROX.	INGREDIENT	GRAMS
½ cup	Bananas, raw, sliced	75
½ cup	Carrots, raw, grated	55
1 large	Egg, hard-boiled	50
3 tbsp	Peanut butter, smooth, unsalted	48
4 small	Potatoes, baked in skin	559
3 tsp	Safflower oil	13
1 tsp	Salmon oil	5
	Sardines, canned in water, drained	180
1½ scoops	HILARY'S BLEND™ supplement	15
	Total	1000

FEEDING GUIDE			
Body weight		Energy intake	Amount to feed
lbs	kg	kcal/day	grams/day
10	4.5	265	175
20	9.1	445	295
40	18.2	748	496
60	27.3	1014	672
80	36.4	1259	834
100	45.5	1488	985

METABOLIZABLE ENERGY

151 kcal/100 grams

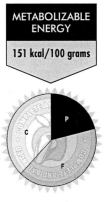

Supplement for home-made meals

R40

Senior Recipe 5

1. Poach sole until it flakes easily.
2. Prepare rice according to package instructions to yield 1 cup of cooked rice.
3. Pulse almonds, blueberries, strawberries, tomatoes, cod liver oil, safflower oil, and salmon oil to small kernels.
4. Sprinkle HILARY'S BLEND™ supplement over the rice and mix in.
5. Stir all ingredients together.

INGREDIENTS

APPROX.	INGREDIENT	GRAMS
1½ cups	Almonds, ground	143
1¼ cups	Blueberries, raw	185
1 tsp	Cod liver oil	5
340 g raw	Flatfish/sole, cooked	239
1 cup	Rice, brown, cooked	195
2 tsp	Safflower oil	9
2 tsp	Salmon oil	9
½ cup	Strawberries, raw, sliced	83
¾ cup	Tomatoes, cherry, raw	112
2 scoops	HILARY'S BLEND™ supplement	20
	Total	1000

METABOLIZABLE ENERGY

168 kcal/100 grams

FEEDING GUIDE

Body weight		Energy intake	Amount to feed
lbs	kg	kcal/day	grams/day
10	4.5	265	158
20	9.1	445	265
40	18.2	748	445
60	27.3	1014	604
80	36.4	1259	749
100	45.5	1488	886

Hilary's Blend™
Supplement for home-made meals

NUTRITION

		Per 100g As Fed	Per 100g Dry Matter	Per 1000 kcal
PROTEIN	g	9.60	28.37	57.01
Arginine	g	0.75	2.21	4.44
Histidine	g	0.27	0.80	1.61
Isoleucine	g	0.39	1.16	2.33
Leucine	g	0.74	2.17	4.36
Lysine	g	0.64	1.90	3.82
Methionine + Cystine	g	0.32	0.96	1.93
Phenylalanine + Tyrosine	g	0.72	2.14	4.30
Threonine	g	0.38	1.11	2.23
Tryptophan	g	0.10	0.30	0.60
Valine	g	0.45	1.33	2.67
FAT (LIPID)	g	10.02	29.59	59.46
Linoleic acid	g	2.51	7.42	14.91
MINERALS				
Calcium	mg	311.56	920.46	1849.76
Phosphorus	mg	249.37	736.72	1480.52
Calcium to Phosphorus ratio		1.25	1.25	1.25
Potassium	mg	394.90	1166.68	2344.57
Sodium	mg	30.54	90.22	181.31
Magnesium	mg	68.25	201.64	405.22
Iron	mg	5.42	16.00	32.15
Copper	mg	0.55	1.63	3.28
Manganese	mg	0.95	2.81	5.65
Zinc	mg	7.22	21.33	42.86
Iodine	mg	0.12	0.35	0.70
Selenium	µg	16.27	48.08	96.62
VITAMINS				
Vitamin A	IU	615	1818	3653
Vitamin D	IU	57	168	338
Vitamin E	mg	10.10	29.85	59.99
Thiamin	mg	0.13	0.38	0.76
Riboflavin	mg	0.35	1.03	2.07
Niacin	mg	1.80	5.31	10.67
Pantothenic acid	mg	1.11	3.26	6.55
Pyridoxine	mg	0.19	0.56	1.13
Folic acid	µg	16.00	47.27	94.99
Choline	mg	110.94	327.75	658.65
Vitamin B12	µg	2.20	6.50	13.06
OTHER (non-essential nutrients)				
Total dietary fiber	g	3.34	9.87	19.83
FATTY ACIDS				
Polyunsaturated fatty acids	g	3.14	9.28	18.65
Eicosapentaenoic acid	mg	210	620	1246
Docosahexaenoic acid	mg	281	830	1668
Omega 6:3 ratio (estimate)		5.4	5.4	5.4
ANTIOXIDANTS				
Vitamin C	mg	8.10	23.92	48.07
Beta-carotene	µg	56.9	168.2	338.0
Lycopene	µg	288.2	851.4	1710.9
Lutein + Zeaxanthin	µg	30.9	91.2	183.3

Senior Recipe 6

NUTRITION				
		Per 100g As Fed	Per 100g Dry Matter	Per 1000 kcal
PROTEIN	g	6.06	24.62	59.09
Arginine	g	0.41	1.66	3.98
Histidine	g	0.16	0.66	1.58
Isoleucine	g	0.28	1.12	2.69
Leucine	g	0.43	1.75	4.20
Lysine	g	0.42	1.70	4.08
Methionine + Cystine	g	0.20	0.82	1.97
Phenylalanine + Tyrosine	g	0.43	1.75	4.20
Threonine	g	0.24	0.98	2.35
Tryptophan	g	0.06	0.26	0.62
Valine	g	0.29	1.19	2.86
FAT (LIPID)	g	2.47	10.03	24.07
Linoleic acid	g	0.92	3.72	8.93
MINERALS				
Calcium	mg	214.19	870.65	2089.54
Phosphorus	mg	158.24	643.21	1543.69
Calcium to Phosphorus ratio		1.35	1.35	1.35
Potassium	mg	269.25	1094.42	2626.59
Sodium	mg	30.14	122.51	294.02
Magnesium	mg	34.32	139.48	334.75
Iron	mg	4.29	17.42	41.81
Copper	mg	0.38	1.55	3.72
Manganese	mg	0.74	2.99	7.18
Zinc	mg	5.59	22.71	54.50
Iodine	mg	0.09	0.37	0.89
Selenium	µg	6.90	28.04	67.30
VITAMINS				
Vitamin A	IU	464	1887	4529
Vitamin D	IU	25	103	246
Vitamin E	mg	4.67	19.00	45.60
Thiamin	mg	0.17	0.68	1.63
Riboflavin	mg	0.19	0.77	1.85
Niacin	mg	2.98	12.10	29.04
Pantothenic acid	mg	0.85	3.47	8.33
Pyridoxine	mg	0.22	0.91	2.18
Folic acid	µg	12.00	48.78	117.07
Choline	mg	64.39	261.73	628.15
Vitamin B12	µg	1.24	5.02	12.05
OTHER (non-essential nutrients)				
Total dietary fiber	g	3.03	12.32	29.57
FATTY ACIDS				
Polyunsaturated fatty acids	g	1.20	4.87	11.69
Eicosapentaenoic acid	mg	80	330	792
Docosahexaenoic acid	mg	115	470	1128
Omega 6:3 ratio (estimate)		5.1	5.1	5.1
ANTIOXIDANTS				
Vitamin C	mg	23.02	93.56	224.54
Beta-carotene	µg	154.0	626.0	1502.5
Lycopene	µg	469.7	1909.3	4582.2
Lutein + Zeaxanthin	µg	811.8	3299.8	7919.6

1. Thaw frozen peas overnight in the refrigerator.
2. Simmer chicken until tender. Dice finely.
3. Prepare rice according to the package instructions to yield 1¾ cups of cooked rice.
4. Pulse peas, strawberries, cod liver oil, safflower oil, and salmon oil until small kernels.
5. Add HILARY'S BLEND™ supplement to the tomato sauce and mix thoroughly.
6. Stir all ingredients together.

INGREDIENTS		
APPROX.	INGREDIENT	GRAMS
200 g raw	Chicken breast, cooked	105
½ tsp	Cod liver oil	2
2¼ cups	Peas, thawed from frozen	326
1¾ cups	Rice, brown, cooked	341
2 tsp	Safflower oil	9
1 tsp	Salmon oil	5
1 cup	Strawberries, raw, sliced	166
⅛ cup	Tomato sauce, canned	31
1½ scoops	HILARY'S BLEND™ supplement	15
	Total	1000

FEEDING GUIDE			
Body weight		Energy intake	Amount to feed
lbs	kg	kcal/day	grams/day
10	4.5	265	257
20	9.1	445	432
40	18.2	748	727
60	27.3	1014	985
80	36.4	1259	1222
100	45.5	1488	1445

METABOLIZABLE ENERGY

103 kcal/100 grams

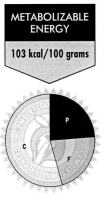

Supplement for home-made meals

Senior Recipe 7

1. Thaw frozen peas overnight in refrigerator.
2. Boil potatoes until soft. Mash.
3. Mash kidney beans and mix with potatoes.
4. Pan-broil lean (10% fat) beef to brown crumbles.
5. Pulse apples, peas, spinach, cod liver oil, safflower oil, and salmon oil until small kernels.
6. Add HILARY'S BLEND™ supplement to the tomato sauce and mix thoroughly.
7. Stir all ingredients together.

INGREDIENTS		
APPROX.	INGREDIENT	GRAMS
2 cups	Apples, raw with skin, sliced	220
½ cup	Beans, kidney, canned	128
210 g raw	Beef, ground, cooked	159
½ tsp	Cod liver oil	2
1½ cups	Peas, thawed from frozen	218
2 small	Potatoes, boiled in skin	206
2 tsp	Safflower oil	9
½ tsp	Salmon oil	2
1 leaf	Spinach, raw	10
⅛ cup	Tomato sauce, canned	31
1½ scoops	HILARY'S BLEND™ supplement	15
	Total	1000

METABOLIZABLE ENERGY

107 kcal/100 grams

FEEDING GUIDE				
Body weight		Energy intake	Amount to feed	
lbs	kg	kcal/day	grams/day	
10	4.5	265	247	
20	9.1	445	416	
40	18.2	748	699	
60	27.3	1014	948	
80	36.4	1259	1176	
100	45.5	1488	1391	

Hilary's Blend™
Supplement for home-made meals

NUTRITION				
		Per 100g As Fed	Per 100g Dry Matter	Per 1000 kcal
PROTEIN	g	6.89	27.47	64.07
Arginine	g	0.44	1.76	4.10
Histidine	g	0.20	0.80	1.87
Isoleucine	g	0.29	1.17	2.73
Leucine	g	0.51	2.03	4.73
Lysine	g	0.52	2.08	4.85
Methionine + Cystine	g	0.22	0.87	2.03
Phenylalanine + Tyrosine	g	0.48	1.91	4.45
Threonine	g	0.26	1.05	2.45
Tryptophan	g	0.06	0.24	0.56
Valine	g	0.34	1.35	3.15
FAT (LIPID)	g	3.45	13.75	32.07
Linoleic acid	g	0.80	3.17	7.39
MINERALS				
Calcium	mg	214.09	854.08	1991.88
Phosphorus	mg	153.59	612.74	1429.03
Calcium to Phosphorus ratio		1.39	1.39	1.39
Potassium	mg	382.33	1525.26	3557.21
Sodium	mg	73.51	293.27	683.96
Magnesium	mg	25.06	99.96	233.13
Iron	mg	4.56	18.20	42.45
Copper	mg	0.39	1.57	3.66
Manganese	mg	0.39	1.54	3.59
Zinc	mg	6.33	25.27	58.93
Iodine	mg	0.09	0.36	0.84
Selenium	µg	3.97	15.85	36.97
VITAMINS				
Vitamin A	IU	484	1930	4502
Vitamin D	IU	25	101	235
Vitamin E	mg	4.71	18.78	43.80
Thiamin	mg	0.14	0.57	1.33
Riboflavin	mg	0.20	0.80	1.87
Niacin	mg	2.18	8.71	20.31
Pantothenic acid	mg	0.89	3.55	8.28
Pyridoxine	mg	0.24	0.94	2.19
Folic acid	µg	12.00	47.87	111.64
Choline	mg	80.07	319.43	744.97
Vitamin B12	µg	1.63	6.51	15.18
OTHER (non-essential nutrients)				
Total dietary fiber	g	2.45	9.79	22.83
FATTY ACIDS				
Polyunsaturated fatty acids	g	0.97	3.87	9.03
Eicosapentaenoic acid	mg	40	160	373
Docosahexaenoic acid	mg	58	230	536
Omega 6:3 ratio (estimate)		8.9	8.9	8.9
ANTIOXIDANTS				
Vitamin C	mg	13.06	52.11	121.53
Beta-carotene	µg	167.0	666.1	1553.5
Lycopene	µg	469.7	1873.9	4370.2
Lutein + Zeaxanthin	µg	670.2	2673.7	6235.6

www.CompleteandBalanced.com

Senior Recipe 8

NUTRITION		Per 100g As Fed	Per 100g Dry Matter	Per 1000 kcal
PROTEIN	g	10.03	28.80	56.63
Arginine	g	0.84	2.42	4.76
Histidine	g	0.25	0.72	1.42
Isoleucine	g	0.40	1.15	2.26
Leucine	g	0.72	2.07	4.07
Lysine	g	0.57	1.64	3.22
Methionine + Cystine	g	0.32	0.91	1.79
Phenylalanine + Tyrosine	g	0.76	2.17	4.27
Threonine	g	0.38	1.10	2.16
Tryptophan	g	0.10	0.28	0.55
Valine	g	0.46	1.33	2.62
FAT (LIPID)	g	11.27	32.34	63.59
Linoleic acid	g	2.30	6.59	12.96
MINERALS				
Calcium	mg	327.54	940.40	1849.22
Phosphorus	mg	262.87	754.70	1484.05
Calcium to Phosphorus ratio		1.25	1.25	1.25
Potassium	mg	452.35	1298.72	2553.82
Sodium	mg	31.67	90.91	178.77
Magnesium	mg	69.10	198.40	390.14
Iron	mg	6.19	17.77	34.94
Copper	mg	0.61	1.75	3.44
Manganese	mg	0.93	2.66	5.23
Zinc	mg	7.74	22.21	43.67
Iodine	mg	0.12	0.34	0.67
Selenium	µg	11.54	33.13	65.15
VITAMINS				
Vitamin A	IU	1133	3254	6399
Vitamin D	IU	57	164	322
Vitamin E	mg	10.34	29.69	58.38
Thiamin	mg	0.21	0.61	1.20
Riboflavin	mg	0.47	1.36	2.67
Niacin	mg	2.52	7.25	14.26
Pantothenic acid	mg	1.17	3.36	6.61
Pyridoxine	mg	0.23	0.66	1.30
Folic acid	µg	16.00	45.94	90.34
Choline	mg	123.70	355.15	698.37
Vitamin B12	µg	1.87	5.36	10.54
OTHER (non-essential nutrients)				
Total dietary fiber	g	4.81	13.82	27.18
FATTY ACIDS				
Polyunsaturated fatty acids	g	2.75	7.89	15.52
Eicosapentaenoic acid	mg	120	340	669
Docosahexaenoic acid	mg	205	590	1160
Omega 6:3 ratio (estimate)		7.4	7.4	7.4
ANTIOXIDANTS				
Vitamin C	mg	19.90	57.13	112.34
Beta-carotene	µg	323.3	928.3	1825.3
Lycopene	µg	0	0	0
Lutein + Zeaxanthin	µg	1616.8	4642.0	9128.0

1. Thaw frozen peas overnight in the refrigerator.
2. Hard boil eggs. Discard shells and mash coarsely.
3. Pulse almonds, peanut butter, peas, spinach, zucchini, cod liver oil, and salmon oil to small kernels.
4. Add HILARY'S BLEND™ supplement to the eggs and mix thoroughly.
5. Stir all ingredients together.

INGREDIENTS		
APPROX.	INGREDIENT	GRAMS
1⅔ cups	Almonds, ground	150
1 tsp	Cod liver oil	5
3 large	Eggs, hard-boiled	150
1 tbsp	Peanut butter, smooth, unsalted	16
3 cups	Peas, thawed from frozen	435
1 tsp	Salmon oil	5
2 leaves	Spinach, raw	20
	Tuna, canned in water, drained	85
1 cup	Zucchini, raw, sliced	114
2 scoops	HILARY'S BLEND™ supplement	20
	Total	1000

FEEDING GUIDE				
Body weight		Energy intake	Amount to feed	
lbs	kg	kcal/day	grams/day	
10	4.5	265	149	
20	9.1	445	251	
40	18.2	748	423	
60	27.3	1014	573	
80	36.4	1259	711	
100	45.5	1488	841	

METABOLIZABLE ENERGY

177 kcal/100 grams

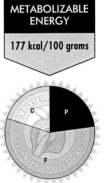

Supplement for home-made meals

Senior Recipe 9

1. Poach fish until it flakes easily.
2. Prepare oatmeal according to package instructions to yield ¾ cup of cooked oatmeal.
3. Pulse almonds, bananas, broccoli, carrots, cod liver oil, safflower oil and salmon oil to small kernels.
4. Add HILARY'S BLEND™ supplement to the yogurt and mix thoroughly.
5. Stir all ingredients together.

INGREDIENTS		
APPROX.	INGREDIENT	GRAMS
½ cup	Almonds, ground	48
1 cup	Bananas, raw, sliced	150
1 cup	Broccoli, raw, chopped	91
1½ cup	Carrots, raw, grated	165
½ tsp	Cod liver oil	2
300 g raw	Flatfish/sole, cooked	208
¾ cup	Oatmeal, cooked	176
4 tsp	Safflower oil	18
1 tsp	Salmon oil	5
½ cup	Yogurt, plain, low fat	122
1½ scoops	HILARY'S BLEND™ supplement	15
	Total	1000

METABOLIZABLE ENERGY

117 kcal/100 grams

FEEDING GUIDE			
Body weight		Energy intake	Amount to feed
lbs	kg	kcal/day	grams/day
10	4.5	265	226
20	9.1	445	380
40	18.2	748	640
60	27.3	1014	867
80	36.4	1259	1076
100	45.5	1488	1272

Hilary's Blend™
Supplement for home-made meals

NUTRITION		Per 100g As Fed	Per 100g Dry Matter	Per 1000 kcal
PROTEIN	g	7.72	30.60	66.09
Arginine	g	0.51	2.02	4.36
Histidine	g	0.23	0.90	1.94
Isoleucine	g	0.34	1.36	2.94
Leucine	g	0.62	2.45	5.29
Lysine	g	0.60	2.39	5.16
Methionine + Cystine	g	0.30	1.17	2.53
Phenylalanine + Tyrosine	g	0.59	2.36	5.10
Threonine	g	0.34	1.34	2.89
Tryptophan	g	0.08	0.32	0.69
Valine	g	0.41	1.61	3.48
FAT (LIPID)	g	5.68	22.52	48.64
Linoleic acid	g	2.03	8.05	17.39
MINERALS				
Calcium	mg	248.62	986.10	2129.62
Phosphorus	mg	195.37	774.89	1673.48
Calcium to Phosphorus ratio		1.27	1.27	1.27
Potassium	mg	391.55	1553.00	3353.92
Sodium	mg	47.77	189.45	409.14
Magnesium	mg	42.36	168.02	362.86
Iron	mg	3.99	15.82	34.17
Copper	mg	0.36	1.43	3.09
Manganese	mg	0.54	2.13	4.60
Zinc	mg	5.41	21.45	46.32
Iodine	mg	0.09	0.36	0.78
Selenium	µg	14.46	57.36	123.88
VITAMINS				
Vitamin A	IU	3056	12119	26173
Vitamin D	IU	25	100	216
Vitamin E	mg	6.11	24.24	52.35
Thiamin	mg	0.11	0.43	0.93
Riboflavin	mg	0.25	1.00	2.16
Niacin	mg	1.21	4.81	10.39
Pantothenic acid	mg	1.00	3.96	8.55
Pyridoxine	mg	0.21	0.81	1.75
Folic acid	µg	12.00	47.60	102.80
Choline	mg	87.13	345.58	746.33
Vitamin B12	µg	1.79	7.10	15.33
OTHER (non-essential nutrients)				
Total dietary fiber	g	2.35	9.31	20.11
FATTY ACIDS				
Polyunsaturated fatty acids	g	2.41	9.56	20.65
Eicosapentaenoic acid	mg	129	510	1101
Docosahexaenoic acid	mg	167	660	1425
Omega 6:3 ratio (estimate)		7.1	7.1	7.1
ANTIOXIDANTS				
Vitamin C	mg	10.49	41.62	89.88
Beta-carotene	µg	1403.8	5567.9	12024.7
Lycopene	µg	0.2	0.7	1.4
Lutein + Zeaxanthin	µg	204.9	812.9	1755.5

Senior Recipe 10

NUTRITION		Per 100g As Fed	Per 100g Dry Matter	Per 1000 kcal
PROTEIN	g	7.52	31.00	61.27
Arginine	g	0.44	1.82	3.60
Histidine	g	0.20	0.84	1.66
Isoleucine	g	0.36	1.48	2.93
Leucine	g	0.61	2.53	5.00
Lysine	g	0.62	2.54	5.02
Methionine + Cystine	g	0.32	1.33	2.63
Phenylalanine + Tyrosine	g	0.60	2.48	4.90
Threonine	g	0.34	1.39	2.75
Tryptophan	g	0.08	0.34	0.67
Valine	g	0.42	1.71	3.38
FAT (LIPID)	g	6.91	28.48	56.29
Linoleic acid	g	2.09	8.63	17.06
MINERALS				
Calcium	mg	233.54	963.27	1903.77
Phosphorus	mg	175.49	723.83	1430.55
Calcium to Phosphorus ratio		1.33	1.33	1.33
Potassium	mg	319.85	1319.25	2607.32
Sodium	mg	47.13	194.39	384.19
Magnesium	mg	21.55	88.90	175.70
Iron	mg	3.92	16.16	31.94
Copper	mg	0.32	1.31	2.59
Manganese	mg	0.42	1.72	3.40
Zinc	mg	5.31	21.89	43.26
Iodine	mg	0.09	0.37	0.73
Selenium	µg	14.46	59.64	117.87
VITAMINS				
Vitamin A	IU	1352	5576	11020
Vitamin D	IU	25	104	206
Vitamin E	mg	4.88	20.12	39.76
Thiamin	mg	0.15	0.60	1.19
Riboflavin	mg	0.27	1.10	2.17
Niacin	mg	2.25	9.29	18.36
Pantothenic acid	mg	1.28	5.27	10.42
Pyridoxine	mg	0.25	1.03	2.04
Folic acid	µg	12.00	49.50	97.83
Choline	mg	99.75	411.44	813.15
Vitamin B12	µg	1.98	8.15	16.11
OTHER (non-essential nutrients)				
Total dietary fiber	g	1.50	6.19	12.23
FATTY ACIDS				
Polyunsaturated fatty acids	g	2.94	12.12	23.95
Eicosapentaenoic acid	mg	153	630	1245
Docosahexaenoic acid	mg	320	1320	2609
Omega 6:3 ratio (estimate)		5.2	5.2	5.2
ANTIOXIDANTS				
Vitamin C	mg	15.98	65.89	130.22
Beta-carotene	µg	527.3	2175.0	4298.6
Lycopene	µg	193.0	796.2	1573.5
Lutein + Zeaxanthin	µg	213.8	881.9	1742.9

1. Poach salmon until it flakes easily.
2. Hard boil eggs. Discard shells and mash coarsely.
3. Prepare rice according to package instructions to yield ½ cup of cooked rice.
4. Pulse blueberries, broccoli, carrots, honey, pears, strawberries, tomatoes, cod liver oil, and safflower oil to small kernels.
5. Add HILARY'S BLEND™ supplement to the yogurt.
6. Stir all ingredients together.

INGREDIENTS		
APPROX.	INGREDIENT	GRAMS
½ cup	Blueberries, raw	74
1 cup	Broccoli, raw, chopped	91
½ cup	Carrots, raw, grated	55
½ tsp	Cod liver oil	2
3 large	Eggs, hard-boiled	150
½ tbsp	Honey	11
¼ cup	Pears, raw, chopped	40
½ cup	Rice, brown, cooked	98
5 tsp	Safflower oil	23
290 g raw	Salmon, Atlantic, cooked	201
½ cup	Strawberries, raw, sliced	83
½ cup	Tomatoes, cherry, raw	75
⅓ cup	Yogurt, plain, low fat	82
1½ scoops	HILARY'S BLEND™ supplement	15
	Total	1000

FEEDING GUIDE			
Body weight		Energy intake	Amount to feed
lbs	kg	kcal/day	grams/day
10	4.5	265	215
20	9.1	445	362
40	18.2	748	608
60	27.3	1014	825
80	36.4	1259	1023
100	45.5	1488	1210

METABOLIZABLE ENERGY

123 kcal/100 grams

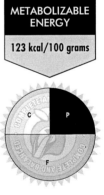

Supplement for home-made meals

Hilary's Blend™

Low Calorie Recipe 1

1. Poach cod until it flakes easily.
2. Hard boil eggs. Discard shells and mash coarsely.
3. Pulse alfalfa sprouts, carrots, celery, cucumber, spinach, cod liver oil, and safflower oil to small kernels.
4. Add HILARY'S BLEND™ supplement to the tomato sauce and mix thoroughly.
5. Stir all ingredients together.

INGREDIENTS		
APPROX.	INGREDIENT	GRAMS
5 cups	Alfalfa sprouts, raw	165
½ cup	Carrots, raw, grated	55
¾ cup	Celery, raw, chopped	75
½ tsp	Cod liver oil	2
385 g raw	Cod, Atlantic, cooked	270
¾ cup	Cucumber, raw with peel, sliced	77
4 large	Eggs, hard-boiled	200
2 tsp	Safflower oil	9
1 leaf	Spinach, raw	10
½ cup	Tomato sauce, canned	122
1 ½ scoops	HILARY'S BLEND™ supplement	15
	Total	1000

METABOLIZABLE ENERGY

81 kcal/100 grams

FEEDING GUIDE			
Body weight		Energy intake*	Amount to feed
lbs	kg	kcal/day	grams/day
10	4.5	171	211
20	9.1	288	355
40	18.2	484	598
60	27.3	656	810
80	36.4	814	1005
100	45.5	963	1189

* Induces approximately 1% loss of body weight each week.

Hilary's Blend™

Supplement for home-made meals

NUTRITION				
		Per 100g As Fed	Per 100g Dry Matter	Per 1000 kcal
PROTEIN	g	9.68	54.15	119.12
Arginine	g	0.54	2.99	6.58
Histidine	g	0.25	1.39	3.06
Isoleucine	g	0.46	2.56	5.63
Leucine	g	0.78	4.35	9.57
Lysine	g	0.80	4.47	9.83
Methionine + Cystine	g	0.40	2.22	4.88
Phenylalanine + Tyrosine	g	0.71	3.98	8.75
Threonine	g	0.43	2.42	5.32
Tryptophan	g	0.11	0.59	1.30
Valine	g	0.51	2.84	6.25
FAT (LIPID)	g	3.63	20.30	44.65
Linoleic acid	g	0.97	5.45	11.99
MINERALS				
Calcium	mg	225.68	1262.36	2776.86
Phosphorus	mg	158.45	886.26	1949.54
Calcium to Phosphorus ratio		1.42	1.42	1.42
Potassium	mg	311.00	1739.56	3826.57
Sodium	mg	124.14	694.38	1527.45
Magnesium	mg	26.22	146.65	322.59
Iron	mg	4.19	23.42	51.52
Copper	mg	0.33	1.87	4.11
Manganese	mg	0.31	1.74	3.83
Zinc	mg	5.42	30.32	66.70
Iodine	mg	0.09	0.50	1.10
Selenium	µg	16.50	92.32	203.08
VITAMINS				
Vitamin A	IU	1458	8156	17940
Vitamin D	IU	25	141	311
Vitamin E	mg	5.18	28.98	63.75
Thiamin	mg	0.10	0.54	1.19
Riboflavin	mg	0.29	1.59	3.50
Niacin	mg	1.22	6.84	15.05
Pantothenic acid	mg	1.08	6.01	13.22
Pyridoxine	mg	0.18	1.01	2.22
Folic acid	µg	12.00	67.12	147.65
Choline	mg	132.65	741.96	1632.12
Vitamin B12	µg	1.71	9.54	20.99
OTHER (non-essential nutrients)				
Total dietary fiber	g	1.21	6.75	14.85
FATTY ACIDS				
Polyunsaturated fatty acids	g	1.17	6.55	14.41
Eicosapentaenoic acid	mg	16	90	198
Docosahexaenoic acid	mg	71	400	880
Omega 6:3 ratio (estimate)		12.5	12.5	12.5
ANTIOXIDANTS				
Vitamin C	mg	3.53	19.75	43.44
Beta-carotene	µg	577.7	3231.4	7108.2
Lycopene	µg	1848.6	10340.1	22745.6
Lutein + Zeaxanthin	µg	229.7	1284.6	2825.7

Low Calorie Recipe 2

NUTRITION		Per 100g As Fed	Per 100g Dry Matter	Per 1000 kcal
PROTEIN	g	10.82	52.34	122.04
Arginine	g	0.61	2.94	6.86
Histidine	g	0.30	1.47	3.43
Isoleucine	g	0.54	2.62	6.11
Leucine	g	0.80	3.85	8.98
Lysine	g	0.87	4.19	9.77
Methionine + Cystine	g	0.39	1.91	4.45
Phenylalanine + Tyrosine	g	0.76	3.67	8.56
Threonine	g	0.45	2.15	5.01
Tryptophan	g	0.12	0.56	1.31
Valine	g	0.54	2.59	6.04
FAT (LIPID)	g	3.16	15.30	35.67
Linoleic acid	g	1.06	5.13	11.96
MINERALS				
Calcium	mg	237.04	1147.24	2674.97
Phosphorus	mg	175.14	847.66	1976.45
Calcium to Phosphorus ratio		1.35	1.35	1.35
Potassium	mg	340.84	1649.65	3846.41
Sodium	mg	79.11	382.86	892.70
Magnesium	mg	32.32	156.42	364.72
Iron	mg	4.22	20.40	47.57
Copper	mg	0.35	1.69	3.94
Manganese	mg	0.32	1.55	3.61
Zinc	mg	5.48	26.50	61.79
Iodine	mg	0.09	0.44	1.03
Selenium	µg	8.83	42.73	99.63
VITAMINS				
Vitamin A	IU	730	3535	8242
Vitamin D	IU	25	122	285
Vitamin E	mg	4.91	23.76	55.40
Thiamin	mg	0.11	0.54	1.26
Riboflavin	mg	0.23	1.12	2.61
Niacin	mg	4.61	22.31	52.02
Pantothenic acid	mg	1.08	5.22	12.17
Pyridoxine	mg	0.28	1.34	3.12
Folic acid	µg	12.00	58.08	135.42
Choline	mg	67.82	328.25	765.37
Vitamin B12	µg	1.34	6.49	15.13
OTHER (non-essential nutrients)				
Total dietary fiber	g	1.87	9.03	21.05
FATTY ACIDS				
Polyunsaturated fatty acids	g	1.39	6.73	15.69
Eicosapentaenoic acid	mg	82	400	933
Docosahexaenoic acid	mg	119	570	1329
Omega 6:3 ratio (estimate)		5.9	5.9	5.9
ANTIOXIDANTS				
Vitamin C	mg	20.37	98.61	229.92
Beta-carotene	µg	305.8	1479.8	3450.5
Lycopene	µg	1242.5	6013.4	14021.2
Lutein + Zeaxanthin	µg	749.5	3627.5	8458.0

1. Thaw frozen peas overnight in the refrigerator.
2. Simmer chicken until tender. Dice finely.
3. Pulse alfalfa sprouts, beans, broccoli, peas, spinach, strawberries, cod liver oil, safflower oil, and salmon oil to small kernels.
4. Add HILARY'S BLEND™ supplement to the tomato sauce and mix thoroughly.
5. Stir all ingredients together.

INGREDIENTS		
APPROX.	INGREDIENT	GRAMS
4 cups	Alfalfa sprouts, raw	132
1 cup	Beans, green, raw, chopped	110
1 cup	Broccoli, raw, chopped	91
540 g raw	Chicken breast, cooked	282
½ tsp	Cod liver oil	2
½ cup	Peas, thawed from frozen	74
2½ tsp	Safflower oil	11
1 tsp	Salmon oil	5
3 leaves	Spinach, raw	30
½ cup	Strawberries, raw, sliced	84
⅓ cup	Tomato sauce, canned	82
⅓ cup	Yogurt, plain, low fat	82
1½ scoops	HILARY'S BLEND™ supplement	15
	Total	1000

FEEDING GUIDE			
Body weight		Energy intake*	Amount to feed
lbs	kg	kcal/day	grams/day
10	4.5	171	192
20	9.1	288	324
40	18.2	484	544
60	27.3	656	738
80	36.4	814	915
100	45.5	963	1082

* Induces approximately 1% loss of body weight each week.

METABOLIZABLE ENERGY

89 kcal/100 grams

Supplement for home-made meals

Low Calorie Recipe 3

1. Poach fish until it flakes easily.
2. Pulse blueberries, broccoli, carrots, celery, honey, cod liver oil, and safflower oil to small kernels.
3. Add HILARY'S BLEND™ supplement to the tomato sauce and mix thoroughly.
4. Stir all ingredients together.

INGREDIENTS		
APPROX.	INGREDIENT	GRAMS
1 ¼ cups	Blueberries, raw	185
1 cup	Broccoli, raw, chopped	91
1 cup	Carrots, raw, grated	110
1 cup	Celery, raw, chopped	101
½ tsp	Cod liver oil	2
460 g raw	Flatfish/sole, cooked	323
3 tbsp	Honey	63
4 tsp	Safflower oil	18
¼ cup	Tomato sauce, canned	61
⅛ cup	Yogurt, plain, low fat	31
1 ½ scoops	HILARY'S BLEND™ supplement	15
	Total	1000

METABOLIZABLE ENERGY

98 kcal/100 grams

FEEDING GUIDE			
Body weight		Energy intake*	Amount to feed
lbs	kg	kcal/day	grams/day
10	4.5	171	175
20	9.1	288	294
40	18.2	484	494
60	27.3	656	670
80	36.4	814	831
100	45.5	963	982

* Induces approximately 1% loss of body weight each week.

Hilary's Blend™
Supplement for home-made meals

NUTRITION		Per 100g As Fed	Per 100g Dry Matter	Per 1000 kcal
PROTEIN	g	8.63	35.93	87.69
Arginine	g	0.51	2.12	5.17
Histidine	g	0.25	1.03	2.51
Isoleucine	g	0.39	1.63	3.98
Leucine	g	0.69	2.86	6.98
Lysine	g	0.76	3.18	7.76
Methionine + Cystine	g	0.35	1.44	3.51
Phenylalanine + Tyrosine	g	0.63	2.62	6.39
Threonine	g	0.39	1.61	3.93
Tryptophan	g	0.10	0.40	0.98
Valine	g	0.45	1.85	4.52
FAT (LIPID)	g	2.69	11.20	27.34
Linoleic acid	g	1.39	5.80	14.16
MINERALS				
Calcium	mg	223.72	931.14	2272.57
Phosphorus	mg	180.15	749.81	1830.01
Calcium to Phosphorus ratio		1.24	1.24	1.24
Potassium	mg	358.79	1493.37	3644.77
Sodium	mg	89.93	374.31	913.55
Magnesium	mg	28.27	117.65	287.14
Iron	mg	3.83	15.93	38.88
Copper	mg	0.31	1.31	3.20
Manganese	mg	0.35	1.46	3.56
Zinc	mg	5.20	21.64	52.82
Iodine	mg	0.09	0.37	0.90
Selenium	µg	19.26	80.17	195.67
VITAMINS				
Vitamin A	IU	2198	9148	22327
Vitamin D	IU	25	105	257
Vitamin E	mg	5.08	21.13	51.57
Thiamin	mg	0.09	0.36	0.88
Riboflavin	mg	0.20	0.83	2.03
Niacin	mg	1.29	5.37	13.11
Pantothenic acid	mg	0.94	3.91	9.54
Pyridoxine	mg	0.18	0.75	1.83
Folic acid	µg	12.00	49.95	121.91
Choline	mg	91.63	381.40	930.86
Vitamin B12	µg	2.03	8.44	20.60
OTHER (non-essential nutrients)				
Total dietary fiber	g	1.63	6.78	16.55
FATTY ACIDS				
Polyunsaturated fatty acids	g	1.65	6.88	16.79
Eicosapentaenoic acid	mg	92	380	927
Docosahexaenoic acid	mg	105	440	1074
Omega 6:3 ratio (estimate)		7.4	7.4	7.4
ANTIOXIDANTS				
Vitamin C	mg	11.36	47.27	115.37
Beta-carotene	µg	990.1	4121.1	10058.2
Lycopene	µg	924.4	3847.4	9390.2
Lutein + Zeaxanthin	µg	199.2	829.2	2023.7

Low Calorie Recipe 4

NUTRITION		Per 100g As Fed	Per 100g Dry Matter	Per 1000 kcal
PROTEIN	g	8.63	44.55	90.70
Arginine	g	0.43	2.22	4.52
Histidine	g	0.20	1.03	2.10
Isoleucine	g	0.43	2.24	4.56
Leucine	g	0.72	3.74	7.61
Lysine	g	0.62	3.18	6.47
Methionine + Cystine	g	0.34	1.76	3.58
Phenylalanine + Tyrosine	g	0.68	3.50	7.13
Threonine	g	0.37	1.89	3.85
Tryptophan	g	0.09	0.44	0.90
Valine	g	0.49	2.53	5.15
FAT (LIPID)	g	5.55	28.64	58.31
Linoleic acid	g	0.53	2.73	5.56
MINERALS				
Calcium	mg	256.97	1326.65	2700.89
Phosphorus	mg	205.26	1059.71	2157.43
Calcium to Phosphorus ratio		1.25	1.25	1.25
Potassium	mg	262.90	1357.29	2763.27
Sodium	mg	77.24	398.74	811.78
Magnesium	mg	23.18	119.69	243.67
Iron	mg	5.45	28.13	57.27
Copper	mg	0.39	2.00	4.07
Manganese	mg	0.40	2.05	4.17
Zinc	mg	6.00	30.97	63.05
Iodine	mg	0.09	0.46	0.94
Selenium	µg	18.27	94.32	192.02
VITAMINS				
Vitamin A	IU	2194	11326	23057
Vitamin D	IU	26	133	270
Vitamin E	mg	5.04	26.00	52.93
Thiamin	mg	0.12	0.61	1.24
Riboflavin	mg	0.55	2.85	5.80
Niacin	mg	1.62	8.36	17.02
Pantothenic acid	mg	1.90	9.80	19.95
Pyridoxine	mg	0.21	1.06	2.16
Folic acid	µg	12.00	61.95	126.12
Choline	mg	162.52	839.07	1708.24
Vitamin B12	µg	3.25	16.78	34.16
OTHER (non-essential nutrients)				
Total dietary fiber	g	1.31	6.75	13.74
FATTY ACIDS				
Polyunsaturated fatty acids	g	0.78	4.01	8.16
Eicosapentaenoic acid	mg	15	80	163
Docosahexaenoic acid	mg	33	170	346
Omega 6:3 ratio (estimate)		15.2	15.2	15.2
ANTIOXIDANTS				
Vitamin C	mg	8.68	44.80	91.21
Beta-carotene	µg	275.7	1423.3	2897.7
Lycopene	µg	2.1	10.8	22.1
Lutein + Zeaxanthin	µg	846.3	4369.3	8895.3

1. Simmer chicken liver until cooked. Mash.
2. Hard boil eggs. Discard shells and mash coarsely.
3. Pulse alfalfa sprouts, blueberries, spinach, zucchini, and cod liver oil to small kernels,
4. Add HILARY'S BLEND™ supplement to the eggs and mix thoroughly.
5. Stir all ingredients together.

INGREDIENTS		
APPROX.	INGREDIENT	GRAMS
9 cups	Alfalfa sprouts, raw	294
¼ cup	Applesauce, canned	61
¼ cup	Blueberries, raw	37
⅓ cup	Cheese, cheddar, shredded	38
½ tsp	Cod liver oil	2
6 large	Eggs, hard-boiled	300
160 g raw	Liver, chicken, cooked	100
4 leaves	Spinach, raw	40
1 cup	Zucchini, raw, sliced	113
1½ scoops	HILARY'S BLEND™ supplement	15
	Total	1000

FEEDING GUIDE			
Body weight		Energy intake*	Amount to feed
lbs	kg	kcal/day	grams/day
10	4.5	171	180
20	9.1	288	303
40	18.2	484	510
60	27.3	656	691
80	36.4	814	857
100	45.5	963	1013

* Induces approximately 1% loss of body weight each week.

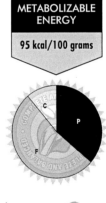

METABOLIZABLE ENERGY

95 kcal/100 grams

Hilary's

Supplement for home-made meals Blend ™

R50

Low Calorie Recipe 5

1. Thaw frozen peas overnight in the refrigerator.
2. Hard boil egg. Discard shell and mash coarsely.
3. Pulse bananas, lettuce, peas, strawberries, cod liver oil, and safflower oil to small kernels.
4. Add HILARY'S BLEND™ supplement to the tomato sauce and mix thoroughly.
5. Stir all ingredients together.

INGREDIENTS

APPROX.	INGREDIENT	GRAMS
¼ cup	Applesauce, canned, unsweetened	61
⅓ cup	Bananas, raw, sliced	50
½ cup	Cheese, cottage, low fat	113
½ tsp	Cod liver oil	2
1 large	Egg, hard-boiled	50
¾ cup	Lettuce, raw, shredded	50
1 cup	Peas, thawed from frozen	145
4 tsp	Safflower oil	18
⅓ cup	Strawberries, raw, sliced	55
¼ cup	Tomato sauce, canned	61
	Tuna, canned in water, drained	258
½ cup	Yogurt, plain, low fat	122
1 ½ scoops	HILARY'S BLEND™ supplement	15
	Total	1000

METABOLIZABLE ENERGY

98 kcal/100 grams

FEEDING GUIDE

Body weight		Energy intake*	Amount to feed
lbs	kg	kcal/day	grams/day
10	4.5	171	175
20	9.1	288	294
40	18.2	484	494
60	27.3	656	670
80	36.4	814	831
100	45.5	963	982

* Induces approximately 1% loss of body weight each week.

Hilary's Blend™

Supplement for home-made meals

NUTRITION

		Per 100g As Fed	Per 100g Dry Matter	Per 1000 kcal
PROTEIN	g	9.78	45.38	100.12
Arginine	g	0.55	2.57	5.67
Histidine	g	0.28	1.29	2.85
Isoleucine	g	0.47	2.16	4.77
Leucine	g	0.81	3.78	8.34
Lysine	g	0.83	3.85	8.49
Methionine + Cystine	g	0.38	1.76	3.88
Phenylalanine + Tyrosine	g	0.78	3.62	7.99
Threonine	g	0.42	1.96	4.32
Tryptophan	g	0.10	0.48	1.06
Valine	g	0.53	2.47	5.45
FAT (LIPID)	g	3.71	17.23	38.02
Linoleic acid	g	1.46	6.78	14.96
MINERALS				
Calcium	mg	239.96	1113.73	2457.26
Phosphorus	mg	184.39	855.80	1888.18
Calcium to Phosphorus ratio		1.30	1.30	1.30
Potassium	mg	311.72	1446.80	3192.13
Sodium	mg	109.71	509.18	1123.42
Magnesium	mg	22.47	104.26	230.03
Iron	mg	4.13	19.16	42.27
Copper	mg	0.33	1.53	3.38
Manganese	mg	0.34	1.59	3.51
Zinc	mg	5.38	24.96	55.07
Iodine	mg	0.09	0.42	0.93
Selenium	µg	20.28	94.12	207.66
VITAMINS				
Vitamin A	IU	408	1893	4177
Vitamin D	IU	25	117	259
Vitamin E	mg	4.71	21.84	48.19
Thiamin	mg	0.10	0.44	0.97
Riboflavin	mg	0.24	1.11	2.45
Niacin	mg	2.20	10.22	22.55
Pantothenic acid	mg	0.85	3.93	8.67
Pyridoxine	mg	0.18	0.82	1.81
Folic acid	µg	12.00	55.70	122.89
Choline	mg	75.07	348.42	768.73
Vitamin B12	µg	1.70	7.88	17.39
OTHER (non-essential nutrients)				
Total dietary fiber	g	1.58	7.33	16.17
FATTY ACIDS				
Polyunsaturated fatty acids	g	1.80	8.36	18.44
Eicosapentaenoic acid	mg	74	340	750
Docosahexaenoic acid	mg	186	860	1897
Omega 6:3 ratio (estimate)		5.9	5.9	5.9
ANTIOXIDANTS				
Vitamin C	mg	10.21	47.37	104.51
Beta-carotene	µg	96.2	446.4	984.8
Lycopene	µg	924.3	4289.8	9464.8
Lutein + Zeaxanthin	µg	394.3	1830.0	4037.7

Low Calorie Recipe 6

NUTRITION		Per 100g As Fed	Per 100g Dry Matter	Per 1000 kcal
PROTEIN	g	6.81	35.19	86.87
Arginine	g	0.41	2.13	5.26
Histidine	g	0.18	0.94	2.32
Isoleucine	g	0.31	1.59	3.92
Leucine	g	0.54	2.76	6.81
Lysine	g	0.57	2.92	7.21
Methionine + Cystine	g	0.26	1.32	3.26
Phenylalanine + Tyrosine	g	0.51	2.64	6.52
Threonine	g	0.32	1.63	4.02
Tryptophan	g	0.07	0.34	0.84
Valine	g	0.37	1.93	4.76
FAT (LIPID)	g	2.35	12.11	29.89
Linoleic acid	g	1.12	5.76	14.22
MINERALS				
Calcium	mg	256.24	1323.43	3266.84
Phosphorus	mg	183.15	945.93	2335.00
Calcium to Phosphorus ratio		1.40	1.40	1.40
Potassium	mg	393.20	2030.83	5013.03
Sodium	mg	55.04	284.25	701.66
Magnesium	mg	29.47	152.19	375.68
Iron	mg	4.04	20.89	51.57
Copper	mg	0.34	1.74	4.30
Manganese	mg	0.39	2.00	4.94
Zinc	mg	5.50	28.41	70.13
Iodine	mg	0.09	0.46	1.14
Selenium	µg	10.97	56.66	139.86
VITAMINS				
Vitamin A	IU	4195	21667	53484
Vitamin D	IU	25	130	322
Vitamin E	mg	4.93	25.46	62.85
Thiamin	mg	0.14	0.74	1.83
Riboflavin	mg	0.24	1.25	3.09
Niacin	mg	1.41	7.25	17.90
Pantothenic acid	mg	0.99	5.12	12.64
Pyridoxine	mg	0.19	0.99	2.44
Folic acid	µg	12.00	61.98	153.00
Choline	mg	81.37	420.26	1037.40
Vitamin B12	µg	1.71	8.85	21.85
OTHER (non-essential nutrients)				
Total dietary fiber	g	2.58	13.30	32.83
FATTY ACIDS				
Polyunsaturated fatty acids	g	1.28	6.59	16.27
Eicosapentaenoic acid	mg	53	280	691
Docosahexaenoic acid	mg	64	330	815
Omega 6:3 ratio (estimate)		9.9	9.9	9.9
ANTIOXIDANTS				
Vitamin C	mg	26.40	136.36	336.60
Beta-carotene	µg	1986.3	10258.9	25323.8
Lycopene	µg	0.2	1.1	2.8
Lutein + Zeaxanthin	µg	851.7	4398.7	10858.0

1. Thaw frozen peas overnight in the refrigerator.
2. Poach fish until it flakes easily.
3. Pulse broccoli, carrots, peas, cod liver oil, and safflower oil to small kernels.
4. Add HILARY'S BLEND™ supplement to the yogurt and mix thoroughly.
5. Stir all ingredients together.

INGREDIENTS		
APPROX.	INGREDIENT	GRAMS
2 cups	Broccoli, raw, chopped	182
2 cups	Carrots, raw, grated	220
½ tsp	Cod liver oil	2
230 g raw	Flatfish/sole, cooked	163
1½ cups	Peas, thawed from frozen	218
3 tsp	Safflower oil	14
¾ cup	Yogurt, plain, low fat	186
1½ scoops	HILARY'S BLEND™ supplement	15
	Total	1000

FEEDING GUIDE			
Body weight		Energy intake*	Amount to feed
lbs	kg	kcal/day	grams/day
10	4.5	171	220
20	9.1	288	369
40	18.2	484	621
60	27.3	656	842
80	36.4	814	1044
100	45.5	963	1234

* Induces approximately 1% loss of body weight each week.

METABOLIZABLE ENERGY

78 kcal/100 grams

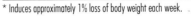

Hilary's BLEND™
Supplement for home-made meals

Low Calorie Recipe 7

1. Thaw frozen peas overnight in the refrigerator.
2. Gently simmer chicken liver and turkey breast until tender. Dice finely.
3. Hard boil egg. Discard shell and mash coarsely.
4. Pulse blueberries, carrots, peas, strawberries, zucchini, cod liver oil, and safflower oil to small kernels.
5. Add HILARY'S BLEND™ supplement to the tomato sauce and mix thoroughly.
6. Stir all ingredients together.

INGREDIENTS

APPROX.	INGREDIENT	GRAMS
¾ cup	Blueberries, raw	111
½ cup	Carrots, raw, grated	55
½ tsp	Cod liver oil	2
1 large	Egg, hard-boiled	50
100 g raw	Liver, chicken, cooked	60
⅞ cup	Peas, thawed from frozen	127
1 tsp	Safflower oil	5
⅔ cup	Strawberries, raw, sliced	111
½ cup	Tomato sauce, canned	122
350 g raw	Turkey breast, cooked	199
⅛ cup	Yogurt, plain, low fat	30
1 cup	Zucchini, raw, sliced	113
1½ scoops	HILARY'S BLEND™ supplement	15
	Total	1000

METABOLIZABLE ENERGY

81 kcal/100 grams

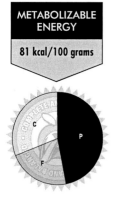

FEEDING GUIDE

Body weight		Energy intake*	Amount to feed
lbs	kg	kcal/day	grams/day
10	4.5	171	211
20	9.1	288	355
40	18.2	484	598
60	27.3	656	810
80	36.4	814	1005
100	45.5	963	1189

* Induces approximately 1% loss of body weight each week.

Hilary's Blend™
Supplement for home-made meals

NUTRITION				
		Per 100g As Fed	Per 100g Dry Matter	Per 1000 kcal
PROTEIN	g	9.43	47.24	117.15
Arginine	g	0.63	3.15	7.81
Histidine	g	0.27	1.36	3.37
Isoleucine	g	0.46	2.32	5.75
Leucine	g	0.74	3.72	9.22
Lysine	g	0.80	4.00	9.92
Methionine + Cystine	g	0.37	1.82	4.51
Phenylalanine + Tyrosine	g	0.75	3.77	9.35
Threonine	g	0.41	2.07	5.13
Tryptophan	g	0.10	0.51	1.26
Valine	g	0.50	2.51	6.22
FAT (LIPID)	g	1.99	9.97	24.72
Linoleic acid	g	0.56	2.81	6.97
MINERALS				
Calcium	mg	219.75	1100.74	2729.60
Phosphorus	mg	174.90	876.07	2172.47
Calcium to Phosphorus ratio		1.26	1.26	1.26
Potassium	mg	343.81	1722.17	4270.62
Sodium	mg	95.69	479.31	1188.59
Magnesium	mg	21.57	108.03	267.89
Iron	mg	4.96	24.86	61.65
Copper	mg	0.37	1.87	4.64
Manganese	mg	0.43	2.13	5.28
Zinc	mg	5.76	28.85	71.54
Iodine	mg	0.09	0.45	1.12
Selenium	µg	13.31	66.66	165.30
VITAMINS				
Vitamin A	IU	2125	10642	26391
Vitamin D	IU	25	126	314
Vitamin E	mg	4.96	24.82	61.55
Thiamin	mg	0.12	0.60	1.49
Riboflavin	mg	0.35	1.75	4.34
Niacin	mg	2.98	14.94	37.05
Pantothenic acid	mg	1.30	6.52	16.17
Pyridoxine	mg	0.29	1.43	3.55
Folic acid	µg	12.00	60.11	149.06
Choline	mg	109.72	549.60	1362.89
Vitamin B12	µg	2.36	11.83	29.34
OTHER (non-essential nutrients)				
Total dietary fiber	g	1.97	9.88	24.50
FATTY ACIDS				
Polyunsaturated fatty acids	g	0.69	3.45	8.56
Eicosapentaenoic acid	mg	14	70	174
Docosahexaenoic acid	mg	32	160	397
Omega 6:3 ratio (estimate)		14.0	14.0	14.0
ANTIOXIDANTS				
Vitamin C	mg	17.48	87.56	217.13
Beta-carotene	µg	558.4	2797.2	6936.5
Lycopene	µg	1849.9	9266.0	22977.7
Lutein + Zeaxanthin	µg	603.2	3021.4	7492.3

Low Calorie Recipe 8

NUTRITION		Per 100g As Fed	Per 100g Dry Matter	Per 1000 kcal
PROTEIN	g	7.73	37.40	84.09
Arginine	g	0.45	2.15	4.83
Histidine	g	0.22	1.05	2.36
Isoleucine	g	0.37	1.79	4.02
Leucine	g	0.64	3.11	6.99
Lysine	g	0.60	2.91	6.54
Methionine + Cystine	g	0.27	1.32	2.97
Phenylalanine + Tyrosine	g	0.63	3.04	6.83
Threonine	g	0.33	1.58	3.55
Tryptophan	g	0.08	0.38	0.85
Valine	g	0.41	1.99	4.47
FAT (LIPID)	g	3.67	17.74	39.88
Linoleic acid	g	1.21	5.87	13.20
MINERALS				
Calcium	mg	227.35	1100.56	2474.39
Phosphorus	mg	171.50	830.21	1866.56
Calcium to Phosphorus ratio		1.33	1.33	1.33
Potassium	mg	296.75	1436.51	3229.71
Sodium	mg	105.85	512.42	1152.08
Magnesium	mg	22.52	109.03	245.13
Iron	mg	4.15	20.10	45.19
Copper	mg	0.35	1.70	3.82
Manganese	mg	0.43	2.08	4.68
Zinc	mg	5.41	26.20	58.91
Iodine	mg	0.09	0.44	0.99
Selenium	µg	8.52	41.23	92.70
VITAMINS				
Vitamin A	IU	569	2756	6195
Vitamin D	IU	25	122	275
Vitamin E	mg	4.63	22.40	50.36
Thiamin	mg	0.18	0.89	2.00
Riboflavin	mg	0.23	1.10	2.47
Niacin	mg	2.03	9.84	22.12
Pantothenic acid	mg	0.91	4.40	9.89
Pyridoxine	mg	0.21	1.01	2.27
Folic acid	µg	12.00	58.09	130.60
Choline	mg	62.89	304.42	684.43
Vitamin B12	µg	1.71	8.27	18.59
OTHER (non-essential nutrients)				
Total dietary fiber	g	2.50	12.08	27.16
FATTY ACIDS				
Polyunsaturated fatty acids	g	1.77	8.59	19.31
Eicosapentaenoic acid	mg	104	500	1124
Docosahexaenoic acid	mg	213	1030	2316
Omega 6:3 ratio (estimate)		4.6	4.6	4.6
ANTIOXIDANTS				
Vitamin C	mg	14.20	68.74	154.55
Beta-carotene	µg	206.6	1000.0	2248.4
Lycopene	µg	0	0	0
Lutein + Zeaxanthin	µg	824.7	3992.4	8976.1

1. Thaw frozen peas overnight in refrigerator.
2. Poach salmon until it flakes easily.
3. Prepare oatmeal according to package directions to yield ¼ cup of cooked oatmeal.
4. Pulse beans, blueberries, lettuce, peas, cod liver oil, and safflower oil to small kernels.
5. Sprinkle HILARY'S BLEND™ supplement over the cottage cheese and mix thoroughly.
6. Stir all ingredients together.

INGREDIENTS		
APPROX.	INGREDIENT	GRAMS
¾ cup	Beans, green, raw, chopped	83
¼ cup	Blueberries, raw	37
1 cup	Cheese, cottage, low fat	226
½ tsp	Cod liver oil	2
2 cups	Lettuce, raw, shredded	144
¼ cup	Oatmeal, cooked	58
2 cups	Peas, thawed from frozen	290
3 tsp	Safflower oil	14
190 g raw	Salmon, Atlantic, cooked	131
1½ scoops	HILARY'S BLEND™ supplement	15
	Total	1000

FEEDING GUIDE			
Body weight		Energy intake*	Amount to feed
lbs	kg	kcal/day	grams/day
10	4.5	171	186
20	9.1	288	313
40	18.2	484	526
60	27.3	656	713
80	36.4	814	885
100	45.5	963	1047

* Induces approximately 1% loss of body weight each week.

METABOLIZABLE ENERGY

92 kcal/100 grams

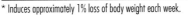

Hilary's Blend™
Supplement for home-made meals

Low Calorie Recipe 9

1. Thaw frozen peas overnight in refrigerator.
2. Poach chicken until tender. Dice finely.
3. Hard boil egg. Discard shell and mash coarsely.
4. Pulse alfalfa sprouts, beans, broccoli, carrots, peas, tomatoes, cod liver oil, safflower oil, and salmon oil to small kernels.
5. Add HILARY'S BLEND™ supplement to the tomato sauce and mix thoroughly.
6. Stir all ingredients together.

INGREDIENTS

APPROX.	INGREDIENT	GRAMS
2 cups	Alfalfa sprouts, raw	66
1 cup	Beans, green, raw, chopped	110
1½ cups	Broccoli, raw, chopped	137
½ cup	Carrots, raw, grated	55
400 g raw	Chicken breast, cooked	210
1 tsp	Cod liver oil	5
1 large	Egg, hard-boiled	50
¾ cup	Peas, thawed from frozen	109
4 tsp	Safflower oil	18
1 tsp	Salmon oil	5
¼ cup	Tomato sauce, canned	61
¼ cup	Tomatoes, cherry, raw	37
½ cup	Yogurt, plain, low fat	122
1½ scoops	HILARY'S BLEND™ supplement	15
	Total	1000

METABOLIZABLE ENERGY

98 kcal/100 grams

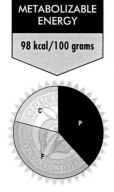

FEEDING GUIDE

Body weight		Energy intake*	Amount to feed
lbs	kg	kcal/day	grams/day
10	4.5	171	175
20	9.1	288	294
40	18.2	484	494
60	27.3	656	670
80	36.4	814	831
100	45.5	963	982

* Induces approximately 1% loss of body weight each week.

NUTRITION

		Per 100g As Fed	Per 100g Dry Matter	Per 1000 kcal
PROTEIN	g	9.39	43.81	95.39
Arginine	g	0.54	2.51	5.47
Histidine	g	0.26	1.22	2.66
Isoleucine	g	0.47	2.19	4.77
Leucine	g	0.70	3.26	7.10
Lysine	g	0.74	3.46	7.53
Methionine + Cystine	g	0.36	1.66	3.61
Phenylalanine + Tyrosine	g	0.69	3.22	7.01
Threonine	g	0.40	1.85	4.03
Tryptophan	g	0.10	0.47	1.02
Valine	g	0.48	2.25	4.90
FAT (LIPID)	g	4.45	20.78	45.24
Linoleic acid	g	1.59	7.43	16.18
MINERALS				
Calcium	mg	244.30	1140.05	2482.25
Phosphorus	mg	174.06	812.27	1768.57
Calcium to Phosphorus ratio		1.40	1.40	1.40
Potassium	mg	345.76	1613.53	3513.17
Sodium	mg	74.97	349.85	761.74
Magnesium	mg	24.91	116.24	253.09
Iron	mg	4.27	19.92	43.37
Copper	mg	0.34	1.59	3.46
Manganese	mg	0.36	1.67	3.64
Zinc	mg	5.52	25.74	56.04
Iodine	mg	0.09	0.42	0.91
Selenium	µg	8.40	39.20	85.35
VITAMINS				
Vitamin A	IU	1771	8266	17997
Vitamin D	IU	55	258	561
Vitamin E	mg	4.92	22.97	50.01
Thiamin	mg	0.12	0.55	1.20
Riboflavin	mg	0.25	1.18	2.57
Niacin	mg	3.70	17.28	37.62
Pantothenic acid	mg	1.10	5.13	11.17
Pyridoxine	mg	0.25	1.18	2.57
Folic acid	µg	12.00	56.00	121.93
Choline	mg	79.65	371.70	809.31
Vitamin B12	µg	1.40	6.51	14.17
OTHER (non-essential nutrients)				
Total dietary fiber	g	2.08	9.69	21.10
FATTY ACIDS				
Polyunsaturated fatty acids	g	1.97	9.18	19.99
Eicosapentaenoic acid	mg	102	480	1045
Docosahexaenoic acid	mg	152	710	1546
Omega 6:3 ratio (estimate)		6.7	6.7	6.7
ANTIOXIDANTS				
Vitamin C	mg	20.23	94.42	205.58
Beta-carotene	µg	631.4	2946.6	6415.6
Lycopene	µg	1019.5	4757.7	10359.1
Lutein + Zeaxanthin	µg	568.9	2654.8	5780.3

Supplement for home-made meals

Low Calorie Recipe 10

NUTRITION		Per 100g As Fed	Per 100g Dry Matter	Per 1000 kcal
PROTEIN	g	8.35	36.11	88.76
Arginine	g	0.60	2.57	6.32
Histidine	g	0.21	0.89	2.19
Isoleucine	g	0.40	1.72	4.23
Leucine	g	0.65	2.83	6.96
Lysine	g	0.55	2.37	5.83
Methionine + Cystine	g	0.28	1.22	3.00
Phenylalanine + Tyrosine	g	0.70	3.04	7.47
Threonine	g	0.34	1.48	3.64
Tryptophan	g	0.10	0.43	1.06
Valine	g	0.44	1.91	4.70
FAT (LIPID)	g	3.34	14.44	35.50
Linoleic acid	g	1.26	5.46	13.42
MINERALS				
Calcium	mg	244.56	1057.17	2598.68
Phosphorus	mg	176.73	763.94	1877.88
Calcium to Phosphorus ratio		1.38	1.38	1.38
Potassium	mg	408.43	1765.54	4339.96
Sodium	mg	77.54	335.17	823.90
Magnesium	mg	43.30	187.19	460.14
Iron	mg	5.50	23.79	58.48
Copper	mg	0.46	1.98	4.87
Manganese	mg	0.65	2.81	6.91
Zinc	mg	5.62	24.30	59.73
Iodine	mg	0.09	0.39	0.96
Selenium	µg	6.05	26.14	64.26
VITAMINS				
Vitamin A	IU	795	3437	8448
Vitamin D	IU	25	109	268
Vitamin E	mg	4.84	20.93	51.45
Thiamin	mg	0.15	0.66	1.62
Riboflavin	mg	0.33	1.40	3.44
Niacin	mg	0.98	4.22	10.37
Pantothenic acid	mg	0.82	3.54	8.70
Pyridoxine	mg	0.21	0.91	2.24
Folic acid	µg	12.00	51.87	127.50
Choline	mg	78.34	338.62	832.38
Vitamin B12	µg	1.21	5.25	12.91
OTHER (non-essential nutrients)				
Total dietary fiber	g	3.93	16.98	41.74
FATTY ACIDS				
Polyunsaturated fatty acids	g	1.69	7.29	17.92
Eicosapentaenoic acid	mg	79	340	836
Docosahexaenoic acid	mg	113	490	1204
Omega 6:3 ratio (estimate)		7.8	7.8	7.8
ANTIOXIDANTS				
Vitamin C	mg	19.43	83.97	206.41
Beta-carotene	µg	353.2	1526.8	3753.2
Lycopene	µg	469.7	2030.4	4991.1
Lutein + Zeaxanthin	µg	1104.6	4774.7	11737.0

1. Thaw frozen peas overnight in the refrigerator.
2. Boil soybeans until tender.
3. Heat slightly beaten egg whites until they are cooked. Mash coarsely.
4. Pulse alfalfa sprouts, broccoli, chickpeas, lettuce, peas, soybeans, spinach, cod liver oil, and salmon oil to small kernels.
5. Add HILARY'S BLEND™ supplement to the tomato sauce and mix thoroughly.
6. Stir all ingredients together.

INGREDIENTS		
APPROX.	INGREDIENT	GRAMS
2 cups	Alfalfa sprouts, raw	66
1 cup	Broccoli, raw, chopped	91
⅓ cup	Chickpeas, canned	80
½ tsp	Cod liver oil	2
⅔ cup	Egg whites, cooked	161
½ cup	Lettuce, raw, shredded	36
1½ cups	Peas, thawed from frozen	218
1 tsp	Salmon oil	5
1½ cups	Soybeans, mature, boiled	260
3½ leaves	Spinach, raw	35
⅛ cup	Tomato sauce, canned	31
1½ scoops	HILARY'S BLEND™ supplement	15
	Total	1000

FEEDING GUIDE			
Body weight		Energy intake*	Amount to feed
lbs	kg	kcal/day	grams/day
10	4.5	171	182
20	9.1	288	306
40	18.2	484	515
60	27.3	656	698
80	36.4	814	866
100	45.5	963	1024

* Induces approximately 1% loss of body weight each week.

METABOLIZABLE ENERGY

94 kcal/100 grams

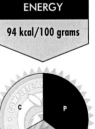

Hilary's Blend™

Supplement for home-made meals

R56

High Calorie Recipe 1

1. Poach chicken liver. Crumble with a fork.
2. Hard boil eggs. Discard shells and mash coarsely.
3. Add HILARY'S BLEND™ supplement to the mashed eggs and mix thoroughly.
4. Fold ingredients together until well blended.

INGREDIENTS

APPROX.	INGREDIENT	GRAMS
1 ⅓ cup	Almonds, ground	126
5 tbsp	Butter	71
½ cup	Cheese, cheddar, shredded	57
2 tsp	Cod liver oil	9
2 large	Eggs, hard-boiled	100
895 g raw	Liver, chicken, cooked	555
3 tsp	Safflower oil	14
4 tsp	Salmon oil	18
5 scoops	HILARY'S BLEND™ supplement	50
	Total	1000

METABOLIZABLE ENERGY

293 kcal/100 grams

FEEDING GUIDE

Body weight		Energy intake*	Amount to feed
lbs	kg	kcal/day	grams/day
10	4.5	436	149
20	9.1	733	250
40	18.2	1233	421
60	27.3	1671	570
80	36.4	2073	708
100	45.5	2451	836

* assumes very active working/endurance dog.

Hilary's Blend™
Supplement for home-made meals

NUTRITION

		Per 100g As Fed	Per 100g Dry Matter	Per 1000 kcal
PROTEIN	g	18.99	36.92	64.74
Arginine	g	1.30	2.52	4.42
Histidine	g	0.55	1.07	1.88
Isoleucine	g	0.88	1.72	3.02
Leucine	g	1.62	3.14	5.51
Lysine	g	1.33	2.59	4.54
Methionine + Cystine	g	0.72	1.40	2.46
Phenylalanine + Tyrosine	g	1.63	3.17	5.56
Threonine	g	0.77	1.49	2.61
Tryptophan	g	0.20	0.38	0.67
Valine	g	1.06	2.05	3.59
FAT (LIPID)	g	22.65	44.04	77.23
Linoleic acid	g	3.35	6.50	11.40
MINERALS				
Calcium	mg	747.17	1452.99	2547.94
Phosphorus	mg	553.85	1077.05	1888.70
Calcium to Phosphorus ratio		1.35	1.35	1.35
Potassium	mg	629.69	1224.53	2147.32
Sodium	mg	99.63	193.74	339.74
Magnesium	mg	61.03	118.68	208.12
Iron	mg	18.60	36.16	63.41
Copper	mg	1.31	2.55	4.47
Manganese	mg	1.27	2.47	4.33
Zinc	mg	19.00	36.95	64.80
Iodine	mg	0.30	0.58	1.02
Selenium	µg	50.03	97.29	170.61
VITAMINS				
Vitamin A	IU	8591	16706	29296
Vitamin D	IU	112	218	382
Vitamin E	mg	19.04	37.03	64.94
Thiamin	mg	0.32	0.62	1.09
Riboflavin	mg	1.71	3.32	5.82
Niacin	mg	7.37	14.33	25.13
Pantothenic acid	mg	5.93	11.53	20.22
Pyridoxine	mg	0.60	1.17	2.05
Folic acid	µg	40.00	77.79	136.41
Choline	mg	389.93	758.29	1329.73
Vitamin B12	µg	13.52	26.30	46.12
OTHER (non-essential nutrients)				
Total dietary fiber	g	2.79	5.42	9.50
FATTY ACIDS				
Polyunsaturated fatty acids	g	4.62	8.99	15.76
Eicosapentaenoic acid	mg	297	580	1017
Docosahexaenoic acid	mg	431	840	1473
Omega 6:3 ratio (estimate)		5.3	5.3	5.3
ANTIOXIDANTS				
Vitamin C	mg	15.49	30.11	52.80
Beta-carotene	µg	33.9	66.0	115.7
Lycopene	µg	11.7	22.7	39.8
Lutein + Zeaxanthin	µg	81.5	158.5	277.9

High Calorie Recipe 2

NUTRITION		Per 100g As Fed	Per 100g Dry Matter	Per 1000 kcal
PROTEIN	g	20.57	33.79	59.42
Arginine	g	1.46	2.40	4.22
Histidine	g	0.63	1.03	1.81
Isoleucine	g	0.93	1.53	2.69
Leucine	g	1.68	2.76	4.85
Lysine	g	1.49	2.45	4.31
Methionine + Cystine	g	0.81	1.32	2.32
Phenylalanine + Tyrosine	g	1.65	2.72	4.78
Threonine	g	0.83	1.36	2.39
Tryptophan	g	0.21	0.34	0.60
Valine	g	1.12	1.85	3.25
FAT (LIPID)	g	26.33	43.24	76.03
Linoleic acid	g	2.74	4.50	7.91
MINERALS				
Calcium	mg	724.01	1189.19	2091.10
Phosphorus	mg	576.21	946.42	1664.21
Calcium to Phosphorus ratio		1.26	1.26	1.26
Potassium	mg	780.76	1282.39	2254.99
Sodium	mg	63.68	104.59	183.91
Magnesium	mg	104.12	171.02	300.73
Iron	mg	15.47	25.40	44.66
Copper	mg	5.75	9.45	16.62
Manganese	mg	1.40	2.31	4.06
Zinc	mg	20.59	33.81	59.45
Iodine	mg	0.30	0.49	0.86
Selenium	µg	20.83	34.20	60.14
VITAMINS				
Vitamin A	IU	9281	15244	26805
Vitamin D	IU	112	184	324
Vitamin E	mg	16.78	27.56	48.46
Thiamin	mg	0.47	0.78	1.37
Riboflavin	mg	1.61	2.64	4.64
Niacin	mg	8.89	14.61	25.69
Pantothenic acid	mg	4.60	7.56	13.29
Pyridoxine	mg	0.68	1.12	1.97
Folic acid	µg	40.00	65.70	115.53
Choline	mg	374.31	614.81	1081.10
Vitamin B12	µg	30.81	50.60	88.98
OTHER (non-essential nutrients)				
Total dietary fiber	g	6.42	10.55	18.55
FATTY ACIDS				
Polyunsaturated fatty acids	g	8.14	13.38	23.53
Eicosapentaenoic acid	mg	479	790	1389
Docosahexaenoic acid	mg	682	1120	1969
Omega 6:3 ratio (estimate)		6.0	6.0	6.0
ANTIOXIDANTS				
Vitamin C	mg	0.32	0.53	0.93
Beta-carotene	µg	70.6	116.0	203.9
Lycopene	µg	0	0	0
Lutein + Zeaxanthin	µg	109.4	179.7	316.0

1. Pan-broil lean (10% fat) beef to brown crumbles.
2. Poach liver until tender. Dice finely.
3. Add HILARY'S BLEND™ supplement to the beef crumbles and mix thoroughly.
4. Fold ingredients together until well blended.

INGREDIENTS		
APPROX.	INGREDIENT	GRAMS
½ cup	Almonds, ground	48
380 g raw	Beef, ground, cooked	285
6 tbsp	Butter	86
2 tsp	Cod liver oil	9
1 cup	Flaxseeds, whole, ground	168
450 g raw	Liver, beef, cooked	313
2 tsp	Safflower oil	9
8 tsp	Salmon oil	32
5 scoops	HILARY'S BLEND™ supplement	50
	Total	1000

FEEDING GUIDE			
Body weight		Energy intake*	Amount to feed
lbs	kg	kcal/day	grams/day
10	4.5	436	126
20	9.1	733	212
40	18.2	1233	356
60	27.3	1671	483
80	36.4	2073	599
100	45.5	2451	708

* assumes very active working/endurance dog.

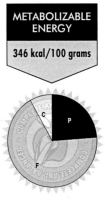

METABOLIZABLE ENERGY

346 kcal/100 grams

Hilary's Blend™

Supplement for home-made meals

R58

High Calorie Recipe 3

1. Poach turkey breast and liver until tender. Dice finely.
2. Prepare oatmeal according to package directions to yield ½ cup of cooked oatmeal.
3. Add HILARY'S BLEND™ supplement to the oatmeal and mix thoroughly.
4. Stir all ingredients together.

INGREDIENTS

APPROX.	INGREDIENT	GRAMS
2 tbsp	Butter	28
1½ tsp	Cod liver oil	7
420 g raw	Liver, beef, cooked	294
½ cup	Oatmeal, cooked	117
8½ tbsp	Safflower oil	116
3½ tbsp	Salmon oil	48
615 g raw	Turkey breast, cooked	350
4 scoops	HILARY'S BLEND™ supplement	40
	Total	1000

METABOLIZABLE ENERGY

280 kcal/100 grams

FEEDING GUIDE

Body weight		Energy intake*	Amount to feed
lbs	kg	kcal/day	grams/day
10	4.5	436	156
20	9.1	733	262
40	18.2	1233	440
60	27.3	1671	597
80	36.4	2073	740
100	45.5	2451	875

* assumes very active working/endurance dog.

NUTRITION

		Per 100g As Fed	Per 100g Dry Matter	Per 1000 kcal
PROTEIN	g	18.65	39.43	66.61
Arginine	g	1.22	2.58	4.36
Histidine	g	0.57	1.21	2.04
Isoleucine	g	0.92	1.95	3.29
Leucine	g	1.58	3.34	5.64
Lysine	g	1.61	3.40	5.74
Methionine + Cystine	g	0.77	1.64	2.77
Phenylalanine + Tyrosine	g	1.58	3.33	5.63
Threonine	g	0.81	1.70	2.87
Tryptophan	g	0.22	0.47	0.79
Valine	g	1.05	2.22	3.75
FAT (LIPID)	g	21.12	44.67	75.47
Linoleic acid	g	9.01	19.05	32.18
MINERALS				
Calcium	g	535.57	1132.61	1913.45
Phosphorus	g	406.55	859.77	1452.51
Calcium to Phosphorus ratio		1.32	1.32	1.32
Potassium	g	512.62	1084.07	1831.45
Sodium	g	48.26	102.06	172.42
Magnesium	g	30.90	65.35	110.40
Iron	mg	11.64	24.62	41.59
Copper	mg	5.04	10.67	18.03
Manganese	mg	0.78	1.65	2.79
Zinc	mg	15.10	31.93	53.94
Iodine	mg	0.24	0.51	0.86
Selenium	µg	21.85	46.22	78.08
VITAMINS				
Vitamin A	IU	8440	17848	30153
Vitamin D	IU	86	181	306
Vitamin E	mg	12.24	25.89	43.74
Thiamin	mg	0.18	0.37	0.63
Riboflavin	mg	1.38	2.91	4.92
Niacin	mg	8.42	17.80	30.07
Pantothenic acid	mg	3.92	8.28	13.99
Pyridoxine	mg	0.62	1.31	2.21
Folic acid	µg	32.00	67.67	114.32
Choline	mg	313.88	663.79	1121.42
Vitamin B12	µg	27.78	58.75	99.25
OTHER (non-essential nutrients)				
Total dietary fiber	g	1.20	2.54	4.29
FATTY ACIDS				
Polyunsaturated fatty acids	g	11.12	23.52	39.74
Eicosapentaenoic acid	mg	673	1420	2399
Docosahexaenoic acid	mg	966	2040	3446
Omega 6:3 ratio (estimate)		5.8	5.8	5.8
ANTIOXIDANTS				
Vitamin C	mg	0.21	0.44	0.74
Beta-carotene	µg	57.9	122.5	207.0
Lycopene	µg	0	0	0
Lutein + Zeaxanthin	µg	21.1	44.5	75.2

Hilary's Blend™

Supplement for home-made meals

High Calorie Recipe 4

NUTRITION		Per 100g As Fed	Per 100g Dry Matter	Per 1000 kcal
PROTEIN	g	14.35	29.05	53.26
Arginine	g	1.00	2.01	3.68
Histidine	g	0.41	0.83	1.52
Isoleucine	g	0.67	1.36	2.49
Leucine	g	1.12	2.26	4.14
Lysine	g	1.17	2.36	4.33
Methionine + Cystine	g	0.58	1.17	2.14
Phenylalanine + Tyrosine	g	1.07	2.17	3.98
Threonine	g	0.64	1.29	2.36
Tryptophan	g	0.18	0.36	0.66
Valine	g	0.77	1.55	2.84
FAT (LIPID)	g	19.70	39.87	73.09
Linoleic acid	g	3.76	7.60	13.93
MINERALS				
Calcium	mg	612.27	1239.00	2271.44
Phosphorus	mg	470.00	951.10	1743.63
Calcium to Phosphorus ratio		1.30	1.30	1.30
Potassium	mg	663.07	1341.80	2459.90
Sodium	mg	239.76	485.18	889.47
Magnesium	mg	95.46	193.18	354.15
Iron	mg	9.36	18.95	34.74
Copper	mg	0.86	1.73	3.17
Manganese	mg	0.97	1.96	3.59
Zinc	mg	11.06	22.38	41.03
Iodine	mg	0.18	0.36	0.66
Selenium	µg	27.32	55.28	101.34
VITAMINS				
Vitamin A	IU	2005	4058	7440
Vitamin D	IU	131	266	487
Vitamin E	mg	10.12	20.48	37.55
Thiamin	mg	0.40	0.81	1.48
Riboflavin	mg	0.38	0.77	1.41
Niacin	mg	3.63	7.35	13.47
Pantothenic acid	mg	1.75	3.53	6.47
Pyridoxine	mg	0.31	0.63	1.15
Folic acid	µg	24.00	48.57	89.04
Choline	mg	171.97	348.01	638.00
Vitamin B12	µg	6.30	12.74	23.36
OTHER (non-essential nutrients)				
Total dietary fiber	g	6.03	12.19	22.35
FATTY ACIDS				
Polyunsaturated fatty acids	g	9.35	18.93	34.70
Eicosapentaenoic acid	mg	557	1130	2072
Docosahexaenoic acid	mg	714	1440	2640
Omega 6:3 ratio (estimate)		6.4	6.4	6.4
ANTIOXIDANTS				
Vitamin C	mg	2.41	4.88	8.95
Beta-carotene	µg	919.2	1860.1	3410.1
Lycopene	µg	0.1	0.2	0.4
Lutein + Zeaxanthin	µg	142.7	288.8	529.5

1. Prick potato with a fork, microwave until soft. Mash coarsely.
2. Mash sardines. Add HILARY'S BLEND™ supplement to the sardines and mix thoroughly.
3. Fold ingredients together until well blended.

INGREDIENTS		
APPROX.	**INGREDIENT**	**GRAMS**
3 tbsp	Butter	43
1 cup	Carrots, raw, grated	110
1 cup	Flaxseeds, whole, ground	168
1 medium	Potato, baked in skin	173
3 tsp	Safflower oil	14
6 tsp	Salmon oil	27
	Sardines, canned in water, drained	435
3 scoops	HILARY'S BLEND™ supplement	30
	Total	1000

FEEDING GUIDE			
Body weight		Energy intake*	Amount to feed
lbs	kg	kcal/day	grams/day
10	4.5	436	161
20	9.1	733	271
40	18.2	1233	457
60	27.3	1671	619
80	36.4	2073	768
100	45.5	2451	908

* assumes very active working/endurance dog.

METABOLIZABLE ENERGY

270 kcal/100 grams

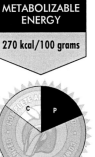

Supplement for home-made meals

R60

High Calorie Recipe 5

1. Mash sardines and tuna together.
2. Add HILARY'S BLEND™ supplement to the fish and mix thoroughly.
3. Fold in the Cheerios.
4. For extra hydration, add warm water AFTER weighing out the amount to feed.

INGREDIENTS		
APPROX.	INGREDIENT	GRAMS
14½ cups	GENERAL MILLS'® Honey Nut Cheerios	532
	Sardines, canned in water, drained	276
	Tuna, canned in water, drained	172
2 scoops	HILARY'S BLEND™ supplement	20
	Total	1000

METABOLIZABLE ENERGY

289 kcal/100 grams

FEEDING GUIDE			
Body weight		Energy intake*	Amount to feed
lbs	kg	kcal/day	grams/day
10	4.5	436	151
20	9.1	733	254
40	18.2	1233	427
60	27.3	1671	578
80	36.4	2073	717
100	45.5	2451	848

* for weight gain.

Hilary's
Supplement for home-made meals
BLEND™

NUTRITION				
		Per 100g As Fed	Per 100g Dry Matter	Per 1000 kcal
PROTEIN	g	16.56	23.78	57.22
Arginine	g	0.65	0.93	2.24
Histidine	g	0.32	0.46	1.11
Isoleucine	g	0.50	0.72	1.73
Leucine	g	0.88	1.27	3.06
Lysine	g	1.00	1.43	3.44
Methionine + Cystine	g	0.44	0.63	1.52
Phenylalanine + Tyrosine	g	0.79	1.14	2.74
Threonine	g	0.48	0.68	1.64
Tryptophan	g	0.14	0.20	0.48
Valine	g	0.56	0.80	1.93
FAT (LIPID)	g	6.52	9.37	22.55
Linoleic acid	g	1.90	2.73	6.57
MINERALS				
Calcium	mg	561.76	806.95	1941.79
Phosphorus	mg	450.49	647.11	1557.16
Calcium to Phosphorus ratio		1.25	1.25	1.25
Potassium	mg	518.99	745.50	1793.92
Sodium	mg	512.90	736.76	1772.89
Magnesium	mg	80.36	115.43	277.76
Iron	mg	14.13	20.29	48.82
Copper	mg	0.61	0.88	2.11
Manganese	mg	1.79	2.58	6.21
Zinc	mg	14.01	20.13	48.44
Iodine	mg	0.13	0.19	0.45
Selenium	µg	38.35	55.08	132.54
VITAMINS				
Vitamin A	IU	983	1412	3399
Vitamin D	IU	158	227	547
Vitamin E	mg	7.07	10.16	24.45
Thiamin	mg	0.78	1.13	2.72
Riboflavin	mg	1.04	1.50	3.61
Niacin	mg	12.27	17.62	42.40
Pantothenic acid	mg	1.45	2.08	5.01
Pyridoxine	mg	1.09	1.57	3.78
Folic acid	µg	385.74	554.10	1333.35
Choline	mg	117.19	168.33	405.06
Vitamin B12	µg	7.12	10.23	24.62
OTHER (non-essential nutrients)				
Total dietary fiber	g	4.28	6.14	14.77
FATTY ACIDS				
Polyunsaturated fatty acids	g	2.56	3.68	8.86
Eicosapentaenoic acid	mg	171	250	602
Docosahexaenoic acid	mg	249	360	866
Omega 6:3 ratio (estimate)		5.1	5.1	5.1
ANTIOXIDANTS				
Vitamin C	mg	11.4	16.4	39.3
Beta-carotene	µg	0.0	0.0	0.0
Lycopene	µg	0.0	0.0	0.0
Lutein + Zeaxanthin	µg	61.7	88.7	213.3

Low Oxalate Recipe 1

NUTRITION		Per 100g As Fed	Per 100g Dry Matter	Per 1000 kcal
PROTEIN	g	12.70	38.54	84.17
Arginine	g	0.80	2.42	5.29
Histidine	g	0.38	1.16	2.53
Isoleucine	g	0.65	1.96	4.28
Leucine	g	0.95	2.90	6.33
Lysine	g	1.01	3.05	6.66
Methionine + Cystine	g	0.50	1.51	3.30
Phenylalanine + Tyrosine	g	0.94	2.86	6.25
Threonine	g	0.53	1.60	3.49
Tryptophan	g	0.15	0.45	0.98
Valine	g	0.64	1.94	4.24
FAT (LIPID)	g	5.03	15.27	33.35
Linoleic acid	g	2.10	6.38	13.93
MINERALS				
Calcium	mg	276.84	839.87	1834.22
Phosphorus	mg	220.05	667.59	1457.97
Calcium to Phosphorus ratio		1.26	1.26	1.26
Potassium	mg	286.98	870.63	1901.40
Sodium	mg	32.38	98.24	214.55
Magnesium	mg	39.00	118.32	258.40
Iron	mg	5.33	16.18	35.34
Copper	mg	0.45	1.36	2.97
Manganese	mg	0.79	2.41	5.26
Zinc	mg	7.24	21.96	47.96
Iodine	mg	0.12	0.36	0.79
Selenium	µg	14.65	44.43	97.03
VITAMINS				
Vitamin A	IU	590	1789	3907
Vitamin D	IU	57	173	378
Vitamin E	mg	6.12	18.58	40.58
Thiamin	mg	0.15	0.45	0.98
Riboflavin	mg	0.23	0.69	1.51
Niacin	mg	6.09	18.48	40.36
Pantothenic acid	mg	1.29	3.91	8.54
Pyridoxine	mg	0.36	1.09	2.38
Folic acid	µg	16.00	48.54	106.01
Choline	mg	84.50	256.35	559.85
Vitamin B12	µg	1.72	5.22	11.40
OTHER (non-essential nutrients)				
Total dietary fiber	g	1.93	5.86	12.80
FATTY ACIDS				
Polyunsaturated fatty acids	g	2.48	7.52	16.42
Eicosapentaenoic acid	mg	103	310	677
Docosahexaenoic acid	mg	153	460	1005
Omega 6:3 ratio (estimate)		8.7	8.7	8.7
ANTIOXIDANTS				
Vitamin C	mg	4.32	13.11	28.63
Beta-carotene	µg	48.5	147.1	321.3
Lycopene	µg	0	0	0
Lutein + Zeaxanthin	µg	267.5	811.6	1772.5

1. Thaw frozen peas overnight in the refrigerator.
2. Poach chicken until tender. Dice finely.
3. Prepare rice according to package directions to yield 2½ cups of cooked rice.
4. Sprinkle HILARY'S BLEND™ supplement over the cooked rice and blend in.
5. Stir all ingredients together.

INGREDIENTS		
APPROX.	INGREDIENT	GRAMS
675 g raw	Chicken breast, cooked	350
1 tsp	Cod liver oil	5
¾ cup	Peas, thawed from frozen	108
2½ cups	Rice, brown, cooked	489
5 tsp	Safflower oil	23
1 tsp	Salmon oil	5
2 scoops	HILARY'S BLEND™ supplement	20
	Total	1000

FEEDING GUIDE			
Body weight		Energy intake	Amount to feed
lbs	kg	kcal/day	grams/day
10	4.5	296	196
20	9.1	497	329
40	18.2	836	554
60	27.3	1134	751
80	36.4	1407	932
100	45.5	1663	1101

METABOLIZABLE ENERGY

151 kcal/100 grams

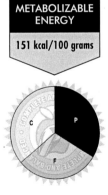

Hilary's
Blend™
Supplement for home-made meals

Low Oxalate Recipe 2

1. Thaw frozen peas overnight in the refrigerator.
2. Poach chicken until tender. Dice finely.
3. Prepare rice according to package directions to yield 2 cups of cooked rice.
4. Hard boil egg. Discard shell and mash coarsely.
5. Pulse bananas, grapefruit, peas, cod liver oil, safflower oil, and salmon oil to small kernels.
6. Sprinkle HILARY'S BLEND™ supplement over the rice and mix thoroughly.
7. Stir all ingredients together.

INGREDIENTS

APPROX.	INGREDIENT	GRAMS
¼ cup	Bananas, raw, sliced	38
540 g raw	Chicken breast, cooked	280
1 tsp	Cod liver oil	5
1 large	Egg, hard-boiled	50
¼ cup	Grapefruit, raw with juice	58
1 cup	Peas, thawed from frozen	145
2 cups	Rice, brown, cooked	390
2½ tsp	Safflower oil	12
½ tsp	Salmon oil	2
2 scoops	HILARY'S BLEND™ supplement	20
	Total	1000

METABOLIZABLE ENERGY

133 kcal/100 grams

FEEDING GUIDE

Body weight		Energy intake	Amount to feed
lbs	kg	kcal/day	grams/day
10	4.5	296	222
20	9.1	497	374
40	18.2	836	629
60	27.3	1134	852
80	36.4	1407	1058
100	45.5	1663	1250

Hilary's BLEND™

Supplement for home-made meals

NUTRITION

		Per 100g As Fed	Per 100g Dry Matter	Per 1000 kcal
PROTEIN	g	11.19	37.13	84.46
Arginine	g	0.71	2.35	5.35
Histidine	g	0.33	1.09	2.48
Isoleucine	g	0.57	1.88	4.28
Leucine	g	0.84	2.78	6.32
Lysine	g	0.87	2.89	6.57
Methionine + Cystine	g	0.44	1.46	3.32
Phenylalanine + Tyrosine	g	0.84	2.78	6.32
Threonine	g	0.47	1.54	3.50
Tryptophan	g	0.13	0.42	0.96
Valine	g	0.57	1.87	4.25
FAT (LIPID)	g	3.86	12.80	29.12
Linoleic acid	g	1.27	4.22	9.60
MINERALS				
Calcium	mg	279.69	927.81	2110.48
Phosphorus	mg	210.35	697.79	1587.26
Calcium to Phosphorus ratio		1.33	1.33	1.33
Potassium	mg	301.56	1000.37	2275.53
Sodium	mg	33.13	109.90	249.99
Magnesium	mg	35.98	119.37	271.53
Iron	mg	5.35	17.74	40.35
Copper	mg	0.45	1.48	3.37
Manganese	mg	0.73	2.42	5.50
Zinc	mg	7.21	23.93	54.43
Iodine	mg	0.12	0.40	0.91
Selenium	µg	13.40	44.43	101.06
VITAMINS				
Vitamin A	IU	715	2372	5395
Vitamin D	IU	57	189	430
Vitamin E	mg	6.17	20.46	46.54
Thiamin	mg	0.15	0.50	1.14
Riboflavin	mg	0.25	0.83	1.89
Niacin	mg	5.10	16.91	38.47
Pantothenic acid	mg	1.29	4.29	9.76
Pyridoxine	mg	0.33	1.10	2.50
Folic acid	µg	16.00	53.08	120.74
Choline	mg	95.67	317.37	721.92
Vitamin B12	µg	1.75	5.81	13.22
OTHER (non-essential nutrients)				
Total dietary fiber	g	2.13	7.08	16.10
FATTY ACIDS				
Polyunsaturated fatty acids	g	1.53	5.08	11.56
Eicosapentaenoic acid	mg	64	210	478
Docosahexaenoic acid	mg	99	330	751
Omega 6:3 ratio (estimate)		8.4	8.4	8.4
ANTIOXIDANTS				
Vitamin C	mg	7.94	26.34	59.92
Beta-carotene	µg	106.4	353.1	803.1
Lycopene	µg	82.3	273.0	621.0
Lutein + Zeaxanthin	µg	377.9	1253.7	2851.9

www.CompleteandBalanced.com

Low Oxalate Recipe 3

NUTRITION		Per 100g As Fed	Per 100g Dry Matter	Per 1000 kcal
PROTEIN	g	11.71	45.88	111.49
Arginine	g	0.73	2.85	6.93
Histidine	g	0.33	1.30	3.16
Isoleucine	g	0.58	2.28	5.54
Leucine	g	0.85	3.33	8.09
Lysine	g	0.93	3.62	8.80
Methionine + Cystine	g	0.44	1.73	4.20
Phenylalanine + Tyrosine	g	0.85	3.32	8.07
Threonine	g	0.49	1.90	4.62
Tryptophan	g	0.13	0.51	1.24
Valine	g	0.58	2.28	5.54
FAT (LIPID)	g	2.07	8.12	19.73
Linoleic acid	g	0.42	1.65	4.01
MINERALS				
Calcium	mg	217.59	852.33	2071.12
Phosphorus	mg	180.89	708.58	1721.82
Calcium to Phosphorus ratio		1.20	1.20	1.20
Potassium	mg	354.97	1390.49	3378.83
Sodium	mg	56.92	222.96	541.78
Magnesium	mg	25.84	101.24	246.01
Iron	mg	4.57	17.90	43.50
Copper	mg	0.35	1.36	3.30
Manganese	mg	0.38	1.51	3.67
Zinc	mg	5.47	21.44	52.10
Iodine	mg	0.09	0.35	0.85
Selenium	µg	9.77	38.28	93.02
VITAMINS				
Vitamin A	IU	910	3566	8664
Vitamin D	IU	25	99	240
Vitamin E	mg	4.65	18.23	44.30
Thiamin	mg	0.17	0.66	1.60
Riboflavin	mg	0.23	0.89	2.16
Niacin	mg	4.90	19.21	46.68
Pantothenic acid	mg	1.08	4.22	10.25
Pyridoxine	mg	0.33	1.30	3.16
Folic acid	µg	12.00	47.01	114.23
Choline	mg	84.09	329.38	800.38
Vitamin B12	µg	1.35	5.29	12.85
OTHER (non-essential nutrients)				
Total dietary fiber	g	2.92	11.44	27.80
FATTY ACIDS				
Polyunsaturated fatty acids	g	0.55	2.14	5.20
Eicosapentaenoic acid	mg	17	70	170
Docosahexaenoic acid	mg	29	120	292
Omega 6:3 ratio (estimate)		10.9	10.9	10.9
ANTIOXIDANTS				
Vitamin C	mg	8.94	35.02	85.10
Beta-carotene	µg	402.5	1576.8	3831.6
Lycopene	µg	0	0	0
Lutein + Zeaxanthin	µg	794.8	3113.5	7565.8

1. Thaw frozen peas overnight in the refrigerator.
2. Poach chicken until tender. Dice finely.
3. Boil chopped cauliflower until cooked.
4. Hard boil egg. Discard shell and mash coarsely.
5. Prick potato with a fork, microwave until soft. Mash coarsely.
6. Pulse cauliflower, peas, cod liver oil, and safflower oil to small kernels.
7. Add HILARY'S BLEND™ supplement to the mashed egg and mix thoroughly.
8. Stir all ingredients together.

INGREDIENTS		
APPROX.	INGREDIENT	GRAMS
⅔ cup	Cauliflower, boiled, chopped	120
540 g raw	Chicken breast, cooked	281
½ tsp	Cod liver oil	2
1 large	Egg, hard-boiled	50
2 cups	Peas, thawed from frozen	320
1 med./large	Potato, baked in skin	210
½ tsp	Safflower oil	2
1½ scoops	HILARY'S BLEND™ supplement	15
	Total	1000

FEEDING GUIDE			
Body weight		Energy intake	Amount to feed
lbs	kg	kcal/day	grams/day
10	4.5	296	282
20	9.1	497	474
40	18.2	836	797
60	27.3	1134	1080
80	36.4	1407	1340
100	45.5	1663	1584

METABOLIZABLE ENERGY

105 kcal/100 grams

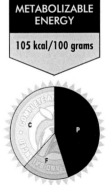

Hilory's Blend

Supplement for home-made meals

Low Oxalate Recipe 4

1. Thaw frozen peas overnight in the refrigerator.
2. Poach turkey breast until tender. Dice finely.
3. Prepare the rice according to the package directions to yield 1½ cups of cooked rice.
4. Pulse bananas, peas, cod liver oil, and safflower oil.
5. Sprinkle HILARY'S BLEND™ supplement over the rice and mix in.
6. Stir all ingredients together.

INGREDIENTS		
APPROX.	INGREDIENT	GRAMS
1⅔ cups	Bananas, raw, sliced	250
1 tsp	Cod liver oil	5
2 cups	Peas, thawed from frozen	290
1½ cups	Rice, brown, cooked	295
1 tsp	Safflower oil	5
1 pinch	Salt	<1
250 g raw	Turkey breast, cooked	140
1½ scoops	HILARY'S BLEND™ supplement	15
	Total	1000

NUTRITION				
		Per 100g As Fed	Per 100g Dry Matter	Per 1000 kcal
PROTEIN	g	6.81	25.01	63.73
Arginine	g	0.49	1.79	4.56
Histidine	g	0.20	0.74	1.89
Isoleucine	g	0.32	1.15	2.93
Leucine	g	0.51	1.87	4.76
Lysine	g	0.53	1.95	4.97
Methionine + Cystine	g	0.23	0.85	2.17
Phenylalanine + Tyrosine	g	0.51	1.86	4.74
Threonine	g	0.28	1.03	2.62
Tryptophan	g	0.07	0.26	0.66
Valine	g	0.35	1.28	3.26
FAT (LIPID)	g	1.57	5.75	14.65
Linoleic acid	g	0.54	1.99	5.07
MINERALS				
Calcium	g	211.13	774.99	1974.75
Phosphorus	g	158.67	582.41	1484.04
Calcium to Phosphorus ratio		1.33	1.33	1.33
Potassium	g	326.33	1197.83	3052.18
Sodium	g	28.56	104.73	266.86
Magnesium	g	36.26	133.10	339.15
Iron	mg	4.28	15.72	40.06
Copper	mg	0.38	1.40	3.57
Manganese	mg	0.68	2.50	6.37
Zinc	mg	5.66	20.78	52.95
Iodine	mg	0.09	0.33	0.84
Selenium	µg	8.16	29.94	76.29
VITAMINS				
Vitamin A	IU	738	2708	6901
Vitamin D	IU	55	203	517
Vitamin E	mg	4.58	16.83	42.88
Thiamin	mg	0.16	0.57	1.45
Riboflavin	mg	0.20	0.74	1.89
Niacin	mg	2.51	9.22	23.49
Pantothenic acid	mg	0.90	3.29	8.38
Pyridoxine	mg	0.31	1.13	2.88
Folic acid	µg	12.00	44.05	112.24
Choline	mg	76.98	282.57	720.02
Vitamin B12	µg	1.26	4.61	11.75
OTHER (non-essential nutrients)				
Total dietary fiber	g	3.04	11.14	28.39
FATTY ACIDS				
Polyunsaturated fatty acids	g	0.68	2.50	6.37
Eicosapentaenoic acid	mg	34	130	331
Docosahexaenoic acid	mg	60	220	561
Omega 6:3 ratio (estimate)		6.2	6.2	6.2
ANTIOXIDANTS				
Vitamin C	mg	13.78	50.56	128.83
Beta-carotene	µg	136.7	501.8	1278.7
Lycopene	µg	0	0	0
Lutein + Zeaxanthin	µg	723.8	2656.9	6770.1

METABOLIZABLE ENERGY

107 kcal/100 grams

FEEDING GUIDE			
Body weight		Energy intake	Amount to feed
lbs	kg	kcal/day	grams/day
10	4.5	296	276
20	9.1	497	465
40	18.2	836	782
60	27.3	1134	1060
80	36.4	1407	1315
100	45.5	1663	1554

Hilary's Blend™

Supplement for home-made meals

NUTRITION

		Per 100g As Fed	Per 100g Dry Matter	Per 1000 kcal
PROTEIN	g	9.96	32.15	73.33
Arginine	g	0.67	2.18	4.97
Histidine	g	0.22	0.71	1.62
Isoleucine	g	0.38	1.23	2.81
Leucine	g	0.66	2.12	4.84
Lysine	g	0.53	1.70	3.88
Methionine + Cystine	g	0.23	0.76	1.73
Phenylalanine + Tyrosine	g	0.73	2.36	5.38
Threonine	g	0.34	1.10	2.51
Tryptophan	g	0.11	0.36	0.82
Valine	g	0.41	1.33	3.03
FAT (LIPID)	g	6.65	21.48	48.99
Linoleic acid	g	2.55	8.22	18.75
MINERALS				
Calcium	mg	342.00	1103.81	2517.70
Phosphorus	mg	248.93	803.41	1832.51
Calcium to Phosphorus ratio		1.37	1.37	1.37
Potassium	mg	506.35	1634.24	3727.57
Sodium	mg	92.04	297.05	677.55
Magnesium	mg	80.96	261.29	595.98
Iron	mg	7.72	24.92	56.84
Copper	mg	0.63	2.03	4.63
Manganese	mg	0.82	2.64	6.02
Zinc	mg	7.46	24.08	54.92
Iodine	mg	0.12	0.39	0.89
Selenium	µg	5.47	17.64	40.24
VITAMINS				
Vitamin A	IU	1118	3608	8228
Vitamin D	IU	57	184	420
Vitamin E	mg	6.73	21.73	49.56
Thiamin	mg	0.16	0.53	1.21
Riboflavin	mg	0.32	1.03	2.35
Niacin	mg	1.31	4.24	9.67
Pantothenic acid	mg	1.00	3.22	7.34
Pyridoxine	mg	0.26	0.83	1.89
Folic acid	µg	16.00	51.64	117.79
Choline	mg	115.13	371.57	847.52
Vitamin B12	µg	1.60	5.16	11.77
OTHER (non-essential nutrients)				
Total dietary fiber	g	4.12	13.31	30.36
FATTY ACIDS				
Polyunsaturated fatty acids	g	3.12	10.08	22.99
Eicosapentaenoic acid	mg	34	110	251
Docosahexaenoic acid	mg	55	180	411
Omega 6:3 ratio (estimate)		11.5	11.5	11.5
ANTIOXIDANTS				
Vitamin C	mg	12.16	39.24	89.50
Beta-carotene	µg	368.0	1187.8	2709.2
Lycopene	µg	469.7	1516.0	3457.8
Lutein + Zeaxanthin	µg	914.3	2951.0	6731.0

Vegetarian Adult 1

1. Boil soybeans until tender.
2. Pulse beans, broccoli, lettuce, peas, spinach, peanut butter, and cod liver oil to small kernels.
3. Add HILARY'S BLEND™ supplement to the tomato sauce and mix thoroughly.
4. Mix kidney beans, chickpeas, flaxseeds, curd cheese and tomato sauce.
5. Stir all ingredients together.

INGREDIENTS

APPROX.	INGREDIENT	GRAMS
¼ cup	Beans, green, raw, chopped	27
½ cup	Beans, kidney, canned	128
¾ cup	Broccoli, raw, chopped	68
⅓ cup	Chickpeas, canned	80
1 tsp	Cod liver oil	5
1 tbsp	Flaxseeds, ground	7
⅓ cup	Lettuce, raw, shredded	23
2 tbsp	Peanut butter, smooth, unsalted	32
½ cup	Peas, thawed from frozen	73
½ cup	Soybean, curd cheese	112
2 cups	Soybeans, boiled	344
5 leaves	Spinach, raw	50
⅛ cup	Tomato sauce, canned	31
2 scoops	HILARY'S BLEND™ supplement	20
	Total	1000

FEEDING GUIDE

Body weight		Energy intake	Amount to feed
lbs	kg	kcal/day	grams/day
10	4.5	296	217
20	9.1	497	366
40	18.2	836	615
60	27.3	1134	834
80	36.4	1407	1034
100	45.5	1663	1223

METABOLIZABLE ENERGY

136 kcal/100 grams

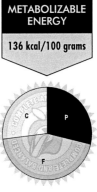

Supplement for home-made meals

R66

Vegetarian Adult 2

1. Thaw frozen peas overnight in the refrigerator.
2. Hard boil eggs. Discard shells and mash coarsely.
3. Pulse almonds, kidney beans, broccoli, carrots, flaxseeds, peas, spinach, zucchini, cod liver oil, and safflower oil to small kernels.
4. Add HILARY'S BLEND™ supplement to the eggs and mix thoroughly.
5. Stir the eggs and tomato sauce into the pulsed mixture.

INGREDIENTS

APPROX.	INGREDIENT	GRAMS
1 cup	Almonds, ground	95
1½ cups	Beans, kidney, boiled	266
1 cup	Broccoli, raw, chopped	91
¼ cup	Carrots, raw, grated	28
1 tsp	Cod liver oil	5
5 large	Eggs, hard-boiled	250
1 tbsp	Flaxseeds, ground	7
1 cup	Peas, thawed from frozen	145
1 tsp	Safflower oil	5
2 leaves	Spinach, raw	20
⅛ cup	Tomato sauce, canned	31
⅓ cup	Zucchini, raw	37
2 scoops	HILARY'S BLEND™ supplement	20
	Total	1000

METABOLIZABLE ENERGY

158 kcal/100 grams

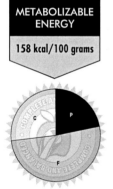

FEEDING GUIDE

Body weight		Energy intake	Amount to feed
lbs	kg	kcal/day	grams/day
10	4.5	296	187
20	9.1	497	315
40	18.2	836	529
60	27.3	1134	718
80	36.4	1407	890
100	45.5	1663	1053

Supplement for home-made meals

NUTRITION

		Per 100g As Fed	Per 100g Dry Matter	Per 1000 kcal
PROTEIN	g	8.81	26.83	55.61
Arginine	g	0.67	2.03	4.21
Histidine	g	0.22	0.68	1.41
Isoleucine	g	0.39	1.18	2.45
Leucine	g	0.67	2.04	4.23
Lysine	g	0.52	1.57	3.25
Methionine + Cystine	g	0.31	0.94	1.95
Phenylalanine + Tyrosine	g	0.73	2.22	4.60
Threonine	g	0.37	1.11	2.30
Tryptophan	g	0.10	0.29	0.60
Valine	g	0.45	1.37	2.84
FAT (LIPID)	g	8.89	27.09	56.14
Linoleic acid	g	1.92	5.85	12.12
MINERALS				
Calcium	mg	322.58	982.57	2036.37
Phosphorus	mg	245.08	746.53	1547.18
Calcium to Phosphorus ratio		1.32	1.32	1.32
Potassium	mg	465.58	1418.14	2939.09
Sodium	mg	59.39	180.89	374.89
Magnesium	mg	55.68	169.60	351.50
Iron	mg	6.47	19.69	40.81
Copper	mg	0.57	1.75	3.63
Manganese	mg	0.80	2.44	5.06
Zinc	mg	7.57	23.05	47.77
Iodine	mg	0.12	0.37	0.77
Selenium	µg	8.99	27.38	56.74
VITAMINS				
Vitamin A	IU	1491	4542	9413
Vitamin D	IU	57	174	360
Vitamin E	mg	8.96	27.28	56.54
Thiamin	mg	0.19	0.58	1.20
Riboflavin	mg	0.44	1.35	2.80
Niacin	mg	1.28	3.91	8.10
Pantothenic acid	mg	1.34	4.09	8.48
Pyridoxine	mg	0.20	0.60	1.24
Folic acid	µg	16.00	48.74	101.01
Choline	mg	152.55	464.65	962.99
Vitamin B12	µg	1.88	5.72	11.85
OTHER (non-essential nutrients)				
Total dietary fiber	g	5.00	15.24	31.58
FATTY ACIDS				
Polyunsaturated fatty acids	g	2.30	7.01	14.53
Eicosapentaenoic acid	mg	36	110	228
Docosahexaenoic acid	mg	64	200	414
Omega 6:3 ratio (estimate)		7.9	7.9	7.9
ANTIOXIDANTS				
Vitamin C	mg	15.81	48.17	99.83
Beta-carotene	µg	456.2	1389.7	2880.0
Lycopene	µg	469.7	1430.8	2965.4
Lutein + Zeaxanthin	µg	909.5	2770.3	5741.5

Vegetarian Adult 3

NUTRITION		Per 100g As Fed	Per 100g Dry Matter	Per 1000 kcal
PROTEIN	g	9.65	32.26	72.04
Arginine	g	0.65	2.17	4.85
Histidine	g	0.25	0.85	1.90
Isoleucine	g	0.47	1.56	3.48
Leucine	g	0.77	2.59	5.78
Lysine	g	0.66	2.19	4.89
Methionine + Cystine	g	0.32	1.06	2.37
Phenylalanine + Tyrosine	g	0.83	2.78	6.21
Threonine	g	0.42	1.39	3.10
Tryptophan	g	0.12	0.41	0.92
Valine	g	0.52	1.72	3.84
FAT (LIPID)	g	5.89	19.70	43.99
Linoleic acid	g	1.62	5.41	12.08
MINERALS				
Calcium	mg	268.32	897.18	2003.48
Phosphorus	mg	222.82	745.04	1663.74
Calcium to Phosphorus ratio		1.20	1.20	1.20
Potassium	mg	443.38	1482.53	3310.62
Sodium	mg	46.84	156.63	349.77
Magnesium	mg	46.61	155.84	348.00
Iron	mg	5.93	19.84	44.30
Copper	mg	0.47	1.56	3.48
Manganese	mg	0.65	2.18	4.87
Zinc	mg	5.86	19.60	43.77
Iodine	mg	0.09	0.30	0.67
Selenium	µg	7.51	25.09	56.03
VITAMINS				
Vitamin A	IU	1514	5063	11307
Vitamin D	IU	56	186	415
Vitamin E	mg	4.91	16.42	36.67
Thiamin	mg	0.18	0.61	1.36
Riboflavin	mg	0.32	1.08	2.41
Niacin	mg	0.93	3.12	6.97
Pantothenic acid	mg	0.99	3.31	7.39
Pyridoxine	mg	0.20	0.66	1.47
Folic acid	µg	12.00	40.12	89.59
Choline	mg	115.03	384.63	858.91
Vitamin B12	µg	1.39	4.65	10.38
OTHER (non-essential nutrients)				
Total dietary fiber	g	4.93	16.49	36.82
FATTY ACIDS				
Polyunsaturated fatty acids	g	2.07	6.91	15.43
Eicosapentaenoic acid	mg	35	120	268
Docosahexaenoic acid	mg	61	200	447
Omega 6:3 ratio (estimate)		8.8	8.8	8.8
ANTIOXIDANTS				
Vitamin C	mg	14.31	47.83	106.81
Beta-carotene	µg	488.2	1632.5	3645.6
Lycopene	µg	0.03	0.09	0.20
Lutein + Zeaxanthin	µg	858.1	2869.2	6407.2

1. Thaw frozen peas overnight in the refrigerator.
2. Hard boil eggs. Discard shells and mash coarsely.
3. Boil soybeans until soft.
4. Pulse beans, kidney beans, broccoli, carrots, flaxseeds, peas, soybeans, spinach, cod liver oil, and safflower oil to small kernels.
5. Add HILARY'S BLEND™ supplement to the eggs and mix thoroughly.
6. Stir the eggs and cheese into the pulsed mixture.

INGREDIENTS		
APPROX.	INGREDIENT	GRAMS
½ cup	Beans, green, raw, chopped	55
1 cup	Beans, kidney, canned	256
¾ cup	Broccoli, raw, chopped	68
¼ cup	Carrots, raw, grated	28
¼ cup	Cheese, cheddar, shredded	28
1 tsp	Cod liver oil	5
3 large	Eggs, hard-boiled	150
2 tsp	Flaxseeds, ground	5
1 cup	Peas, thawed from frozen	145
1 tsp	Safflower oil	5
1¼ cup	Soybeans, boiled	215
2½ leaves	Spinach, raw	25
1½ scoops	HILARY'S BLEND™ supplement	15
	Total	1000

FEEDING GUIDE			
Body weight		Energy intake	Amount to feed
lbs	kg	kcal/day	grams/day
10	4.5	296	221
20	9.1	497	371
40	18.2	836	624
60	27.3	1134	846
80	36.4	1407	1050
100	45.5	1663	1241

METABOLIZABLE ENERGY

134 kcal/100 grams

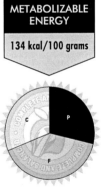

Hilary's BLEND™

Supplement for home-made meals

Vegetarian Adult 4

1. Thaw frozen peas overnight in the refrigerator.
2. Hard boil eggs. Discard shells and mash coarsely.
3. Prepare egg noodles according to package directions to yield 1 cup of cooked noodles.
4. Pulse alfalfa sprouts, kidney beans, carrots, flaxseeds, peas, cod liver oil, and safflower oil to small kernels.
5. Add HILARY'S BLEND™ supplement to the eggs and mix thoroughly.
6. Stir all ingredients together.

INGREDIENTS

APPROX.	INGREDIENT	GRAMS
2 cups	Alfalfa sprouts, raw	66
½ cup	Beans, kidney, canned	128
¼ cup	Carrots, raw, grated	28
1 tsp	Cod liver oil	5
1 cup	Egg noodles, cooked	160
6 large	Eggs, hard-boiled	300
1 tsp	Flaxseeds, ground	3
2 cups	Peas, thawed from frozen	290
1 tsp	Safflower oil	5
1½ scoops	HILARY'S BLEND™ supplement	15
	Total	1000

METABOLIZABLE ENERGY

117 kcal/100 grams

FEEDING GUIDE

Body weight		Energy intake	Amount to feed
lbs	kg	kcal/day	grams/day
10	4.5	296	253
20	9.1	497	425
40	18.2	836	715
60	27.3	1134	969
80	36.4	1407	1202
100	45.5	1663	1421

NUTRITION

		Per 100g As Fed	Per 100g Dry Matter	Per 1000 kcal
PROTEIN	g	7.09	28.03	60.75
Arginine	g	0.43	1.69	3.66
Histidine	g	0.16	0.64	1.39
Isoleucine	g	0.34	1.34	2.90
Leucine	g	0.56	2.20	4.77
Lysine	g	0.45	1.79	3.88
Methionine + Cystine	g	0.29	1.13	2.45
Phenylalanine + Tyrosine	g	0.56	2.22	4.81
Threonine	g	0.30	1.20	2.60
Tryptophan	g	0.07	0.29	0.63
Valine	g	0.39	1.53	3.32
FAT (LIPID)	g	4.89	19.33	41.90
Linoleic acid	g	0.91	3.62	7.85
MINERALS				
Calcium	mg	230.32	911.19	1974.97
Phosphorus	mg	180.13	712.61	1544.55
Calcium to Phosphorus ratio		1.28	1.28	1.28
Potassium	mg	274.09	1084.34	2350.26
Sodium	mg	82.53	326.49	707.65
Magnesium	mg	25.13	99.43	215.51
Iron	mg	4.57	18.09	39.21
Copper	mg	0.38	1.49	3.23
Manganese	mg	0.45	1.77	3.84
Zinc	mg	5.75	22.76	49.33
Iodine	mg	0.09	0.36	0.78
Selenium	µg	13.82	54.67	118.49
VITAMINS				
Vitamin A	IU	1382	5467	11850
Vitamin D	IU	55	219	474
Vitamin E	mg	4.90	19.37	41.98
Thiamin	mg	0.16	0.65	1.41
Riboflavin	mg	0.33	1.31	2.84
Niacin	mg	1.05	4.16	9.02
Pantothenic acid	mg	1.16	4.58	9.93
Pyridoxine	mg	0.16	0.61	1.32
Folic acid	µg	12.00	47.47	102.89
Choline	mg	133.49	528.11	1144.66
Vitamin B12	µg	1.55	6.12	13.26
OTHER (non-essential nutrients)				
Total dietary fiber	g	2.33	9.22	19.98
FATTY ACIDS				
Polyunsaturated fatty acids	g	1.21	4.78	10.36
Eicosapentaenoic acid	mg	36	140	303
Docosahexaenoic acid	mg	66	260	564
Omega 6:3 ratio (estimate)		6.1	6.1	6.1
ANTIOXIDANTS				
Vitamin C	mg	12.46	49.30	106.86
Beta-carotene	µg	371.4	1469.3	3184.6
Lycopene	µg	0.03	0.11	0.24
Lutein + Zeaxanthin	µg	839.4	3320.9	7198.0

Hilary's Blend™

Supplement for home-made meals

Vegetarian Diabetic 1

NUTRITION				
		Per 100g As Fed	Per 100g Dry Matter	Per 1000 kcal
PROTEIN	g	7.69	26.98	61.56
Arginine	g	0.56	1.98	4.52
Histidine	g	0.18	0.63	1.44
Isoleucine	g	0.30	1.04	2.37
Leucine	g	0.53	1.87	4.27
Lysine	g	0.40	1.40	3.19
Methionine + Cystine	g	0.20	0.69	1.57
Phenylalanine + Tyrosine	g	0.62	2.17	4.95
Threonine	g	0.27	0.93	2.12
Tryptophan	g	0.09	0.32	0.73
Valine	g	0.33	1.17	2.67
FAT (LIPID)	g	6.38	22.38	51.07
Linoleic acid	g	2.07	7.25	16.54
MINERALS				
Calcium	mg	256.94	901.61	2057.30
Phosphorus	mg	190.87	669.75	1528.24
Calcium to Phosphorus ratio		1.35	1.35	1.35
Potassium	mg	455.03	1596.68	3643.31
Sodium	mg	105.38	369.78	843.76
Magnesium	mg	49.01	171.97	392.40
Iron	mg	5.46	19.16	43.72
Copper	mg	0.46	1.62	3.70
Manganese	mg	0.73	2.56	5.84
Zinc	mg	5.60	19.65	44.84
Iodine	mg	0.09	0.32	0.73
Selenium	µg	5.06	17.75	40.50
VITAMINS				
Vitamin A	IU	722	2532	5777
Vitamin D	IU	55	194	442
Vitamin E	mg	5.53	19.40	44.27
Thiamin	mg	0.13	0.45	1.03
Riboflavin	mg	0.28	0.96	2.19
Niacin	mg	1.81	6.34	14.47
Pantothenic acid	mg	0.89	3.11	7.10
Pyridoxine	mg	0.22	0.78	1.78
Folic acid	µg	12.00	42.11	96.09
Choline	mg	84.77	297.47	678.77
Vitamin B12	µg	1.24	4.33	9.88
OTHER (non-essential nutrients)			.	
Total dietary fiber	g	4.41	15.46	35.28
FATTY ACIDS				
Polyunsaturated fatty acids	g	2.35	8.23	18.78
Eicosapentaenoic acid	mg	34	120	274
Docosahexaenoic acid	mg	55	190	434
Omega 6:3 ratio (estimate)		25.3	25.3	25.3
ANTIOXIDANTS				
Vitamin C	mg	15.55	54.57	124.52
Beta-carotene	µg	125.2	439.5	1002.8
Lycopene	µg	1848.5	6486.5	14801.0
Lutein + Zeaxanthin	µg	476.8	1673.2	3818.0

1. Boil soybeans until tender.
2. Pulse apples, beans, broccoli, peanut butter, zucchini, and cod liver oil to small kernels.
3. Add HILARY'S BLEND supplement to the tomato sauce and mix thoroughly.
4. Shred the slices of bread. Stir bread pieces and Metamucil® into the yogurt.
5. Stir all ingredients together.

INGREDIENTS		
APPROX.	**INGREDIENT**	**GRAMS**
⅔ cups	Apples, raw with skin, sliced	73
1 cup	Beans, green, raw, chopped	110
2 slices	Bread, whole wheat	56
1¼ cups	Broccoli, raw, chopped	114
1 tsp	Cod liver oil	5
2 tsp	Metamucil®	14
4 tbsp	Peanut butter, smooth, unsalted	64
1½ cups	Soybeans, mature, boiled	252
½ cup	Tomato sauce, canned	122
½ cup	Yogurt, plain, low fat	62
1 cup	Zucchini, raw, sliced	113
1½ scoops	HILARY'S BLEND™ supplement	15
	Total	1000

FEEDING GUIDE			
Body weight		Energy intake	Amount to feed
lbs	kg	kcal/day	grams/day
10	4.5	296	237
20	9.1	497	398
40	18.2	836	670
60	27.3	1134	908
80	36.4	1407	1126
100	45.5	1663	1332

METABOLIZABLE ENERGY

125 kcal/100 grams

Hilary's
Supplement for home-made meals *Blend* ™

R70

Vegetarian Diabetic 2

1. Prepare barley according to package directions to yield 1⅛ cups of cooked barley.
2. Hard boil eggs. Discard shells and mash coarsely.
3. Lightly boil peas until tender.
4. Pulse broccoli, peas, and cod liver oil to small kernels.
5. Add Metamucil®, flaxseeds and HILARY'S BLEND supplement to the yogurt and blend thoroughly.
6. Stir all ingredients together.

INGREDIENTS

APPROX.	INGREDIENT	GRAMS
1⅛ cups	Barley, pearled, cooked	182
½ cup	Broccoli, raw, chopped	46
½ tsp	Cod liver oil	3
8 large	Eggs, hard-boiled	400
1 tbsp	Flaxseeds, ground	10
3 tsp	Metamucil®	21
1 cup	Peas, green, boiled	160
⅔ cup	Yogurt, plain, low fat	163
1½ scoops	HILARY'S BLEND™ supplement	15
	Total	1000

METABOLIZABLE ENERGY

125 kcal/100 grams

FEEDING GUIDE

Body weight		Energy intake	Amount to feed
lbs	kg	kcal/day	grams/day
10	4.5	296	237
20	9.1	497	398
40	18.2	836	670
60	27.3	1134	908
80	36.4	1407	1126
100	45.5	1663	1332

Hilary's Blend™
Supplement for home-made meals

NUTRITION

		Per 100g As Fed	Per 100g Dry Matter	Per 1000 kcal
PROTEIN	g	7.44	27.73	59.57
Arginine	g	0.44	1.65	3.54
Histidine	g	0.17	0.65	1.40
Isoleucine	g	0.38	1.41	3.03
Leucine	g	0.61	2.28	4.90
Lysine	g	0.52	1.93	4.15
Methionine + Cystine	g	0.35	1.30	2.79
Phenylalanine + Tyrosine	g	0.67	2.49	5.35
Threonine	g	0.33	1.24	2.66
Tryptophan	g	0.08	0.31	0.67
Valine	g	0.45	1.68	3.61
FAT (LIPID)	g	5.36	19.98	42.92
Linoleic acid	g	0.60	2.22	4.77
MINERALS				
Calcium	mg	258.38	963.40	2069.69
Phosphorus	mg	189.88	707.97	1520.95
Calcium to Phosphorus ratio		1.36	1.36	1.36
Potassium	mg	267.24	996.40	2140.59
Sodium	mg	79.17	295.17	634.12
Magnesium	mg	21.63	80.66	173.28
Iron	mg	4.64	17.30	37.17
Copper	mg	0.33	1.23	2.64
Manganese	mg	0.36	1.35	2.90
Zinc	mg	5.72	21.32	45.80
Iodine	mg	0.09	0.34	0.73
Selenium	µg	14.95	55.75	119.77
VITAMINS				
Vitamin A	IU	909	3388	7278
Vitamin D	IU	35	131	282
Vitamin E	mg	4.96	18.50	39.74
Thiamin	mg	0.15	0.56	1.20
Riboflavin	mg	0.39	1.47	3.16
Niacin	mg	0.96	3.57	7.67
Pantothenic acid	mg	1.34	4.99	10.72
Pyridoxine	mg	0.15	0.57	1.22
Folic acid	µg	12.00	44.74	96.12
Choline	mg	161.08	600.61	1290.30
Vitamin B12	µg	1.74	6.47	13.90
OTHER (non-essential nutrients)				
Total dietary fiber	g	3.24	12.08	25.95
FATTY ACIDS				
Polyunsaturated fatty acids	g	0.99	3.69	7.93
Eicosapentaenoic acid	mg	23	80	172
Docosahexaenoic acid	mg	48	180	387
Omega 6:3 ratio (estimate)		12.9	12.9	12.9
ANTIOXIDANTS				
Vitamin C	mg	5.82	21.71	46.64
Beta-carotene	µg	221.0	824.0	1770.3
Lycopene	µg	0	0	0
Lutein + Zeaxanthin	µg	606.4	2261.2	4857.7

Vegetarian Urate 1

NUTRITION		Per 100g As Fed	Per 100g Dry Matter	Per 1000 kcal
PROTEIN	**g**	**6.75**	**26.47**	**62.27**
Arginine	g	0.43	1.69	3.98
Histidine	g	0.20	0.77	1.81
Isoleucine	g	0.34	1.33	3.13
Leucine	g	0.58	2.27	5.34
Lysine	g	0.49	1.90	4.47
Methionine + Cystine	g	0.22	0.88	2.07
Phenylalanine + Tyrosine	g	0.61	2.40	5.65
Threonine	g	0.28	1.09	2.56
Tryptophan	g	0.07	0.27	0.64
Valine	g	0.36	1.42	3.34
FAT (LIPID)	**g**	**3.71**	**14.57**	**34.28**
Linoleic acid	g	1.98	7.75	18.23
MINERALS				
Calcium	mg	237.57	932.11	2192.84
Phosphorus	mg	166.98	655.17	1541.32
Calcium to Phosphorus ratio		1.42	1.42	1.42
Potassium	mg	281.24	1103.46	2595.95
Sodium	mg	240.40	943.22	2218.98
Magnesium	mg	25.35	99.46	233.98
Iron	mg	4.35	17.05	40.11
Copper	mg	0.39	1.53	3.60
Manganese	mg	0.55	2.17	5.11
Zinc	mg	5.60	21.96	51.66
Iodine	mg	0.09	0.35	0.82
Selenium	µg	4.37	17.13	40.30
VITAMINS				
Vitamin A	IU	414	1625	3824
Vitamin D	IU	25	99	233
Vitamin E	mg	4.77	18.70	43.99
Thiamin	mg	0.12	0.48	1.13
Riboflavin	mg	0.22	0.85	2.00
Niacin	mg	0.83	3.24	7.62
Pantothenic acid	mg	0.83	3.27	7.69
Pyridoxine	mg	0.27	1.06	2.49
Folic acid	µg	12.00	47.08	110.76
Choline	mg	73.09	286.78	674.67
Vitamin B12	µg	1.39	5.45	12.82
OTHER (non-essential nutrients)				
Total dietary fiber	g	3.32	13.03	30.65
FATTY ACIDS				
Polyunsaturated fatty acids	g	2.27	8.89	20.91
Eicosapentaenoic acid	mg	14	50	118
Docosahexaenoic acid	mg	22	90	212
Omega 6:3 ratio (estimate)		7.6	7.6	7.6
ANTIOXIDANTS				
Vitamin C	mg	15.22	59.72	140.49
Beta-carotene	µg	119.9	470.4	1106.6
Lycopene	µg	469.7	1842.9	4335.6
Lutein + Zeaxanthin	µg	554.2	2174.3	5115.2

1. Thaw frozen peas overnight in the refrigerator.
2. Pulse blueberries, broccoli, chickpeas, flaxseeds, peas, cod liver oil, and safflower oil to small kernels.
3. Add HILARY'S BLEND™ supplement to the tomato sauce and mix thoroughly.
4. Stir the cottage cheese and tomato sauce into the pulsed mixture.

INGREDIENTS		
APPROX.	INGREDIENT	GRAMS
⅓ cup	Blueberries, raw	49
¾ cup	Broccoli, raw, chopped	68
1 cup	Chickpeas, canned	320
½ tsp	Cod liver oil	2
1⅓ cups	Cottage cheese, low fat	301
4 tsp	Flaxseeds, ground	10
1¼ cups	Peas, thawed from frozen	181
5 tsp	Safflower oil	23
⅛ cup	Tomato sauce, canned	31
1½ scoops	HILARY'S BLEND™ supplement	15
	Total	1000

FEEDING GUIDE			
Body weight		Energy intake	Amount to feed
lbs	kg	kcal/day	grams/day
10	4.5	296	274
20	9.1	497	461
40	18.2	836	775
60	27.3	1134	1050
80	36.4	1407	1303
100	45.5	1663	1540

METABOLIZABLE ENERGY

108 kcal/100 grams

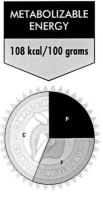

Hilary's Blend™

Supplement for home-made meals

Vegetarian Urate 2

1. Thaw frozen peas overnight in the refrigerator.
2. Boil soybeans until soft.
3. Pulse almonds, kidney beans, broccoli, carrots, flaxseeds, peas, soybeans, spinach, and cod liver oil to small kernels.
4. Add HILARY'S BLEND™ supplement to the tomato sauce and mix thoroughly.
5. Stir the cottage cheese and tomato sauce into the pulsed mixture.

INGREDIENTS

APPROX.	INGREDIENT	GRAMS
1½ cups	Almonds, ground	143
½ cup	Beans, kidney, canned	128
½ cup	Broccoli, raw, chopped	46
¼ cup	Carrots, raw, grated	28
1 tsp	Cod liver oil	5
1 cup	Cottage cheese, low fat	226
5 tsp	Flaxseeds, ground	12
½ cup	Peas, thawed from frozen	73
1½ cup	Soybeans, boiled	258
3 leaves	Spinach, raw	30
⅛ cup	Tomato sauce, canned	31
2 scoops	HILARY'S BLEND™ supplement	20
	Total	1000

METABOLIZABLE ENERGY

181 kcal/100 grams

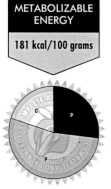

FEEDING GUIDE

Body weight		Energy intake	Amount to feed
lbs	kg	kcal/day	grams/day
10	4.5	296	163
20	9.1	497	275
40	18.2	836	462
60	27.3	1134	626
80	36.4	1407	777
100	45.5	1663	919

NUTRITION

		Per 100g As Fed	Per 100g Dry Matter	Per 1000 kcal
PROTEIN	g	12.14	31.96	66.98
Arginine	g	0.95	2.51	5.26
Histidine	g	0.34	0.91	1.91
Isoleucine	g	0.56	1.47	3.08
Leucine	g	0.99	2.61	5.47
Lysine	g	0.72	1.91	4.00
Methionine + Cystine	g	0.36	0.95	1.99
Phenylalanine + Tyrosine	g	1.08	2.84	5.95
Threonine	g	0.49	1.30	2.72
Tryptophan	g	0.14	0.38	0.80
Valine	g	0.60	1.59	3.33
FAT (LIPID)	g	10.75	28.32	59.35
Linoleic acid	g	2.99	7.87	16.49
MINERALS				
Calcium	mg	356.78	939.69	1969.38
Phosphorus	mg	290.76	765.81	1604.97
Calcium to Phosphorus ratio		1.23	1.23	1.23
Potassium	mg	532.77	1403.21	2940.82
Sodium	mg	118.90	313.15	656.29
Magnesium	mg	81.95	215.85	452.37
Iron	mg	7.20	18.97	39.76
Copper	mg	0.69	1.81	3.79
Manganese	mg	1.04	2.74	5.74
Zinc	mg	7.60	20.01	41.94
Iodine	mg	0.12	0.32	0.67
Selenium	µg	5.86	15.43	32.35
VITAMINS				
Vitamin A	IU	1360	3581	7505
Vitamin D	IU	57	150	315
Vitamin E	mg	10.02	26.39	55.31
Thiamin	mg	0.19	0.50	1.05
Riboflavin	mg	0.45	1.18	2.47
Niacin	mg	1.31	3.45	7.23
Pantothenic acid	mg	1.05	2.75	5.76
Pyridoxine	mg	0.21	0.55	1.15
Folic acid	µg	16.00	42.14	88.32
Choline	mg	105.97	279.10	584.93
Vitamin B12	µg	1.74	4.59	9.62
OTHER (non-essential nutrients)				
Total dietary fiber	g	5.75	15.14	31.73
FATTY ACIDS				
Polyunsaturated fatty acids	g	3.56	9.37	19.64
Eicosapentaenoic acid	mg	34	90	189
Docosahexaenoic acid	mg	55	140	293
Omega 6:3 ratio (estimate)		8.8	8.8	8.8
ANTIOXIDANTS				
Vitamin C	mg	8.85	23.30	48.83
Beta-carotene	µg	458.7	1208.2	2532.1
Lycopene	µg	469.7	1237.2	2592.9
Lutein + Zeaxanthin	µg	626.4	1649.9	3457.8

Hilary's Blend™
Supplement for home-made meals

Limited Antigen Fish 1

1. Gently poach the fish until it flakes easily.
2. Prepare barley according to package directions to yield 3 cups of cooked barley.
3. Sprinkle HILARY'S BLEND™ supplement over the barley then mix in.
4. Stir all ingredients together.

NUTRITION

		Per 100g As Fed	Per 100g Dry Matter	Per 1000 kcal
PROTEIN	g	12.86	37.01	79.73
Arginine	g	0.76	2.18	4.70
Histidine	g	0.37	1.07	2.31
Isoleucine	g	0.58	1.68	3.62
Leucine	g	1.03	2.97	6.40
Lysine	g	1.12	3.23	6.96
Methionine + Cystine	g	0.52	1.49	3.21
Phenylalanine + Tyrosine	g	0.95	2.73	5.88
Threonine	g	0.55	1.59	3.43
Tryptophan	g	0.15	0.43	0.93
Valine	g	0.66	1.90	4.09
FAT (LIPID)	g	6.01	17.29	37.25
Linoleic acid	g	1.90	5.47	11.78
MINERALS				
Calcium	mg	310.98	895.01	1928.07
Phosphorus	mg	242.71	698.53	1504.80
Calcium to Phosphorus ratio		1.28	1.28	1.28
Potassium	mg	408.13	1174.62	2530.42
Sodium	mg	40.83	117.40	252.91
Magnesium	mg	30.17	86.84	187.07
Iron	mg	5.39	15.52	33.43
Copper	mg	0.44	1.27	2.74
Manganese	mg	0.43	1.24	2.67
Zinc	mg	7.07	20.35	43.84
Iodine	mg	0.12	0.35	0.75
Selenium	µg	11.34	32.64	70.31
VITAMINS				
Vitamin A	IU	643	1850	3985
Vitamin D	IU	57	164	353
Vitamin E	mg	6.01	17.28	37.23
Thiamin	mg	0.20	0.58	1.25
Riboflavin	mg	0.23	0.66	1.42
Niacin	mg	5.56	16.01	34.49
Pantothenic acid	mg	1.50	4.32	9.31
Pyridoxine	mg	0.31	0.88	1.90
Folic acid	µg	16.00	46.05	99.20
Choline	mg	86.31	248.41	535.14
Vitamin B12	µg	4.02	11.56	24.90
OTHER (non-essential nutrients)				
Total dietary fiber	g	2.29	6.59	14.20
FATTY ACIDS				
Polyunsaturated fatty acids	g	2.69	7.74	16.67
Eicosapentaenoic acid	mg	197	570	1228
Docosahexaenoic acid	mg	453	1300	2801
Omega 6:3 ratio (estimate)		3.1	3.1	3.1
ANTIOXIDANTS				
Vitamin C	mg	1.60	4.62	9.95
Beta-carotene	µg	0	0	0
Lycopene	µg	0	0	0
Lutein + Zeaxanthin	µg	26.4	75.9	163.5

INGREDIENTS

APPROX.	INGREDIENT	GRAMS
3 cups	Barley, pearled, cooked	471
1 tsp	Cod liver oil	5
4 tsp	Safflower oil	18
1 pinch	Salt	<1
695 g raw	Trout, rainbow, cooked	486
2 scoops	HILARY'S BLEND™ supplement	20
	Total	1000

FEEDING GUIDE

Body weight		Energy intake	Amount to feed
lbs	kg	kcal/day	grams/day
10	4.5	296	184
20	9.1	497	309
40	18.2	836	520
60	27.3	1134	704
80	36.4	1407	874
100	45.5	1663	1033

METABOLIZABLE ENERGY

161 kcal/100 grams

Supplement for home-made meals

Limited Antigen Fish 2

1. Prick potatoes with a fork, then microwave until soft. Mash.
2. Gently poach catfish until it flakes easily.
3. Add HILARY'S BLEND™ supplement to the mashed potatoes and mix thoroughly.
4. Stir all ingredients together.

INGREDIENTS

APPROX.	INGREDIENT	GRAMS
595 g raw	Catfish, farmed, cooked	415
1 tsp	Cod liver oil	5
3 medium	Potatoes, baked in skin	519
6 tsp	Safflower oil	27
3 tsp	Salmon oil	14
2 scoops	HILARY'S BLEND™ supplement	20
	Total	1000

METABOLIZABLE ENERGY

153 kcal/100 grams

FEEDING GUIDE

Body weight		Energy intake	Amount to feed
lbs	kg	kcal/day	grams/day
10	4.5	296	193
20	9.1	497	325
40	18.2	836	547
60	27.3	1134	741
80	36.4	1407	919
100	45.5	1663	1087

Hilary's Blend™ — Supplement for home-made meals

NUTRITION

		Per 100g As Fed	Per 100g Dry Matter	Per 1000 kcal
PROTEIN	g	9.07	28.88	59.20
Arginine	g	0.52	1.67	3.42
Histidine	g	0.26	0.82	1.68
Isoleucine	g	0.41	1.31	2.69
Leucine	g	0.71	2.26	4.63
Lysine	g	0.79	2.52	5.17
Methionine + Cystine	g	0.35	1.12	2.30
Phenylalanine + Tyrosine	g	0.67	2.14	4.39
Threonine	g	0.39	1.24	2.54
Tryptophan	g	0.11	0.34	0.70
Valine	g	0.47	1.51	3.10
FAT (LIPID)	g	8.00	25.47	52.21
Linoleic acid	g	2.49	7.93	16.26
MINERALS				
Calcium	mg	275.52	877.55	1799.00
Phosphorus	mg	226.01	719.84	1475.69
Calcium to Phosphorus ratio		1.22	1.22	1.22
Potassium	mg	560.88	1786.45	3662.26
Sodium	mg	41.89	133.42	273.51
Magnesium	mg	29.58	94.22	193.15
Iron	mg	5.51	17.54	35.96
Copper	mg	0.48	1.51	3.10
Manganese	mg	0.42	1.34	2.75
Zinc	mg	7.07	22.51	46.15
Iodine	mg	0.12	0.38	0.78
Selenium	µg	6.23	19.83	40.65
VITAMINS				
Vitamin A	IU	526	1675	3434
Vitamin D	IU	57	182	372
Vitamin E	mg	6.02	19.18	39.32
Thiamin	mg	0.26	0.81	1.66
Riboflavin	mg	0.22	0.69	1.41
Niacin	mg	2.10	6.67	13.67
Pantothenic acid	mg	1.25	3.99	8.18
Pyridoxine	mg	0.29	0.92	1.89
Folic acid	µg	16.00	50.96	104.47
Choline	mg	80.00	254.81	522.37
Vitamin B12	µg	2.76	8.80	18.04
OTHER (non-essential nutrients)				
Total dietary fiber	g	1.64	5.23	10.72
FATTY ACIDS				
Polyunsaturated fatty acids	g	3.30	10.51	21.55
Eicosapentaenoic acid	mg	237	760	1558
Docosahexaenoic acid	mg	363	1160	2378
Omega 6:3 ratio (estimate)		4.5	4.5	4.5
ANTIOXIDANTS				
Vitamin C	mg	5.31	16.93	34.71
Beta-carotene	µg	3.1	9.9	20.3
Lycopene	µg	0	0	0
Lutein + Zeaxanthin	µg	15.6	49.6	101.7

NUTRITION		Per 100g As Fed	Per 100g Dry Matter	Per 1000 kcal
PROTEIN	g	7.15	29.21	56.11
Arginine	g	0.45	1.82	3.50
Histidine	g	0.20	0.82	1.58
Isoleucine	g	0.32	1.31	2.52
Leucine	g	0.57	2.33	4.48
Lysine	g	0.56	2.30	4.42
Methionine + Cystine	g	0.29	1.19	2.29
Phenylalanine + Tyrosine	g	0.55	2.23	4.28
Threonine	g	0.30	1.21	2.32
Tryptophan	g	0.09	0.35	0.67
Valine	g	0.38	1.53	2.94
FAT (LIPID)	g	7.38	30.13	57.87
Linoleic acid	g	2.81	11.46	22.01
MINERALS				
Calcium	mg	273.23	1115.93	2143.50
Phosphorus	mg	202.08	825.35	1585.35
Calcium to Phosphorus ratio		1.35	1.35	1.35
Potassium	mg	281.86	1151.15	2211.16
Sodium	mg	34.40	140.32	269.53
Magnesium	mg	28.34	115.74	222.32
Iron	mg	5.17	21.09	40.51
Copper	mg	0.41	1.69	3.25
Manganese	mg	0.72	2.92	5.61
Zinc	mg	6.89	28.15	54.07
Iodine	mg	0.12	0.49	0.94
Selenium	µg	15.66	63.97	122.88
VITAMINS				
Vitamin A	IU	512	2091	4017
Vitamin D	IU	57	233	447
Vitamin E	mg	6.07	24.79	47.62
Thiamin	mg	0.21	0.85	1.63
Riboflavin	mg	0.21	0.84	1.61
Niacin	mg	2.35	9.60	18.44
Pantothenic acid	mg	1.30	5.29	10.16
Pyridoxine	mg	0.23	0.94	1.81
Folic acid	µg	16.00	65.35	125.53
Choline	mg	85.20	347.95	668.35
Vitamin B12	µg	2.28	9.29	17.84
OTHER (non-essential nutrients)				
Total dietary fiber	g	1.69	6.92	13.29
FATTY ACIDS				
Polyunsaturated fatty acids	g	3.83	15.66	30.08
Eicosapentaenoic acid	mg	201	820	1575
Docosahexaenoic acid	mg	406	1660	3189
Omega 6:3 ratio (estimate)		5.3	5.3	5.3
ANTIOXIDANTS				
Vitamin C	mg	0.89	3.64	6.99
Beta-carotene	µg	0	0	0
Lycopene	µg	0	0	0
Lutein + Zeaxanthin	µg	126.4	516.1	991.3

Limited Antigen Fish 3

1. Gently poach salmon until it flakes easily.
2. Prepare oatmeal according to package directions to yield 3 cups of cooked oatmeal.
3. Sprinkle HILARY'S BLEND™ supplement over the oatmeal and mix thoroughly.
4. Stir all ingredients together.

INGREDIENTS		
APPROX.	INGREDIENT	GRAMS
1 tsp	Cod liver oil	5
3 cups	Oatmeal, cooked	702
7 tsp	Safflower oil	32
345 g raw	Salmon, Atlantic, cooked	241
1 pinch	Salt	<1
2 scoops	HILARY'S BLEND™ supplement	20
	Total	1000

FEEDING GUIDE			
Body weight		Energy intake	Amount to feed
lbs	kg	kcal/day	grams/day
10	4.5	296	233
20	9.1	497	392
40	18.2	836	659
60	27.3	1134	893
80	36.4	1407	1108
100	45.5	1663	1309

METABOLIZABLE ENERGY

127 kcal/100 grams

Hilary's
Supplement for home-made meals
Blend™

R76

Limited Antigen Fish 4

1. Prick the potatoes with a fork, then microwave until soft. Mash.
2. Add HILARY'S BLEND™ supplement to the tuna and mix thoroughly.
3. Stir all ingredients together.

INGREDIENTS

APPROX.	INGREDIENT	GRAMS
1 tsp	Cod liver oil	5
3 small	Potatoes, baked in skin	414
10 tsp	Safflower oil	45
	Tuna, canned in water, drained	516
2 scoops	HILARY'S BLEND™ supplement	20
	Total	1000

METABOLIZABLE ENERGY

150 kcal/100 grams

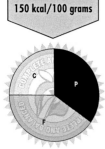

FEEDING GUIDE

Body weight		Energy intake	Amount to feed
lbs	kg	kcal/day	grams/day
10	4.5	296	197
20	9.1	497	332
40	18.2	836	558
60	27.3	1134	756
80	36.4	1407	938
100	45.5	1663.	1109

Hilary's Blend
Supplement for home-made meals

NUTRITION

		Per 100g As Fed	Per 100g Dry Matter	Per 1000 kcal
PROTEIN	g	13.22	42.97	88.36
Arginine	g	0.78	2.52	5.18
Histidine	g	0.38	1.24	2.55
Isoleucine	g	0.60	1.96	4.03
Leucine	g	1.05	3.42	7.03
Lysine	g	1.18	3.84	7.90
Methionine + Cystine	g	0.52	1.69	3.48
Phenylalanine + Tyrosine	g	0.97	3.16	6.50
Threonine	g	0.57	1.86	3.82
Tryptophan	g	0.15	0.50	1.03
Valine	g	0.69	2.23	4.59
FAT (LIPID)	g	6.59	21.40	44.01
Linoleic acid	g	3.41	11.07	22.76
MINERALS				
Calcium	mg	277.43	901.60	1854.00
Phosphorus	mg	228.95	744.05	1530.02
Calcium to Phosphorus ratio		1.21	1.21	1.21
Potassium	mg	493.78	1604.69	3299.79
Sodium	mg	33.44	108.67	223.46
Magnesium	mg	32.88	106.85	219.72
Iron	mg	5.55	18.05	37.12
Copper	mg	0.43	1.40	2.88
Manganese	mg	0.40	1.30	2.67
Zinc	mg	6.84	22.24	45.73
Iodine	mg	0.12	0.39	0.80
Selenium	µg	34.07	110.71	227.66
VITAMINS				
Vitamin A	IU	514	1670	3435
Vitamin D	IU	57	185	381
Vitamin E	mg	6.02	19.55	40.20
Thiamin	mg	0.08	0.26	0.53
Riboflavin	mg	0.21	0.70	1.44
Niacin	mg	3.90	12.66	26.03
Pantothenic acid	mg	1.02	3.31	6.81
Pyridoxine	mg	0.30	0.98	2.02
Folic acid	µg	16.00	52.00	106.93
Choline	mg	80.00	259.98	534.61
Vitamin B12	µg	2.20	7.16	14.72
OTHER (non-essential nutrients)				
Total dietary fiber	g	1.41	4.58	9.42
FATTY ACIDS				
Polyunsaturated fatty acids	g	4.07	13.21	27.16
Eicosapentaenoic acid	mg	155	500	1028
Docosahexaenoic acid	mg	379	1230	2529
Omega 6:3 ratio (estimate)		6.6	6.6	6.6
ANTIOXIDANTS				
Vitamin C	mg	3.97	12.92	26.57
Beta-carotene	µg	2.5	8.1	16.6
Lycopene	µg	0	0	0
Lutein + Zeaxanthin	µg	12.4	40.4	83.0

Limited Antigen Fish 5

NUTRITION				
		Per 100g As Fed	Per 100g Dry Matter	Per 1000 kcal
PROTEIN	g	10.20	30.75	70.59
Arginine	g	0.60	1.80	4.13
Histidine	g	0.29	0.88	2.02
Isoleucine	g	0.46	1.38	3.17
Leucine	g	0.81	2.44	5.60
Lysine	g	0.86	2.59	5.95
Methionine + Cystine	g	0.41	1.24	2.85
Phenylalanine + Tyrosine	g	0.76	2.29	5.26
Threonine	g	0.43	1.31	3.01
Tryptophan	g	0.12	0.37	0.85
Valine	g	0.52	1.57	3.60
FAT (LIPID)	g	3.54	10.68	24.52
Linoleic acid	g	1.48	4.46	10.24
MINERALS				
Calcium	mg	290.65	876.04	2011.06
Phosphorus	mg	215.68	650.07	1492.32
Calcium to Phosphorus ratio		1.35	1.35	1.35
Potassium	mg	397.91	1199.33	2753.22
Sodium	mg	28.08	84.64	194.30
Magnesium	mg	53.28	160.59	368.66
Iron	mg	5.79	17.46	40.08
Copper	mg	0.60	1.82	4.18
Manganese	mg	0.47	1.41	3.24
Zinc	mg	7.14	21.51	49.38
Iodine	mg	0.12	0.36	0.83
Selenium	µg	20.80	62.69	143.91
VITAMINS				
Vitamin A	IU	563	1698	3898
Vitamin D	IU	57	172	394
Vitamin E	mg	6.01	18.10	41.55
Thiamin	mg	0.12	0.37	0.85
Riboflavin	mg	0.23	0.69	1.58
Niacin	mg	3.96	11.93	27.39
Pantothenic acid	mg	1.01	3.04	6.98
Pyridoxine	mg	0.26	0.79	1.81
Folic acid	µg	16.00	48.23	110.72
Choline	mg	88.42	266.49	611.76
Vitamin B12	µg	2.05	6.18	14.19
OTHER (non-essential nutrients)				
Total dietary fiber	g	2.89	8.70	19.97
FATTY ACIDS				
Polyunsaturated fatty acids	g	1.90	5.72	13.13
Eicosapentaenoic acid	mg	64	190	436
Docosahexaenoic acid	mg	178	540	1240
Omega 6:3 ratio (estimate)		6.8	6.8	6.8
ANTIOXIDANTS				
Vitamin C	mg	0	0	0
Beta-carotene	µg	0	0	0
Lycopene	µg	0	0	0
Lutein + Zeaxanthin	µg	35.2	106.0	243.3

1. Gently poach halibut until it flakes easily.
2. Prepare barley according to package directions to yield 4 cups of cooked barley.
3. Add HILARY'S BLEND™ supplement to the halibut and mix thoroughly.
4. Stir all ingredients together.

INGREDIENTS		
APPROX.	INGREDIENT	GRAMS
4 cups	Barley, pearled, cooked	628
1 tsp	Cod liver oil	5
470 g raw	Halibut, cooked	329
4 tsp	Safflower oil	18
2 scoops	HILARY'S BLEND™ supplement	20
	Total	1000

FEEDING GUIDE			
Body weight		Energy intake	Amount to feed
lbs	kg	kcal/day	grams/day
10	4.5	296	204
20	9.1	497	343
40	18.2	836	577
60	27.3	1134	782
80	36.4	1407	970
100	45.5	1663	1147

METABOLIZABLE ENERGY

145 kcal/100 grams

Supplement for home-made meals

Hilary's Blend™

R78

Limited Antigen Novel 1

1. Poach pork chops until tender. Dice finely.
2. Prick potatoes with a fork, then microwave until soft. Mash coarsely.
3. Sprinkle HILARY'S BLEND™ supplement over the mashed potatoes and mix thoroughly.
4. Stir all ingredients together.

INGREDIENTS		
APPROX.	INGREDIENT	GRAMS
1 tsp	Cod liver oil	5
722 g raw	Pork, boneless loin chops	426
4 medium	Potatoes, boiled in skin	544
1 tsp	Safflower oil	5
2 scoops	HILARY'S BLEND™ supplement	20
	Total	1000

METABOLIZABLE ENERGY

149 kcal/100 grams

FEEDING GUIDE			
Body weight		Energy intake	Amount to feed
lbs	kg	kcal/day	grams/day
10	4.5	296	198
20	9.1	497	334
40	18.2	836	561
60	27.3	1134	761
80	36.4	1407	944
100	45.5	1663	1116

Hilary's Blend™
Supplement for home-made meals

NUTRITION		Per 100g As Fed	Per 100g Dry Matter	Per 1000 kcal
PROTEIN	g	13.57	40.10	91.01
Arginine	g	0.83	2.44	5.54
Histidine	g	0.52	1.55	3.52
Isoleucine	g	0.63	1.86	4.22
Leucine	g	1.07	3.16	7.17
Lysine	g	1.19	3.52	7.99
Methionine + Cystine	g	0.52	1.54	3.49
Phenylalanine + Tyrosine	g	1.02	3.01	6.83
Threonine	g	0.61	1.80	4.09
Tryptophan	g	0.18	0.52	1.18
Valine	g	0.74	2.18	4.95
FAT (LIPID)	g	5.34	15.77	35.79
Linoleic acid	g	0.63	1.85	4.20
MINERALS				
Calcium	mg	279.93	827.40	1877.77
Phosphorus	mg	216.31	639.35	1450.99
Calcium to Phosphorus ratio		1.29	1.29	1.29
Potassium	mg	535.10	1581.62	3589.45
Sodium	mg	33.36	98.62	223.82
Magnesium	mg	28.16	83.22	188.87
Iron	mg	5.12	15.14	34.36
Copper	mg	0.50	1.46	3.31
Manganese	mg	0.38	1.13	2.56
Zinc	mg	7.62	22.53	51.13
Iodine	mg	0.12	0.35	0.79
Selenium	µg	20.31	60.04	136.26
VITAMINS				
Vitamin A	IU	504	1490	3382
Vitamin D	IU	57	168	382
Vitamin E	mg	6.01	17.75	40.28
Thiamin	mg	0.49	1.44	3.27
Riboflavin	mg	0.31	0.91	2.07
Niacin	mg	3.33	9.85	22.35
Pantothenic acid	mg	1.40	4.14	9.40
Pyridoxine	mg	0.39	1.16	2.63
Folic acid	µg	16.00	47.29	107.32
Choline	mg	80.00	236.46	536.64
Vitamin B12	µg	1.90	5.61	12.73
OTHER (non-essential nutrients)				
Total dietary fiber	g	1.48	4.37	9.92
FATTY ACIDS				
Polyunsaturated fatty acids	g	0.78	2.31	5.24
Eicosapentaenoic acid	mg	34	100	227
Docosahexaenoic acid	mg	55	160	363
Omega 6:3 ratio (estimate)		7.8	7.8	7.8
ANTIOXIDANTS				
Vitamin C	mg	7.20	21.28	48.29
Beta-carotene	µg	1.1	3.2	7.3
Lycopene	µg	0	0	0
Lutein + Zeaxanthin	µg	4.9	14.5	32.8

Limited Antigen Novel 2

NUTRITION		Per 100g As Fed	Per 100g Dry Matter	Per 1000 kcal
PROTEIN	g	8.71	33.56	65.22
Arginine	g	0.56	2.14	4.16
Histidine	g	0.32	1.23	2.39
Isoleucine	g	0.40	1.53	2.97
Leucine	g	0.69	2.66	5.17
Lysine	g	0.69	2.67	5.19
Methionine + Cystine	g	0.35	1.34	2.60
Phenylalanine + Tyrosine	g	0.67	2.59	5.03
Threonine	g	0.38	1.45	2.82
Tryptophan	g	0.11	0.43	0.84
Valine	g	0.47	1.83	3.56
FAT (LIPID)	g	7.27	28.01	54.43
Linoleic acid	g	1.07	4.12	8.01
MINERALS				
Calcium	mg	275.51	1061.61	2062.98
Phosphorus	mg	201.92	778.04	1511.93
Calcium to Phosphorus ratio		1.36	1.36	1.36
Potassium	mg	286.33	1103.28	2143.96
Sodium	mg	23.76	91.57	177.94
Magnesium	mg	27.54	106.12	206.22
Iron	mg	5.43	20.92	40.65
Copper	mg	0.41	1.59	3.09
Manganese	mg	0.71	2.75	5.34
Zinc	mg	7.65	29.48	57.29
Iodine	mg	0.12	0.46	0.89
Selenium	µg	15.17	58.47	113.62
VITAMINS				
Vitamin A	IU	502	1935	3760
Vitamin D	IU	57	220	427
Vitamin E	mg	6.13	23.61	45.88
Thiamin	mg	0.31	1.21	2.35
Riboflavin	mg	0.23	0.90	1.75
Niacin	mg	1.54	5.93	11.52
Pantothenic acid	mg	1.08	4.16	8.08
Pyridoxine	mg	0.18	0.69	1.34
Folic acid	µg	16.00	61.65	119.80
Choline	mg	108.86	419.46	815.12
Vitamin B12	µg	1.75	6.72	13.06
OTHER (non-essential nutrients)				
Total dietary fiber	g	1.69	6.53	12.69
FATTY ACIDS				
Polyunsaturated fatty acids	g	1.25	4.83	9.39
Eicosapentaenoic acid	mg	34	130	253
Docosahexaenoic acid	mg	55	210	408
Omega 6:3 ratio (estimate)		13.1	13.1	13.1
ANTIOXIDANTS				
Vitamin C	mg	0.19	0.72	1.40
Beta-carotene	µg	0	0	0
Lycopene	µg	0	0	0
Lutein + Zeaxanthin	µg	126.4	486.9	946.2

1. Pan-broil pork to crumbles.
2. Prepare oatmeal according to package directions to yield 3 cups of cooked oatmeal.
3. Add HILARY'S BLEND™ supplement to the pork and mix thoroughly.
4. Stir all ingredients together.

INGREDIENTS		
APPROX.	INGREDIENT	GRAMS
1 tsp	Cod liver oil	5
3 cups	Oatmeal, cooked	702
360 g raw	Pork, ground, cooked	268
1 tsp	Safflower oil	5
2 scoops	HILARY'S BLEND™ supplement	20
	Total	1000

FEEDING GUIDE			
Body weight		Energy intake	Amount to feed
lbs	kg	kcal/day	grams/day
10	4.5	296	221
20	9.1	497	371
40	18.2	836	624
60	27.3	1134	846
80	36.4	1407	1050
100	45.5	1663	1241

METABOLIZABLE ENERGY

134 kcal/100 grams

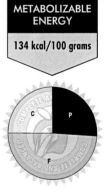

Supplement for home-made meals

R80

Limited Antigen Novel 3

1. Poach rabbit until tender. Dice finely.
2. Prepare oatmeal according to package instructions to yield 2½ cups of cooked oatmeal.
3. Add HILARY'S BLEND™ supplement to the oatmeal and mix thoroughly.
4. Stir all ingredients together.

INGREDIENTS		
APPROX.	INGREDIENT	GRAMS
1 tsp	Cod liver oil	5
2½ cups	Oatmeal, cooked	585
600 g raw	Rabbit, boneless, cooked	376
2 tsp	Safflower oil	9
1 tsp	Salmon oil	5
1 pinch	Salt	<1
2 scoops	HILARY'S BLEND™ supplement	20
	Total	1000

METABOLIZABLE ENERGY

132 kcal/100 grams

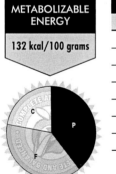

FEEDING GUIDE			
Body weight		Energy intake	Amount to feed
lbs	kg	kcal/day	grams/day
10	4.5	296	224
20	9.1	497	377
40	18.2	836	634
60	27.3	1134	859
80	36.4	1407	1066
100	45.5	1663	1260

Supplement for home-made meals

NUTRITION				
		Per 100g As Fed	Per 100g Dry Matter	Per 1000 kcal
PROTEIN	g	12.94	46.31	98.00
Arginine	g	0.81	2.91	6.16
Histidine	g	0.36	1.28	2.71
Isoleucine	g	0.60	2.16	4.57
Leucine	g	1.01	3.59	7.60
Lysine	g	1.06	3.80	8.04
Methionine + Cystine	g	0.49	1.76	3.72
Phenylalanine + Tyrosine	g	1.01	3.60	7.62
Threonine	g	0.56	2.01	4.25
Tryptophan	g	0.17	0.61	1.29
Valine	g	0.66	2.38	5.04
FAT (LIPID)	g	5.65	20.20	42.75
Linoleic acid	g	1.38	4.95	10.48
MINERALS				
Calcium	mg	276.20	988.08	2091.04
Phosphorus	mg	217.44	777.86	1646.16
Calcium to Phosphorus ratio		1.27	1.27	1.27
Potassium	mg	295.56	1057.34	2237.61
Sodium	mg	33.48	119.68	253.27
Magnesium	mg	25.82	92.37	195.48
Iron	mg	5.90	21.09	44.63
Copper	mg	0.46	1.65	3.49
Manganese	mg	0.65	2.34	4.95
Zinc	mg	7.62	27.27	57.71
Iodine	mg	0.12	0.43	0.91
Selenium	µg	19.21	68.74	145.47
VITAMINS				
Vitamin A	IU	500	1789	3785
Vitamin D	IU	57	204	432
Vitamin E	mg	6.22	22.27	47.13
Thiamin	mg	0.14	0.48	1.02
Riboflavin	mg	0.24	0.84	1.78
Niacin	mg	3.09	11.05	23.38
Pantothenic acid	mg	1.17	4.18	8.85
Pyridoxine	mg	0.20	0.71	1.50
Folic acid	µg	16.00	57.24	121.14
Choline	mg	129.90	464.71	983.45
Vitamin B12	µg	4.05	14.48	30.64
OTHER (non-essential nutrients)				
Total dietary fiber	g	1.50	5.35	11.32
FATTY ACIDS				
Polyunsaturated fatty acids	g	1.82	6.51	13.78
Eicosapentaenoic acid	mg	100	360	762
Docosahexaenoic acid	mg	146	520	1100
Omega 6:3 ratio (estimate)		6.4	6.4	6.4
ANTIOXIDANTS				
Vitamin C	mg	0	0	0
Beta-carotene	µg	0	0	0
Lycopene	µg	0	0	0
Lutein + Zeaxanthin	µg	105.3	376.7	797.2

Limited Antigen Novel 4

NUTRITION		Per 100g As Fed	Per 100g Dry Matter	Per 1000 kcal
PROTEIN	g	13.73	41.75	95.45
Arginine	g	0.83	2.53	5.78
Histidine	g	0.38	1.15	2.63
Isoleucine	g	0.64	1.96	4.48
Leucine	g	1.05	3.20	7.32
Lysine	g	1.18	3.57	8.16
Methionine + Cystine	g	0.51	1.55	3.54
Phenylalanine + Tyrosine	g	1.06	3.21	7.34
Threonine	g	0.61	1.84	4.21
Tryptophan	g	0.18	0.56	1.28
Valine	g	0.70	2.14	4.89
FAT (LIPID)	g	4.57	13.90	31.78
Linoleic acid	g	0.94	2.86	6.54
MINERALS				
Calcium	mg	275.12	836.48	1912.39
Phosphorus	mg	206.76	628.62	1437.17
Calcium to Phosphorus ratio		1.33	1.33	1.33
Potassium	mg	484.61	1473.41	3368.56
Sodium	mg	36.66	111.38	254.64
Magnesium	mg	24.76	75.29	172.13
Iron	mg	5.77	17.54	40.10
Copper	mg	0.54	1.64	3.75
Manganese	mg	0.39	1.18	2.70
Zinc	mg	7.60	23.11	52.83
Iodine	mg	0.12	0.36	0.82
Selenium	µg	16.26	49.43	113.01
VITAMINS				
Vitamin A	IU	502	1525	3487
Vitamin D	IU	57	173	396
Vitamin E	mg	6.19	18.82	43.03
Thiamin	mg	0.13	0.40	0.91
Riboflavin	mg	0.24	0.74	1.69
Niacin	mg	4.11	12.49	28.56
Pantothenic acid	mg	1.37	4.16	9.51
Pyridoxine	mg	0.37	1.12	2.56
Folic acid	µg	16.00	48.65	111.23
Choline	mg	130.66	397.27	908.25
Vitamin B12	µg	4.32	13.14	30.04
OTHER (non-essential nutrients)				
Total dietary fiber	g	1.49	4.54	10.38
FATTY ACIDS				
Polyunsaturated fatty acids	g	1.19	3.62	8.28
Eicosapentaenoic acid	mg	34	100	229
Docosahexaenoic acid	mg	55	170	389
Omega 6:3 ratio (estimate)		12.4	12.4	12.4
ANTIOXIDANTS				
Vitamin C	mg	7.18	21.82	49.89
Beta-carotene	µg	1.1	3.4	7.7
Lycopene	µg	0	0	0
Lutein + Zeaxanthin	µg	5.0	15.1	34.5

1. Boil potatoes until soft. Mash.
2. Poach rabbit until tender. Dice finely.
3. Add HILARY'S BLEND™ supplement to the mashed potatoes and mix thoroughly.
4. Stir all ingredients together.

INGREDIENTS		
APPROX.	INGREDIENT	GRAMS
1 tsp	Cod liver oil	5
4 small	Potatoes, boiled with skin	552
675 g raw	Rabbit, boneless, cooked	418
1 tsp	Safflower oil	5
1 pinch	Salt	<1
2 scoops	HILARY'S BLEND™ supplement	20
	Total	1000

FEEDING GUIDE			
Body weight		Energy intake	Amount to feed
lbs	kg	kcal/day	grams/day
10	4.5	296	205
20	9.1	497	345
40	18.2	836	581
60	27.3	1134	787
80	36.4	1407	977
100	45.5	1663	1155

METABOLIZABLE ENERGY

144 kcal/100 grams

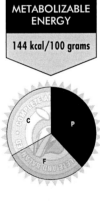

Supplement for home-made meals

Limited Antigen Novel 5

1. Pan-broil venison to crumbles.
2. Prepare barley according to package directions to yield 3 cups of cooked barley.
3. Add HILARY'S BLEND™ supplement to the venison and mix thoroughly.
4. Stir all ingredients together.

INGREDIENTS		
APPROX.	INGREDIENT	GRAMS
3 cups	Barley, pearled, cooked	471
1 tsp	Cod liver oil	5
670 g raw	Venison, ground, cooked	481
4 tsp	Safflower oil	18
2½ scoops	HILARY'S BLEND™ supplement	25
	Total	1000

NUTRITION				
		Per 100g As Fed	Per 100g Dry Matter	Per 1000 kcal
PROTEIN	g	13.79	37.61	81.45
Arginine	g	0.81	2.21	4.79
Histidine	g	0.40	1.10	2.38
Isoleucine	g	0.58	1.59	3.44
Leucine	g	1.04	2.83	6.13
Lysine	g	1.07	2.92	6.32
Methionine + Cystine	g	0.46	1.25	2.71
Phenylalanine + Tyrosine	g	0.97	2.64	5.72
Threonine	g	0.52	1.41	3.05
Tryptophan	g	0.13	0.36	0.78
Valine	g	0.67	1.82	3.94
FAT (LIPID)	g	6.46	17.62	38.16
Linoleic acid	g	1.56	4.27	9.25
MINERALS				
Calcium	mg	341.92	932.59	2019.55
Phosphorus	mg	245.10	668.53	1447.72
Calcium to Phosphorus ratio		1.39	1.39	1.39
Potassium	mg	406.39	1108.44	2400.36
Sodium	mg	43.30	118.11	255.77
Magnesium	mg	27.23	74.27	160.83
Iron	mg	8.00	21.81	47.23
Copper	mg	0.55	1.50	3.25
Manganese	mg	0.50	1.37	2.97
Zinc	mg	10.95	29.85	64.64
Iodine	mg	0.15	0.41	0.89
Selenium	µg	9.01	24.56	53.19
VITAMINS				
Vitamin A	IU	503	1373	2973
Vitamin D	IU	59	160	347
Vitamin E	mg	7.83	21.36	46.26
Thiamin	mg	0.34	0.93	2.01
Riboflavin	mg	0.39	1.05	2.27
Niacin	mg	5.82	15.89	34.41
Pantothenic acid	mg	1.43	3.90	8.45
Pyridoxine	mg	0.35	0.97	2.10
Folic acid	µg	20.00	54.55	118.13
Choline	mg	155.33	423.66	917.45
Vitamin B12	µg	3.12	8.50	18.41
OTHER (non-essential nutrients)				
Total dietary fiber	g	2.42	6.59	14.27
FATTY ACIDS				
Polyunsaturated fatty acids	g	1.77	4.83	10.46
Eicosapentaenoic acid	mg	34	90	195
Docosahexaenoic acid	mg	55	150	325
Omega 6:3 ratio (estimate)		18.9	18.9	18.9
ANTIOXIDANTS				
Vitamin C	mg	0	0	0
Beta-carotene	µg	0	0	0
Lycopene	µg	0	0	0
Lutein + Zeaxanthin	µg	26.4	71.9	155.8

METABOLIZABLE ENERGY
169 kcal/100 grams

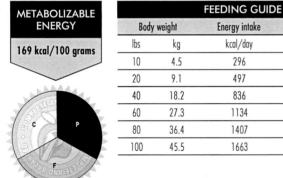

FEEDING GUIDE			
Body weight		Energy intake	Amount to feed
lbs	kg	kcal/day	grams/day
10	4.5	296	175
20	9.1	497	294
40	18.2	836	495
60	27.3	1134	671
80	36.4	1407	832
100	45.5	1663	98

Supplement for home-made meals

Limited Antigen Novel 6

NUTRITION		Per 100g As Fed	Per 100g Dry Matter	Per 1000 kcal
PROTEIN	g	12.33	38.49	86.83
Arginine	g	0.72	2.23	5.03
Histidine	g	0.36	1.11	2.50
Isoleucine	g	0.53	1.64	3.70
Leucine	g	0.91	2.85	6.43
Lysine	g	0.97	3.03	6.84
Methionine + Cystine	g	0.40	1.23	2.77
Phenylalanine + Tyrosine	g	0.87	2.70	6.09
Threonine	g	0.46	1.45	3.27
Tryptophan	g	0.12	0.37	0.83
Valine	g	0.61	1.90	4.29
FAT (LIPID)	g	4.88	15.22	34.34
Linoleic acid	g	0.81	2.52	5.69
MINERALS				
Calcium	mg	278.08	867.92	1957.99
Phosphorus	mg	221.03	689.87	1556.32
Calcium to Phosphorus ratio		1.26	1.26	1.26
Potassium	mg	596.02	1860.25	4196.65
Sodium	mg	41.31	128.93	290.86
Magnesium	mg	29.65	92.55	208.79
Iron	mg	6.59	20.56	46.38
Copper	mg	0.47	1.47	3.32
Manganese	mg	0.43	1.33	3.00
Zinc	mg	8.80	27.46	61.95
Iodine	mg	0.12	0.37	0.83
Selenium	µg	4.49	14.00	31.58
VITAMINS				
Vitamin A	IU	506	1578	3559
Vitamin D	IU	57	178	401
Vitamin E	mg	6.30	19.67	44.37
Thiamin	mg	0.29	0.91	2.05
Riboflavin	mg	0.32	1.00	2.26
Niacin	mg	4.93	15.39	34.72
Pantothenic acid	mg	1.32	4.13	9.32
Pyridoxine	mg	0.43	1.33	3.00
Folic acid	µg	16.00	49.94	112.66
Choline	mg	122.19	381.36	860.33
Vitamin B12	µg	2.56	7.99	18.03
OTHER (non-essential nutrients)			.	
Total dietary fiber	g	1.71	5.35	12.07
FATTY ACIDS				
Polyunsaturated fatty acids	g	1.00	3.12	7.04
Eicosapentaenoic acid	mg	34	110	248
Docosahexaenoic acid	mg	55	170	384
Omega 6:3 ratio (estimate)		10.2	10.2	10.2
ANTIOXIDANTS				
Vitamin C	mg	5.30	16.54	37.31
Beta-carotene	µg	3.3	10.3	23.3
Lycopene	µg	0	0	0
Lutein + Zeaxanthin	µg	16.6	51.7	116.6

1. Pan-broil venison to crumbles.
2. Prick potatoes with a fork, then microwave until soft. Mash coarsely.
3. Add HILARY'S BLEND™ supplement to the venison and mix thoroughly.
4. Stir all ingredients together.

INGREDIENTS			
APPROX.	INGREDIENT		GRAMS
1 tsp	Cod liver oil		5
575 g raw	Venison, ground, cooked		414
4 small	Potatoes, baked in skin		552
2 tsp	Safflower oil		9
2 scoops	HILARY'S BLEND™ supplement		20
		Total	1000

FEEDING GUIDE			
Body weight		Energy intake	Amount to feed
lbs	kg	kcal/day	grams/day
10	4.5	296	208
20	9.1	497	350
40	18.2	836	589
60	27.3	1134	798
80	36.4	1407	991
100	45.5	1663	1171

METABOLIZABLE ENERGY

142 kcal/100 grams

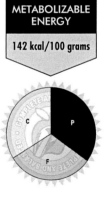

Hilary's Blend™

Supplement for home-made meals

Limited Antigen Novel 7

1. Gently poach goat meat until tender. Dice finely.
2. Boil potatoes until soft. Mash.
3. Add HILARY'S BLEND™ supplement to the mashed potatoes and mix thoroughly.
4. Stir all ingredients together.

INGREDIENTS		
APPROX.	INGREDIENT	GRAMS
1 tsp	Cod liver oil	5
845 g raw	Goat meat, cooked	422
4 medium	Potatoes, boiled in skin	544
2 tsp	Safflower oil	9
2 scoops	HILARY'S BLEND™ supplement	20
	Total	1000

METABOLIZABLE ENERGY

121 kcal/100 grams

NUTRITION				
		Per 100g As Fed	Per 100g Dry Matter	Per 1000 kcal
PROTEIN	g	12.45	42.49	102.97
Arginine	g	0.89	3.02	7.32
Histidine	g	0.26	0.89	2.16
Isoleucine	g	0.62	2.12	5.14
Leucine	g	1.01	3.46	8.38
Lysine	g	0.91	3.11	7.54
Methionine + Cystine	g	0.47	1.61	3.90
Phenylalanine + Tyrosine	g	0.83	2.84	6.88
Threonine	g	0.58	1.98	4.80
Tryptophan	g	0.19	0.63	1.53
Valine	g	0.67	2.29	5.55
FAT (LIPID)	g	2.73	9.33	22.61
Linoleic acid	g	0.75	2.56	6.20
MINERALS				
Calcium	mg	273.89	934.53	2264.70
Phosphorus	mg	196.76	671.34	1626.90
Calcium to Phosphorus ratio		1.39	1.39	1.39
Potassium	mg	527.09	1798.42	4358.22
Sodium	mg	41.97	143.19	347.00
Magnesium	mg	16.23	55.37	134.18
Iron	mg	6.35	21.66	52.49
Copper	mg	0.59	2.02	4.90
Manganese	mg	0.39	1.34	3.25
Zinc	mg	8.83	30.14	73.04
Iodine	mg	0.12	0.41	0.99
Selenium	µg	5.14	17.55	42.53
VITAMINS				
Vitamin A	IU	502	1712	4148
Vitamin D	IU	57	194	471
Vitamin E	mg	6.15	20.98	50.84
Thiamin	mg	0.14	0.49	1.19
Riboflavin	mg	0.43	1.46	3.54
Niacin	mg	2.77	9.45	22.90
Pantothenic acid	mg	1.08	3.69	8.94
Pyridoxine	mg	0.22	0.76	1.84
Folic acid	µg	16.00	54.59	132.29
Choline	mg	124.90	426.16	1032.74
Vitamin B12	µg	2.10	7.17	17.38
OTHER (non-essential nutrients)				
Total dietary fiber	g	1.48	5.05	12.24
FATTY ACIDS				
Polyunsaturated fatty acids	g	0.91	3.09	7.49
Eicosapentaenoic acid	mg	34	120	291
Docosahexaenoic acid	mg	55	190	460
Omega 6:3 ratio (estimate)		9.2	9.2	9.2
ANTIOXIDANTS				
Vitamin C	mg	7.07	24.13	58.48
Beta-carotene	µg	1.1	3.7	9.0
Lycopene	µg	0	0	0
Lutein + Zeaxanthin	µg	4.9	16.7	40.5

FEEDING GUIDE				
Body weight		Energy intake		Amount to feed
lbs	kg	kcal/day		grams/day
10	4.5	296		244
20	9.1	497		411
40	18.2	836		691
60	27.3	1134		937
80	36.4	1407		1163
100	45.5	1663		1374

Hilary's Blend™

Supplement for home-made meals

www.CompleteandBalanced.com

Low Fat Recipe 1

NUTRITION		Per 100g As Fed	Per 100g Dry Matter	Per 1000 kcal
PROTEIN	g	9.42	30.57	73.49
Arginine	g	0.60	1.94	4.66
Histidine	g	0.28	0.92	2.21
Isoleucine	g	0.48	1.55	3.73
Leucine	g	0.72	2.34	5.63
Lysine	g	0.71	2.31	5.55
Methionine + Cystine	g	0.37	1.20	2.88
Phenylalanine + Tyrosine	g	0.72	2.35	5.65
Threonine	g	0.39	1.26	3.03
Tryptophan	g	0.11	0.36	0.87
Valine	g	0.48	1.57	3.77
FAT (LIPID)	g	2.23	7.22	17.36
Linoleic acid	g	0.52	1.70	4.09
MINERALS				
Calcium	mg	274.95	892.12	2144.62
Phosphorus	mg	203.99	661.90	1591.18
Calcium to Phosphorus ratio		1.35	1.35	1.35
Potassium	mg	243.60	790.41	1900.12
Sodium	mg	25.13	81.54	196.02
Magnesium	mg	42.70	138.54	333.04
Iron	mg	5.17	16.76	40.29
Copper	mg	0.45	1.45	3.49
Manganese	mg	0.97	3.13	7.52
Zinc	mg	7.15	23.20	55.77
Iodine	mg	0.12	0.39	0.94
Selenium	µg	13.86	44.97	108.11
VITAMINS				
Vitamin A	IU	505	1638	3938
Vitamin D	IU	57	185	445
Vitamin E	mg	6.09	19.75	47.48
Thiamin	mg	0.14	0.44	1.06
Riboflavin	mg	0.21	0.67	1.61
Niacin	mg	4.77	15.47	37.19
Pantothenic acid	mg	1.24	4.03	9.69
Pyridoxine	mg	0.31	1.01	2.43
Folic acid	µg	16.00	51.92	124.81
Choline	mg	86.72	281.37	676.40
Vitamin B12	µg	1.68	5.46	13.13
OTHER (non-essential nutrients)				
Total dietary fiber	g	1.81	5.89	14.16
FATTY ACIDS				
Polyunsaturated fatty acids	g	0.69	2.22	5.34
Eicosapentaenoic acid	mg	37	120	288
Docosahexaenoic acid	mg	60	190	457
Omega 6:3 ratio (estimate)		6.1	6.1	6.1
ANTIOXIDANTS				
Vitamin C	mg	0	0	0
Beta-carotene	µg	0	0	0
Lycopene	µg	0	0	0
Lutein + Zeaxanthin	µg	0	0	0

1. Poach chicken until tender. Dice finely.
2. Prepare rice according to package directions to yield 3¾ cups of cooked rice.
3. Sprinkle HILARY'S BLEND™ supplement over the rice and mix in.
4. Stir all ingredients together.

INGREDIENTS		
APPROX.	INGREDIENT	GRAMS
1 tsp	Cod liver oil	5
470 g raw	Chicken breast, cooked	243
3¾ cup	Rice, brown, cooked	730
½ tsp	Safflower oil	2
2 scoops	HILARY'S BLEND™ supplement	20
	Total	1000

FEEDING GUIDE			
Body weight		Energy intake	Amount to feed
lbs	kg	kcal/day	grams/day
10	4.5	296	231
20	9.1	497	389
40	18.2	836	653
60	27.3	1134	886
80	36.4	1407	1099
100	45.5	1663	1299

METABOLIZABLE ENERGY

128 kcal/100 grams

Supplement for home-made meals

R86

Low Fat Recipe 2

1. Thaw frozen peas overnight in the refrigerator.
2. Prick potato with a fork, then microwave until soft.
3. Mash potato and sardines coarsely.
4. Add HILARY'S BLEND™ supplement to the yogurt and mix thoroughly.
5. Stir ingredients together.

INGREDIENTS		
APPROX.	INGREDIENT	GRAMS
2 cups	Peas, thawed from frozen	290
1 large	Potato, baked in skin	299
	Sardines, canned in water, drained	92
1¼ cup	Yogurt, plain, low fat	304
1½ scoops	HILARY'S BLEND™ supplement	15
	Total	1000

METABOLIZABLE ENERGY

90 kcal/100 grams

FEEDING GUIDE			
Body weight		Energy intake	Amount to feed
lbs	kg	kcal/day	grams/day
10	4.5	296	329
20	9.1	497	553
40	18.2	836	929
60	27.3	1134	1260
80	36.4	1407	1563
100	45.5	1663	1848

NUTRITION				
		Per 100g As Fed	Per 100g Dry Matter	Per 1000 kcal
PROTEIN	g	6.26	26.66	68.94
Arginine	g	0.35	1.48	3.83
Histidine	g	0.16	0.66	1.71
Isoleucine	g	0.28	1.20	3.10
Leucine	g	0.49	2.08	5.38
Lysine	g	0.50	2.11	5.46
Methionine + Cystine	g	0.21	0.90	2.33
Phenylalanine + Tyrosine	g	0.49	2.09	5.40
Threonine	g	0.25	1.08	2.79
Tryptophan	g	0.06	0.25	0.65
Valine	g	0.36	1.54	3.98
FAT (LIPID)	g	1.72	7.32	18.93
Linoleic acid	g	0.41	1.73	4.47
MINERALS				
Calcium	mg	301.31	1283.66	3319.61
Phosphorus	mg	208.49	888.23	2297.01
Calcium to Phosphorus ratio		1.45	1.45	1.45
Potassium	mg	451.54	1923.69	4974.76
Sodium	mg	76.54	326.10	843.31
Magnesium	mg	29.98	127.73	330.32
Iron	mg	4.51	19.20	49.65
Copper	mg	0.38	1.62	4.19
Manganese	mg	0.42	1.79	4.63
Zinc	mg	5.70	24.26	62.74
Iodine	mg	0.09	0.38	0.98
Selenium	µg	6.69	28.50	73.70
VITAMINS				
Vitamin A	IU	251	1067	2760
Vitamin D	IU	31	134	346
Vitamin E	mg	4.76	20.26	52.39
Thiamin	mg	0.15	0.65	1.68
Riboflavin	mg	0.26	1.10	2.84
Niacin	mg	1.81	7.69	19.89
Pantothenic acid	mg	0.98	4.18	10.81
Pyridoxine	mg	0.22	0.93	2.41
Folic acid	µg	12.00	51.12	132.20
Choline	mg	72.72	309.81	801.18
Vitamin B12	µg	2.23	9.48	24.52
OTHER (non-essential nutrients)				
Total dietary fiber	g	2.51	10.70	27.67
FATTY ACIDS				
Polyunsaturated fatty acids	g	0.58	2.47	6.39
Eicosapentaenoic acid	mg	45	190	491
Docosahexaenoic acid	mg	49	210	543
Omega 6:3 ratio (estimate)		5.2	5.2	5.2
ANTIOXIDANTS				
Vitamin C	mg	14.71	62.67	162.07
Beta-carotene	µg	132.0	562.4	1454.3
Lycopene	µg	0	0	0
Lutein + Zeaxanthin	µg	727.3	3098.5	8013.0

Hilary's Blend™

Supplement for home-made meals

Low Fat Recipe 3

NUTRITION		Per 100g As Fed	Per 100g Dry Matter	Per 1000 kcal
PROTEIN	g	15.81	64.73	157.05
Arginine	g	0.98	4.00	9.70
Histidine	g	0.45	1.84	4.46
Isoleucine	g	0.71	2.91	7.06
Leucine	g	1.25	5.11	12.40
Lysine	g	1.40	5.71	13.85
Methionine + Cystine	g	0.61	2.48	6.02
Phenylalanine + Tyrosine	g	1.13	2.51	6.09
Threonine	g	0.68	2.79	6.77
Tryptophan	g	0.17	0.70	1.70
Valine	g	0.80	3.28	7.96
FAT (LIPID)	g	1.53	6.27	15.21
Linoleic acid	g	0.57	2.31	5.60
MINERALS				
Calcium	mg	214.57	878.63	2131.72
Phosphorus	mg	176.51	722.77	1753.57
Calcium to Phosphorus ratio		1.22	1.22	1.22
Potassium	mg	301.59	1234.95	2996.22
Sodium	mg	73.98	302.95	735.01
Magnesium	mg	36.46	149.28	362.18
Iron	mg	4.25	17.42	42.26
Copper	mg	0.33	1.35	3.28
Manganese	mg	0.34	1.39	3.37
Zinc	mg	5.41	22.17	53.79
Iodine	mg	0.09	0.37	0.90
Selenium	µg	23.60	96.63	234.44
VITAMINS				
Vitamin A	IU	903	3698	8972
Vitamin D	IU	25	103	251
Vitamin E	mg	5.03	20.61	50.00
Thiamin	mg	0.18	0.75	1.82
Riboflavin	mg	0.20	0.83	2.01
Niacin	mg	2.29	9.36	22.71
Pantothenic acid	mg	0.76	3.12	7.57
Pyridoxine	mg	0.26	1.06	2.57
Folic acid	µg	12.00	49.14	119.22
Choline	mg	120.83	494.79	1200.45
Vitamin B12	µg	1.85	7.58	18.39
OTHER (non-essential nutrients)				
Total dietary fiber	g	2.22	9.11	22.10
FATTY ACIDS				
Polyunsaturated fatty acids	g	0.80	3.25	7.89
Eicosapentaenoic acid	mg	16	70	170
Docosahexaenoic acid	mg	117	480	1165
Omega 6:3 ratio (estimate)		5.0	5.0	5.0
ANTIOXIDANTS				
Vitamin C	mg	4.15	16.98	41.20
Beta-carotene	µg	401.2	1642.8	3985.7
Lycopene	µg	0	0	0
Lutein + Zeaxanthin	µg	771.0	3157.0	7659.4

1. Boil peas until tender.
2. Poach the cod until it flakes easily.
3. Pulse blueberries, boiled peas, cod liver oil, and safflower oil.
4. Add HILARY'S BLEND™ supplement to the fish and mix thoroughly.
5. Stir all ingredients together.

INGREDIENTS		
APPROX.	INGREDIENT	GRAMS
¼ cup	Blueberries, raw	37
½ tsp	Cod liver oil	2
885 g raw	Cod, Atlantic, cooked	619
2 cups	Peas, boiled from frozen	320
1½ tsp	Safflower oil	7
1½ scoops	HILARY'S BLEND™ supplement	15
	Total	1000

FEEDING GUIDE			
Body weight		Energy intake	Amount to feed
lbs	kg	kcal/day	grams/day
10	4.5	296	293
20	9.1	497	492
40	18.2	836	828
60	27.3	1134	1123
80	36.4	1407	1393
100	45.5	1663	1647

METABOLIZABLE ENERGY

101 kcal/100 grams

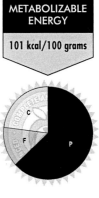

Supplement for home-made meals

R88

Low Fat Recipe 4

1. Thaw frozen peas overnight in the refrigerator.
2. Poach halibut until it flakes easily.
3. Pulse alfalfa sprouts, apple, bananas, broccoli, carrots, honey, pears, peas, cod liver oil, and safflower oil to small kernels.
4. Add HILARY'S BLEND™ supplement to the halibut and mix thoroughly.
5. Stir ingredients together.

INGREDIENTS

APPROX.	INGREDIENT	GRAMS
2 cups	Alfalfa sprouts, raw	66
½ cup	Apple, raw with skin, sliced	55
½ cup	Bananas, raw, sliced	75
⅔ cup	Broccoli, raw, chopped	61
⅔ cup	Carrots, raw, grated	73
1 tsp	Cod liver oil	5
300 g raw	Halibut, cooked	211
3 tbsp	Honey	63
½ cup	Pears, raw, chopped	81
2 cups	Peas, thawed from frozen	290
1 tsp	Safflower oil	5
1½ scoops	HILARY'S BLEND™ supplement	15
	Total	1000

METABOLIZABLE ENERGY

103 kcal/100 grams

FEEDING GUIDE

Body weight		Energy intake	Amount to feed
lbs	kg	kcal/day	grams/day
10	4.5	296	287
20	9.1	497	483
40	18.2	836	812
60	27.3	1134	1101
80	36.4	1407	1366
100	45.5	1663	1615

Hilary's Blend™
Supplement for home-made meals

NUTRITION

		Per 100g As Fed	Per 100g Dry Matter	Per 1000 kcal
PROTEIN	g	7.85	30.46	76.59
Arginine	g	0.49	1.88	4.73
Histidine	g	0.21	0.81	2.04
Isoleucine	g	0.34	1.32	3.32
Leucine	g	0.59	2.30	5.78
Lysine	g	0.65	2.50	6.29
Methionine + Cystine	g	0.27	1.06	2.67
Phenylalanine + Tyrosine	g	0.53	2.04	5.13
Threonine	g	0.34	1.31	3.29
Tryptophan	g	0.08	0.30	0.75
Valine	g	0.39	1.50	3.77
FAT (LIPID)	g	1.87	7.24	18.20
Linoleic acid	g	0.46	1.80	4.53
MINERALS				
Calcium	mg	227.11	880.92	2215.04
Phosphorus	mg	172.05	667.37	1678.07
Calcium to Phosphorus ratio		1.32	1.32	1.32
Potassium	mg	398.30	1544.92	3884.64
Sodium	mg	26.69	103.53	260.32
Magnesium	mg	41.53	161.09	405.05
Iron	mg	4.30	16.69	41.97
Copper	mg	0.47	1.82	4.58
Manganese	mg	0.42	1.61	4.05
Zinc	mg	5.45	21.12	53.11
Iodine	mg	0.09	0.35	0.88
Selenium	µg	10.73	41.62	104.65
VITAMINS				
Vitamin A	IU	2045	7931	19942
Vitamin D	IU	55	214	539
Vitamin E	mg	4.66	18.08	45.46
Thiamin	mg	0.15	0.57	1.43
Riboflavin	mg	0.21	0.81	2.04
Niacin	mg	2.57	9.96	25.04
Pantothenic acid	mg	0.84	3.25	8.17
Pyridoxine	mg	0.23	0.91	2.29
Folic acid	µg	12.00	46.55	117.05
Choline	mg	64.07	248.51	624.87
Vitamin B12	µg	1.49	5.78	14.53
OTHER (non-essential nutrients)				
Total dietary fiber	g	2.93	11.38	28.61
FATTY ACIDS				
Polyunsaturated fatty acids	g	0.79	3.05	7.67
Eicosapentaenoic acid	mg	54	210	528
Docosahexaenoic acid	mg	134	520	1308
Omega 6:3 ratio (estimate)		3.2	3.2	3.2
ANTIOXIDANTS				
Vitamin C	mg	19.29	74.82	188.13
Beta-carotene	µg	767.3	2976.1	7483.2
Lycopene	µg	0.1	0.3	0.7
Lutein + Zeaxanthin	µg	829.5	3217.4	8090.1

Low Fat Recipe 5

NUTRITION		Per 100g As Fed	Per 100g Dry Matter	Per 1000 kcal
PROTEIN	g	8.71	28.43	72.68
Arginine	g	0.53	1.72	4.40
Histidine	g	0.25	0.80	2.05
Isoleucine	g	0.39	1.27	3.25
Leucine	g	0.68	2.22	5.68
Lysine	g	0.75	2.45	6.26
Methionine + Cystine	g	0.33	1.08	2.76
Phenylalanine + Tyrosine	g	0.64	2.07	5.29
Threonine	g	0.37	1.21	3.09
Tryptophan	g	0.10	0.32	0.82
Valine	g	0.45	1.45	3.71
FAT (LIPID)	g	2.14	6.98	17.84
Linoleic acid	g	0.55	1.80	4.60
MINERALS				
Calcium	mg	279.99	913.38	2335.11
Phosphorus	mg	209.56	683.60	1747.67
Calcium to Phosphorus ratio		1.34	1.34	1.34
Potassium	mg	451.36	1472.40	3764.28
Sodium	mg	39.64	129.33	330.64
Magnesium	mg	34.99	114.13	291.78
Iron	mg	5.19	16.94	43.31
Copper	mg	0.44	1.44	3.68
Manganese	mg	0.44	1.43	3.66
Zinc	mg	6.87	22.41	57.29
Iodine	mg	0.12	0.39	1.00
Selenium	µg	18.21	59.42	151.91
VITAMINS				
Vitamin A	IU	559	1824	4663
Vitamin D	IU	57	186	475
Vitamin E	mg	6.58	21.45	54.84
Thiamin	mg	0.11	0.35	0.89
Riboflavin	mg	0.24	0.77	1.97
Niacin	mg	1.57	5.13	13.12
Pantothenic acid	mg	1.12	3.64	9.31
Pyridoxine	mg	0.24	0.78	1.99
Folic acid	µg	16.00	52.19	133.43
Choline	mg	106.52	347.50	888.41
Vitamin B12	µg	2.37	7.73	19.76
OTHER (non-essential nutrients)				
Total dietary fiber	g	2.04	6.64	16.98
FATTY ACIDS				
Polyunsaturated fatty acids	g	0.86	2.80	7.16
Eicosapentaenoic acid	mg	109	360	920
Docosahexaenoic acid	mg	134	440	1125
Omega 6:3 ratio (estimate)		2.5	2.5	2.5
ANTIOXIDANTS				
Vitamin C	mg	5.27	17.18	43.92
Beta-carotene	µg	26.4	86.1	220.0
Lycopene	µg	0	0	0
Lutein + Zeaxanthin	µg	134.8	439.8	1124.5

1. Thaw frozen peas overnight in the refrigerator.
2. Poach sole until it flakes easily.
3. Prick potatoes with a fork, then microwave until soft. Mash.
4. Pulse honey, pears, peas, cod liver oil, and safflower oil to small kernels.
5. Add HILARY'S BLEND™ supplement to the fish and mix thoroughly.
6. Stir all ingredients together.

INGREDIENTS		
APPROX.	INGREDIENT	GRAMS
⅛ cup	Almonds, ground	12
½ cup	Applesauce, unsweetened	122
1 tsp	Cod liver oil	5
440 g raw	Flatfish/sole, cooked	307
4 tbsp	Honey	84
¾ cup	Pears, raw, chopped	121
⅓ cup	Peas, thawed from frozen	48
2 small	Potatoes, baked with skin	276
1 tsp	Safflower oil	5
2 scoops	HILARY'S BLEND™ supplement	20
	Total	1000

FEEDING GUIDE			
Body weight		Energy intake	Amount to feed
lbs	kg	kcal/day	grams/day
10	4.5	296	246
20	9.1	497	414
40	18.2	836	697
60	27.3	1134	945
80	36.4	1407	1172
100	45.5	1663	1386

METABOLIZABLE ENERGY

120 kcal/100 grams

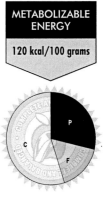

Supplement for home-made meals

Low Fat Recipe 6

1. Poach sole until it flakes easily.
2. Simmer chicken liver to crumbles.
3. Stir liver, sole, cod liver oil, and safflower oil together.
4. Add HILARY'S BLEND™ supplement and mix thoroughly.
5. Sprinkle the cornstarch over the mixture and stir in.
6. Fold in Rice Krispies.

INGREDIENTS

APPROX.	INGREDIENT	GRAMS
10 cups	KELLOGG'S® Rice Krispies	280
1 tsp	Cod liver oil	5
1 tbsp	Cornstarch	8
375 g raw	Flatfish/sole, cooked	262
645 g raw	Liver, chicken, cooked	400
1 tsp	Safflower oil	5
4 scoops	HILARY'S BLEND™ supplement	40
	Total	1000

METABOLIZABLE ENERGY

219 kcal/100 grams

FEEDING GUIDE

Body weight		Energy intake	Amount to feed
lbs	kg	kcal/day	grams/day
10	4.5	296	135
20	9.1	497	227
40	18.2	836	382
60	27.3	1134	518
80	36.4	1407	642
100	45.5	1663	759

Hilary's Blend™
Supplement for home-made meals

NUTRITION

		Per 100g As Fed	Per 100g Dry Matter	Per 1000 kcal
PROTEIN	g	18.03	34.15	82.20
Arginine	g	1.12	2.12	5.10
Histidine	g	0.51	0.97	2.33
Isoleucine	g	0.83	1.56	3.75
Leucine	g	1.51	2.87	6.91
Lysine	g	1.37	2.60	6.26
Methionine + Cystine	g	0.73	1.38	3.32
Phenylalanine + Tyrosine	g	1.44	2.72	6.55
Threonine	g	0.76	1.43	3.44
Tryptophan	g	0.20	0.37	0.89
Valine	g	1.00	1.89	4.55
FAT (LIPID)	g	4.27	8.09	19.47
Linoleic acid	g	0.75	1.41	3.39
MINERALS				
Calcium	mg	539.09	1020.85	2457.22
Phosphorus	mg	449.10	850.44	2047.03
Calcium to Phosphorus ratio		1.20	1.20	1.20
Potassium	mg	526.43	996.87	2399.49
Sodium	mg	319.33	604.70	1455.53
Magnesium	mg	39.04	73.93	177.95
Iron	mg	23.59	44.67	107.52
Copper	mg	0.98	1.86	4.48
Manganese	mg	1.14	2.15	5.18
Zinc	mg	15.00	28.41	68.38
Iodine	mg	0.24	0.45	1.08
Selenium	µg	53.30	100.93	242.94
VITAMINS				
Vitamin A	IU	6371	12065	29041
Vitamin D	IU	64	121	292
Vitamin E	mg	12.53	23.73	57.12
Thiamin	mg	0.74	1.41	3.39
Riboflavin	mg	1.77	3.35	8.06
Niacin	mg	11.60	21.97	52.88
Pantothenic acid	mg	4.59	8.69	20.92
Pyridoxine	mg	1.33	2.51	6.04
Folic acid	µg	32.00	60.60	145.87
Choline	mg	297.85	564.03	1357.64
Vitamin B12	µg	13.25	25.09	60.39
OTHER (non-essential nutrients)				
Total dietary fiber	g	1.23	2.33	5.61
FATTY ACIDS				
Polyunsaturated fatty acids	g	1.26	2.38	5.73
Eicosapentaenoic acid	mg	98	190	457
Docosahexaenoic acid	mg	122	230	554
Omega 6:3 ratio (estimate)		4.7	4.7	4.7
ANTIOXIDANTS				
Vitamin C	mg	18.94	35.87	86.34
Beta-carotene	µg	12.0	22.7	54.7
Lycopene	µg	8.4	15.9	38.3
Lutein + Zeaxanthin	µg	33.2	62.9	151.3

Low Phosphorus/Protein Recipe 1

NUTRITION				
		Per 100g As Fed	Per 100g Dry Matter	Per 1000 kcal
PROTEIN	g	5.98	17.86	31.40
Arginine	g	0.36	1.07	1.88
Histidine	g	0.15	0.46	0.81
Isoleucine	g	0.34	1.01	1.78
Leucine	g	0.52	1.56	2.74
Lysine	g	0.41	1.23	2.16
Methionine + Cystine	g	0.30	0.91	1.60
Phenylalanine + Tyrosine	g	0.58	1.72	3.02
Threonine	g	0.25	0.75	1.32
Tryptophan	g	0.08	0.22	0.39
Valine	g	0.40	1.20	2.11
FAT (LIPID)	g	14.51	43.30	76.13
Linoleic acid	g	4.11	12.28	21.59
MINERALS				
Calcium	mg	327.32	977.13	1717.88
Phosphorus	mg	117.26	350.04	615.40
Calcium to Phosphorus ratio		2.79	2.79	2.79
Potassium	mg	311.94	931.19	1637.11
Sodium	mg	79.23	236.51	415.81
Magnesium	mg	21.58	64.42	113.26
Iron	mg	5.35	15.96	28.06
Copper	mg	0.47	1.39	2.44
Manganese	mg	0.51	1.53	2.69
Zinc	mg	6.68	19.94	35.06
Iodine	mg	0.12	0.36	0.63
Selenium	µg	8.68	25.90	45.53
VITAMINS				
Vitamin A	IU	1862	5559	9773
Vitamin D	IU	101	301	530
Vitamin E	mg	6.42	19.18	33.72
Thiamin	mg	0.10	0.28	0.49
Riboflavin	mg	0.39	1.16	2.04
Niacin	mg	0.65	1.93	3.39
Pantothenic acid	mg	0.94	2.79	4.91
Pyridoxine	mg	0.10	0.29	0.51
Folic acid	µg	16.00	47.76	83.97
Choline	mg	85.31	254.68	447.75
Vitamin B12	µg	1.65	4.91	8.63
OTHER (non-essential nutrients)				
Total dietary fiber	g	1.60	4.79	8.42
FATTY ACIDS				
Polyunsaturated fatty acids	g	5.29	15.79	27.76
Eicosapentaenoic acid	mg	362	1080	1899
Docosahexaenoic acid	mg	518	1550	2725
Omega 6:3 ratio (estimate)		5.0	5.0	5.0
ANTIOXIDANTS				
Vitamin C	mg	3.99	11.89	20.90
Beta-carotene	µg	475.7	1420.0	2496.5
Lycopene	µg	0	0	0
Lutein + Zeaxanthin	µg	970.9	2898.5	5095.7

NOTE: This recipe should be supplemented with potassium citrate (150 mg/kg BW/day).

1. Cook egg whites over medium heat. Mash coarsely.
2. Boil beans until tender.
3. Pulse beans, pears, spinach, cod liver oil, safflower oil and salmon oil to small kernels.
4. Add HILARY'S BLEND™ supplement to the egg whites and mix thoroughly.
5. Stir ingredients together.

INGREDIENTS		
APPROX.	INGREDIENT	GRAMS
1 ⅓ cups	Beans, green, boiled	160
5 tbsp	Butter	71
2 tsp	Cod liver oil	9
1 ½ cups	Egg whites, cooked	364
4 tbsp	Honey	84
½ cup	Pears, raw, cubed	81
3 ½ tbsp	Safflower oil	48
5 tsp	Salmon oil	23
1 tbsp	Seaweed, spirulina, dried	7
7 leaves	Spinach, raw	70
¼ cup	Tofu, firm, with calcium sulfate	63
2 scoops	HILARY'S BLEND™ supplement	20

FEEDING GUIDE			
Body weight		Energy intake	Amount to feed
lbs	kg	kcal/day	grams/day
5	2.3	231	121
10	4.5	389	204
15	6.8	527	277
20	9.1	654	343
25	11.4	774	406
30	13.6	887	466

METABOLIZABLE ENERGY

191 kcal/100 grams

Supplement for home-made meals

Low Phosphorus/Protein Recipe 2

NOTE: This recipe should be supplemented with potassium citrate (150 mg/kg BW/day).

1. Cook egg whites over medium heat. Mash coarsely.
2. Boil beans until tender.
3. Pulse beans, pears, spinach, cod liver oil, safflower oil and salmon oil to small kernels.
4. Add HILARY'S BLEND supplement to the egg whites and mix thoroughly.
5. Stir ingredients together.

INGREDIENTS		
APPROX.	INGREDIENT	GRAMS
1 ⅓ cups	Beans, green, boiled	166
5 tbsp	Butter	71
2 tsp	Cod liver oil	9
1 ⅔ cups	Egg whites, cooked	405
1 ½ tbsp	Honey	31
½ cup	Pears, raw, cubed	81
10 tsp	Safflower oil	45
4 tsp	Salmon oil	18
7 leaves	Spinach, raw	70
⅓ cup	Tofu, firm, with calcium sulfate	84
2 scoops	HILARY'S BLEND™ supplement	20

METABOLIZABLE ENERGY

171 kcal/100 grams

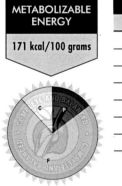

FEEDING GUIDE			
Body weight		Energy intake	Amount to feed
lbs	kg	kcal/day	grams/day
10	4.5	389	228
20	9.1	654	384
30	13.6	887	520
40	18.2	1101	645
50	22.7	1301	763
60	27.3	1492	874

Supplement for home-made meals

NUTRITION				
		Per 100g As Fed	Per 100g Dry Matter	Per 1000 kcal
PROTEIN	g	6.36	22.03	37.24
Arginine	g	0.38	1.31	2.21
Histidine	g	0.17	0.58	0.98
Isoleucine	g	0.36	1.25	2.11
Leucine	g	0.56	1.92	3.25
Lysine	g	0.45	1.55	2.62
Methionine + Cystine	g	0.33	1.14	1.93
Phenylalanine + Tyrosine	g	0.62	2.13	3.60
Threonine	g	0.26	0.91	1.54
Tryptophan	g	0.08	0.27	0.46
Valine	g	0.43	1.48	2.50
FAT (LIPID)	g	13.84	47.99	81.13
Linoleic acid	g	3.97	13.74	23.23
MINERALS				
Calcium	mg	341.06	1182.37	1998.90
Phosphorus	mg	121.00	419.47	709.15
Calcium to Phosphorus ratio		2.82	2.82	2.82
Potassium	mg	312.17	1082.23	1829.61
Sodium	mg	78.78	273.12	461.73
Magnesium	mg	21.89	75.87	128.26
Iron	mg	5.19	17.98	30.40
Copper	mg	0.43	1.50	2.54
Manganese	mg	0.52	1.80	3.04
Zinc	mg	6.69	23.19	39.20
Iodine	mg	0.12	0.42	0.71
Selenium	µg	9.77	33.87	57.26
VITAMINS				
Vitamin A	IU	1866	6468	10935
Vitamin D	IU	101	350	592
Vitamin E	mg	6.39	22.16	37.46
Thiamin	mg	0.08	0.28	0.47
Riboflavin	mg	0.38	1.32	2.23
Niacin	mg	0.57	1.96	3.31
Pantothenic acid	mg	0.92	3.19	5.39
Pyridoxine	mg	0.10	0.33	0.56
Folic acid	µg	16.00	55.47	93.78
Choline	mg	85.00	294.67	498.17
Vitamin B12	µg	1.65	5.71	9.65
OTHER (non-essential nutrients)				
Total dietary fiber	g	1.64	5.67	9.59
FATTY ACIDS				
Polyunsaturated fatty acids	g	4.95	17.17	29.03
Eicosapentaenoic acid	mg	296	1030	1741
Docosahexaenoic acid	mg	427	1480	2502
Omega 6:3 ratio (estimate)		5.9	5.9	5.9
ANTIOXIDANTS				
Vitamin C	mg	3.95	13.69	23.14
Beta-carotene	µg	475.8	1649.5	2788.6
Lycopene	µg	0	0	0
Lutein + Zeaxanthin	µg	975.2	3380.8	5715.5

NUTRITION

		Per 100g As Fed	Per 100g Dry Matter	Per 1000 kcal
PROTEIN	g	7.28	24.48	43.28
Arginine	g	0.42	1.43	2.53
Histidine	g	0.20	0.69	1.22
Isoleucine	g	0.40	1.34	2.37
Leucine	g	0.60	2.00	3.54
Lysine	g	0.56	1.89	3.34
Methionine + Cystine	g	0.35	1.17	2.07
Phenylalanine + Tyrosine	g	0.62	2.10	3.71
Threonine	g	0.30	1.02	1.80
Tryptophan	g	0.08	0.28	0.50
Valine	g	0.44	1.47	2.60
FAT (LIPID)	g	12.42	41.75	73.82
Linoleic acid	g	2.85	9.58	16.94
MINERALS				
Calcium	mg	288.73	970.55	1715.97
Phosphorus	mg	131.73	442.81	782.90
Calcium to Phosphorus ratio		2.19	2.19	2.19
Potassium	mg	322.56	1084.27	1917.03
Sodium	mg	65.84	221.31	391.28
Magnesium	mg	21.51	72.29	127.81
Iron	mg	5.17	17.36	30.69
Copper	mg	0.41	1.38	2.44
Manganese	mg	0.46	1.53	2.71
Zinc	mg	6.70	22.51	39.80
Iodine	mg	0.12	0.40	0.71
Selenium	µg	8.86	29.76	52.62
VITAMINS				
Vitamin A	IU	2072	6965	12314
Vitamin D	IU	101	339	600
Vitamin E	mg	6.49	21.80	38.54
Thiamin	mg	0.08	0.27	0.48
Riboflavin	mg	0.34	1.13	2.00
Niacin	mg	2.13	7.17	12.68
Pantothenic acid	mg	1.00	3.36	5.94
Pyridoxine	mg	0.16	0.55	0.97
Folic acid	µg	16.00	53.78	95.08
Choline	mg	85.77	288.31	509.74
Vitamin B12	µg	1.68	5.63	9.95
OTHER (non-essential nutrients)				
Total dietary fiber	g	1.75	5.87	10.38
FATTY ACIDS				
Polyunsaturated fatty acids	g	3.82	12.83	22.68
Eicosapentaenoic acid	mg	298	1000	1768
Docosahexaenoic acid	mg	429	1440	2546
Omega 6:3 ratio (estimate)		4.3	4.3	4.3
ANTIOXIDANTS				
Vitamin C	mg	5.08	17.06	30.16
Beta-carotene	µg	606.5	2038.7	3604.5
Lycopene	µg	0	0	0
Lutein + Zeaxanthin	µg	1250.7	4204.3	7433.4

Low Phosphorus/Protein Recipe 3

NOTE: This recipe should be supplemented with potassium citrate (150 mg/kg BW/day).

1. Cook egg whites over medium heat. Mash coarsely.
2. Gently simmer chicken until tender. Dice finely.
3. Boil beans until tender.
4. Pulse beans, pears, spinach, cod liver oil, safflower oil and salmon oil to small kernels.
5. Add HILARY'S BLEND supplement to the egg whites and mix thoroughly.
6. Stir all ingredients together.

INGREDIENTS

APPROX.	INGREDIENT	GRAMS
1⅔ cups	Beans, green, boiled	208
5 tbsp	Butter	71
220 g raw	Chicken breast, cooked	114
2 tsp	Cod liver oil	9
1⅛ cups	Egg whites, cooked	273
2 tbsp	Honey	42
¾ cup	Pears, raw, cubed	121
8 tsp	Safflower oil	34
4 tsp	Salmon oil	18
9 leaves	Spinach, raw	90
2 scoops	HILARY'S BLEND™ supplement	20

FEEDING GUIDE

Body weight		Energy intake	Amount to feed
lbs	kg	kcal/day	grams/day
15	6.8	527	313
25	11.4	774	460
40	18.2	1101	654
60	27.3	1492	887
80	36.4	1851	1100
100	45.5	2188	1301

METABOLIZABLE ENERGY

168 kcal/100 grams

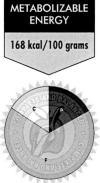

Supplement for home-made meals

Low Phosphorus/Protein Recipe 4

NOTE: This recipe should be supplemented with potassium citrate (150 mg/kg BW/day).

1. Cook egg whites over medium heat. Mash coarsely.
2. Gently simmer chicken until tender. Dice finely.
3. Boil beans until tender.
4. Pulse beans, pears, spinach, cod liver oil, safflower oil and salmon oil to small kernels.
5. Add HILARY'S BLEND™ supplement to the yogurt and mix thoroughly.
6. Stir all ingredients together.

INGREDIENTS

APPROX.	INGREDIENT	GRAMS
1⅓ cups	Beans, green, boiled	159
3 tbsp	Butter	43
330 g raw	Chicken breast, cooked	172
2 tsp	Cod liver oil	9
¾ cup	Egg whites, cooked	182
3 tbsp	Honey	63
1 cup	Pears, raw, cubed	160
10 tsp	Safflower oil	43
4 tsp	Salmon oil	18
7 leaves	Spinach, raw	70
¼ cup	Yogurt, plain, low fat	62
2 scoops	HILARY'S BLEND™ supplement	20
	Total	1000

METABOLIZABLE ENERGY

171 kcal/100 grams

FEEDING GUIDE

Body weight		Energy intake	Amount to feed
lbs	kg	kcal/day	grams/day
30	13.6	887	518
40	18.2	1101	643
50	22.7	1301	760
70	31.8	1675	978
90	40.9	2022	1180
120	54.5	2509	1465

NUTRITION

		Per 100g As Fed	Per 100g Dry Matter	Per 1000 kcal
PROTEIN	g	8.26	25.93	48.19
Arginine	g	0.48	1.50	2.79
Histidine	g	0.24	0.75	1.39
Isoleucine	g	0.45	1.40	2.60
Leucine	g	0.66	2.07	3.85
Lysine	g	0.66	2.08	3.87
Methionine + Cystine	g	0.37	1.16	2.16
Phenylalanine + Tyrosine	g	0.68	2.12	3.94
Threonine	g	0.35	1.09	2.03
Tryptophan	g	0.09	0.29	0.54
Valine	g	0.47	1.48	2.75
FAT (LIPID)	g	11.32	35.55	66.07
Linoleic acid	g	3.48	10.93	20.31
MINERALS				
Calcium	mg	295.79	929.09	1726.84
Phosphorus	mg	149.82	470.57	874.62
Calcium to Phosphorus ratio		1.97	1.97	1.97
Potassium	mg	323.59	1016.42	1889.15
Sodium	mg	57.48	180.55	335.58
Magnesium	mg	21.02	66.03	122.73
Iron	mg	5.15	16.18	30.07
Copper	mg	0.41	1.29	2.40
Manganese	mg	0.43	1.34	2.49
Zinc	mg	6.79	21.32	39.63
Iodine	mg	0.12	0.38	0.71
Selenium	µg	8.80	27.64	51.37
VITAMINS				
Vitamin A	IU	1785	5608	10423
Vitamin D	IU	99	312	580
Vitamin E	mg	6.38	20.04	37.25
Thiamin	mg	0.08	0.26	0.48
Riboflavin	mg	0.31	0.97	1.80
Niacin	mg	2.89	9.07	16.86
Pantothenic acid	mg	1.07	3.36	6.25
Pyridoxine	mg	0.20	0.61	1.13
Folic acid	µg	16.00	50.26	93.41
Choline	mg	85.44	268.37	498.80
Vitamin B12	µg	1.72	5.39	10.02
OTHER (non-essential nutrients)				
Total dietary fiber	g	1.67	5.25	9.76
FATTY ACIDS				
Polyunsaturated fatty acids	g	4.44	13.95	25.93
Eicosapentaenoic acid	mg	298	940	1747
Docosahexaenoic acid	mg	430	1350	2509
Omega 6:3 ratio (estimate)		5.1	5.1	5.1
ANTIOXIDANTS				
Vitamin C	mg	4.26	13.39	24.89
Beta-carotene	µg	469.5	1474.6	2740.8
Lycopene	µg	0	0	0
Lutein + Zeaxanthin	µg	973.8	3058.7	5685.0

Hilary's Blend™

Supplement for home-made meals

NUTRITION		Per 100g As Fed	Per 100g Dry Matter	Per 1000 kcal
PROTEIN	g	9.25	29.30	52.96
Arginine	g	0.53	1.67	3.02
Histidine	g	0.27	0.85	1.54
Isoleucine	g	0.50	1.57	2.84
Leucine	g	0.74	2.34	4.23
Lysine	g	0.75	2.38	4.30
Methionine + Cystine	g	0.40	1.28	2.31
Phenylalanine + Tyrosine	g	0.75	2.38	4.30
Threonine	g	0.39	1.23	2.22
Tryptophan	g	0.10	0.33	0.60
Valine	g	0.53	1.66	3.00
FAT (LIPID)	g	12.01	38.04	68.76
Linoleic acid	g	3.87	12.26	22.16
MINERALS				
Calcium	mg	305.10	966.34	1746.82
Phosphorus	mg	164.08	519.69	939.43
Calcium to Phosphorus ratio		1.86	1.86	1.86
Potassium	mg	326.18	1033.12	1867.53
Sodium	mg	59.09	187.17	338.34
Magnesium	mg	20.90	66.18	119.63
Iron	mg	5.12	16.21	29.30
Copper	mg	0.41	1.29	2.33
Manganese	mg	0.41	1.29	2.33
Zinc	mg	6.86	21.71	39.24
Iodine	mg	0.12	0.38	0.69
Selenium	µg	9.42	29.84	53.94
VITAMINS				
Vitamin A	IU	1602	5074	9173
Vitamin D	IU	99	315	569
Vitamin E	mg	6.35	20.10	36.33
Thiamin	mg	0.09	0.27	0.49
Riboflavin	mg	0.31	0.99	1.79
Niacin	mg	3.30	10.44	18.87
Pantothenic acid	mg	1.13	3.57	6.45
Pyridoxine	mg	0.21	0.67	1.21
Folic acid	µg	16.00	50.68	91.61
Choline	mg	86.19	273.01	493.51
Vitamin B12	µg	1.76	5.57	10.07
OTHER (non-essential nutrients)				
Total dietary fiber	g	1.51	4.78	8.64
FATTY ACIDS				
Polyunsaturated fatty acids	g	4.84	15.32	27.69
Eicosapentaenoic acid	mg	299	950	1717
Docosahexaenoic acid	mg	431	1360	2458
Omega 6:3 ratio (estimate)		5.6	5.6	5.6
ANTIOXIDANTS				
Vitamin C	mg	3.59	11.38	20.57
Beta-carotene	µg	357.3	1131.7	2045.6
Lycopene	µg	0	0	0
Lutein + Zeaxanthin	µg	729.5	2310.6	4176.7

Low Phosphorus/Protein Recipe 5

NOTE: This recipe should be supplemented with potassium citrate (150 mg/kg BW/day).

1. Cook egg whites over medium heat. Mash coarsely.
2. Gently simmer chicken until tender. Dice finely.
3. Boil beans until tender.
4. Pulse beans, pears, spinach, cod liver oil, safflower oil and salmon oil to small kernels.
5. Add HILARY'S BLEND™ supplement to the yogurt and mix thoroughly.
6. Stir all ingredients together.

INGREDIENTS		
APPROX.	INGREDIENT	GRAMS
1 ⅓ cups	Beans, green, boiled	161
3 tbsp	Butter	43
390 g raw	Chicken breast, cooked	203
2 tsp	Cod liver oil	9
⅔ cup	Egg whites, cooked	162
2 tbsp	Honey	42
¾ cup	Pears, raw, cubed	121
3½ tbsp	Safflower oil	48
4 tsp	Salmon oil	18
5 leaves	Spinach, raw	50
½ cup	Yogurt, plain, low fat	123
2 scoops	HILARY'S BLEND™ supplement	20
	Total	1000

FEEDING GUIDE			
Body weight		Energy intake	Amount to feed
lbs	kg	kcal/day	grams/day
60	27.3	1492	854
70	31.8	1675	959
80	36.4	1851	1060
90	40.9	2022	1158
110	50.0	2350	1346
130	59.1	2664	1525

METABOLIZABLE ENERGY

175 kcal/100 grams

Supplement for home-made meals

R96

Low Phosphorus/Protein Recipe 6

NOTE: This recipe should be supplemented with potassium citrate (150 mg/kg BW/day).

1. Cook egg whites over medium heat. Mash coarsely.
2. Gently simmer chicken until tender. Dice finely.
3. Boil beans until tender.
4. Pulse beans, pears, spinach, cod liver oil, safflower oil and salmon oil to small kernels.
5. Add HILARY'S BLEND™ supplement to the yogurt and mix thoroughly.
6. Stir all ingredients together.

INGREDIENTS

APPROX.	INGREDIENT	GRAMS
1¼ cups	Beans, green, boiled	156
3 tbsp	Butter	43
450 g raw	Chicken breast, cooked	234
2 tsp	Cod liver oil	9
½ cup	Egg whites, cooked	122
3 tbsp	Honey	63
¾ cup	Pears, raw, cubed	121
8 tsp	Safflower oil	36
3 tsp	Salmon oil	14
6 leaves	Spinach, raw	60
½ cup	Yogurt, plain, low fat	123
2 scoops	HILARY'S BLEND™ supplement	20
	Total	1000

METABOLIZABLE ENERGY

170 kcal/100 grams

FEEDING GUIDE

Body weight		Energy intake	Amount to feed
lbs	kg	kcal/day	grams/day
110	50.0	2350	1384
120	54.0	2509	1477
130	59.1	2664	1568
140	63.6	2816	1658
150	68.2	2966	1746
160	72.7	3113	1833

Supplement for home-made meals

NUTRITION

		Per 100g As Fed	Per 100g Dry Matter	Per 1000 kcal
PROTEIN	g	9.80	30.32	57.69
Arginine	g	0.56	1.73	3.29
Histidine	g	0.29	0.89	1.69
Isoleucine	g	0.52	1.62	3.08
Leucine	g	0.77	2.39	4.55
Lysine	g	0.80	2.48	4.72
Methionine + Cystine	g	0.42	1.29	2.45
Phenylalanine + Tyrosine	g	0.78	2.41	4.59
Threonine	g	0.41	1.27	2.42
Tryptophan	g	0.11	0.34	0.65
Valine	g	0.54	1.67	3.18
FAT (LIPID)	g	10.52	32.53	61.90
Linoleic acid	g	2.99	9.25	17.60
MINERALS				
Calcium	mg	305.99	946.82	1801.55
Phosphorus	mg	170.83	528.59	1005.77
Calcium to Phosphorus ratio		1.79	1.79	1.79
Potassium	mg	333.30	1031.32	1962.33
Sodium	mg	55.55	171.87	327.02
Magnesium	mg	22.08	68.32	129.99
Iron	mg	5.18	16.03	30.50
Copper	mg	0.41	1.26	2.40
Manganese	mg	0.42	1.28	2.44
Zinc	mg	6.89	21.33	40.59
Iodine	mg	0.12	0.37	0.70
Selenium	µg	9.50	29.39	55.92
VITAMINS				
Vitamin A	IU	1693	5238	9967
Vitamin D	IU	99	308	585
Vitamin E	mg	6.37	19.72	37.52
Thiamin	mg	0.09	0.27	0.51
Riboflavin	mg	0.30	0.93	1.77
Niacin	mg	3.72	11.52	21.92
Pantothenic acid	mg	1.15	3.56	6.77
Pyridoxine	mg	0.23	0.72	1.37
Folic acid	µg	16.00	49.51	94.20
Choline	mg	86.05	266.26	506.62
Vitamin B12	µg	1.77	5.46	10.39
OTHER (non-essential nutrients)				
Total dietary fiber	g	1.52	4.70	8.94
FATTY ACIDS				
Polyunsaturated fatty acids	g	3.81	11.77	22.40
Eicosapentaenoic acid	mg	247	760	1446
Docosahexaenoic acid	mg	359	1110	2112
Omega 6:3 ratio (estimate)		5.3	5.3	5.3
ANTIOXIDANTS				
Vitamin C	mg	3.84	11.87	22.59
Beta-carotene	µg	411.4	1273.1	2422.4
Lycopene	µg	0	0	0
Lutein + Zeaxanthin	µg	847.9	2623.7	4992.2

Low Sodium Recipe 1

NUTRITION		Per 100g As Fed	Per 100g Dry Matter	Per 1000 kcal
PROTEIN	g	7.39	24.73	52.63
Arginine	g	0.46	1.55	3.30
Histidine	g	0.21	0.69	1.47
Isoleucine	g	0.34	1.13	2.41
Leucine	g	0.60	2.01	4.28
Lysine	g	0.58	1.93	4.11
Methionine + Cystine	g	0.30	0.99	2.11
Phenylalanine + Tyrosine	g	0.58	1.92	4.09
Threonine	g	0.32	1.06	2.26
Tryptophan	g	0.09	0.29	0.62
Valine	g	0.40	1.33	2.83
FAT (LIPID)	g	5.81	19.45	41.40
Linoleic acid	g	1.45	4.84	10.30
MINERALS				
Calcium	mg	279.23	934.22	1988.38
Phosphorus	mg	206.50	690.89	1470.48
Calcium to Phosphorus ratio		1.35	1.35	1.35
Potassium	mg	297.11	994.05	2115.72
Sodium	mg	44.22	147.93	314.85
Magnesium	mg	38.49	128.76	274.05
Iron	mg	5.11	17.08	36.35
Copper	mg	0.44	1.48	3.15
Manganese	mg	0.86	2.87	6.11
Zinc	mg	6.99	23.39	49.78
Iodine	mg	0.12	0.40	0.85
Selenium	µg	16.84	56.36	119.96
VITAMINS				
Vitamin A	IU	683	2286	4866
Vitamin D	IU	57	191	406
Vitamin E	mg	6.16	20.60	43.84
Thiamin	mg	0.19	0.64	1.36
Riboflavin	mg	0.24	0.81	1.72
Niacin	mg	3.15	10.53	22.41
Pantothenic acid	mg	1.38	4.62	9.83
Pyridoxine	mg	0.31	1.03	2.19
Folic acid	µg	16.00	53.53	113.93
Choline	mg	97.80	327.20	696.41
Vitamin B12	µg	2.30	7.69	16.37
OTHER (non-essential nutrients)				
Total dietary fiber	g	1.81	6.05	12.88
FATTY ACIDS				
Polyunsaturated fatty acids	g	2.44	8.17	17.39
Eicosapentaenoic acid	mg	193	650	1383
Docosahexaenoic acid	mg	392	1310	2788
Omega 6:3 ratio (estimate)		3.2	3.2	3.2
ANTIOXIDANTS				
Vitamin C	mg	2.25	7.51	15.98
Beta-carotene	µg	84.1	281.5	599.1
Lycopene	µg	469.7	1571.5	3344.8
Lutein + Zeaxanthin	µg	174.8	584.9	1245.0

1. Poach the salmon until it flakes easily.
2. Prepare the rice according to the package to yield 3 cups of cooked rice.
3. Hard boil the egg. Discard shell and mash coarsely.
4. Sprinkle HILARY'S BLEND™ supplement over the rice and mix in.
5. Stir all ingredients together.

INGREDIENTS		
APPROX.	INGREDIENT	GRAMS
½ cup	Beans, green, raw, chopped	55
1 tsp	Cod liver oil	5
1 large	Egg, hard-boiled	50
3 cups	Rice, brown, cooked	585
3 tsp	Safflower oil	14
330 g raw	Salmon, cooked	230
1 leaf	Spinach, raw	10
⅛ cup	Tomato sauce, canned	31
2 scoops	HILARY'S BLEND™ supplement	20
	Total	1000

FEEDING GUIDE			
Body weight		Energy intake	Amount to feed
lbs	kg	kcal/day	grams/day
10	4.5	296	211
20	9.1	497	355
40	18.2	836	597
60	27.3	1134	810
80	36.4	1407	1005
100	45.5	1663	1188

METABOLIZABLE ENERGY

140 kcal/100 grams

Hilary's BLEND™
Supplement for home-made meals

Low Sodium Recipe 2

1. Poach chicken until tender. Dice finely.
2. Cook chicken liver to crumbles.
3. Pulse apples, blueberries, broccoli, brussels sprouts, cabbage, peanut butter, cod liver oil, safflower oil, and salmon oil to small kernels.
4. Add tomato sauce and HILARY'S BLEND™ supplement to the chicken liver crumbles and stir thoroughly.
5. Stir all ingredients together.

INGREDIENTS

APPROX.	INGREDIENT	GRAMS
1½ cups	Apple, raw with skin, sliced	165
⅔ cups	Blueberries, raw	99
1 cup	Broccoli, raw, chopped	91
10 sprouts	Brussels sprouts, raw	190
1 cup	Cabbage, raw, shredded	70
245 g raw	Chicken breast, cooked	127
1 tsp	Cod liver oil	5
145 g raw	Liver, chicken, cooked	90
5 tbsp	Peanut butter, smooth, unsalted	80
3 tsp	Safflower oil	14
4 tsp	Salmon oil	18
⅛ cup	Tomato sauce, canned	31
2 scoops	HILARY'S BLEND™ supplement	20
	Total	1000

METABOLIZABLE ENERGY

145 kcal/100 grams

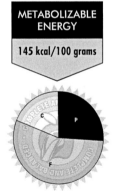

FEEDING GUIDE

Body weight		Energy intake	Amount to feed
lbs	kg	kcal/day	grams/day
10	4.5	296	204
20	9.1	497	343
40	18.2	836	577
60	27.3	1134	782
80	36.4	1407	970
100	45.5	1663	1147

Hilary's Blend™

Supplement for home-made meals

NUTRITION

		Per 100g As Fed	Per 100g Dry Matter	Per 1000 kcal
PROTEIN	g	9.29	31.65	64.12
Arginine	g	0.66	2.25	4.56
Histidine	g	0.25	0.87	1.76
Isoleucine	g	0.40	1.35	2.74
Leucine	g	0.66	2.25	4.56
Lysine	g	0.61	2.06	4.17
Methionine + Cystine	g	0.31	1.05	2.13
Phenylalanine + Tyrosine	g	0.68	2.32	4.70
Threonine	g	0.34	1.15	2.33
Tryptophan	g	0.10	0.34	0.69
Valine	g	0.43	1.47	2.98
FAT (LIPID)	g	8.93	30.43	61.65
Linoleic acid	g	2.35	8.00	16.21
MINERALS				
Calcium	mg	287.38	978.70	1982.90
Phosphorus	mg	206.79	704.25	1426.85
Calcium to Phosphorus ratio		1.39	1.39	1.39
Potassium	mg	408.21	1390.20	2816.62
Sodium	mg	46.82	159.43	323.01
Magnesium	mg	30.56	104.07	210.85
Iron	mg	6.38	21.72	44.01
Copper	mg	0.49	1.65	3.34
Manganese	mg	0.59	2.00	4.05
Zinc	mg	7.32	24.94	50.53
Iodine	mg	0.12	0.41	0.83
Selenium	µg	11.94	40.66	82.38
VITAMINS				
Vitamin A	IU	1934	6586	13344
Vitamin D	IU	57	194	393
Vitamin E	mg	7.21	24.54	49.72
Thiamin	mg	0.13	0.45	0.91
Riboflavin	mg	0.40	1.37	2.78
Niacin	mg	4.43	15.09	30.57
Pantothenic acid	mg	1.76	5.98	12.12
Pyridoxine	mg	0.33	1.12	2.27
Folic acid	µg	16.00	54.49	110.40
Choline	mg	118.30	402.87	816.24
Vitamin B12	µg	3.16	10.76	21.80
OTHER (non-essential nutrients)				
Total dietary fiber	g	2.79	9.51	19.27
FATTY ACIDS				
Polyunsaturated fatty acids	g	3.27	11.12	22.53
Eicosapentaenoic acid	mg	270	920	1864
Docosahexaenoic acid	mg	386	1310	2654
Omega 6:3 ratio (estimate)		4.0	4.0	4.0
ANTIOXIDANTS				
Vitamin C	mg	31.28	106.52	215.82
Beta-carotene	µg	138.1	470.3	952.8
Lycopene	µg	471.6	1606.1	3254.0
Lutein + Zeaxanthin	µg	452.0	1539.5	3119.1

Low Sodium Recipe 3

NUTRITION		Per 100g As Fed	Per 100g Dry Matter	Per 1000 kcal
PROTEIN	g	7.29	31.02	58.93
Arginine	g	0.48	2.06	3.91
Histidine	g	0.20	0.84	1.60
Isoleucine	g	0.33	1.39	2.64
Leucine	g	0.57	2.42	4.60
Lysine	g	0.54	2.31	4.39
Methionine + Cystine	g	0.30	1.26	2.39
Phenylalanine + Tyrosine	g	0.57	2.44	4.64
Threonine	g	0.32	1.34	2.55
Tryptophan	g	0.08	0.35	0.66
Valine	g	0.38	1.60	3.04
FAT (LIPID)	g	7.88	33.56	63.76
Linoleic acid	g	2.38	10.15	19.28
MINERALS				
Calcium	mg	226.40	963.72	1830.95
Phosphorus	mg	183.51	781.15	1484.09
Calcium to Phosphorus ratio		1.23	1.23	1.23
Potassium	mg	319.76	1361.10	2585.92
Sodium	mg	43.37	184.62	350.76
Magnesium	mg	33.83	144.02	273.62
Iron	mg	4.10	17.44	33.13
Copper	mg	0.34	1.46	2.77
Manganese	mg	0.54	2.28	4.33
Zinc	mg	5.38	22.90	43.51
Iodine	mg	0.09	0.38	0.72
Selenium	µg	15.61	66.46	126.27
VITAMINS				
Vitamin A	IU	2156	9179	17439
Vitamin D	IU	55	235	447
Vitamin E	mg	5.81	24.72	46.96
Thiamin	mg	0.11	0.49	0.93
Riboflavin	mg	0.25	1.06	2.01
Niacin	mg	1.00	4.26	8.09
Pantothenic acid	mg	1.01	4.31	8.19
Pyridoxine	mg	0.15	0.64	1.22
Folic acid	µg	12.00	51.08	97.05
Choline	mg	103.83	441.99	839.73
Vitamin B12	µg	1.73	7.38	14.02
OTHER (non-essential nutrients)				
Total dietary fiber	g	1.97	8.39	15.94
FATTY ACIDS				
Polyunsaturated fatty acids	g	3.33	14.17	26.92
Eicosapentaenoic acid	mg	310	1320	2508
Docosahexaenoic acid	mg	430	1830	3477
Omega 6:3 ratio (estimate)		3.5	3.5	3.5
ANTIOXIDANTS				
Vitamin C	mg	12.55	53.42	101.49
Beta-carotene	µg	796.8	3391.9	6444.2
Lycopene	µg	383.5	1632.3	3101.1
Lutein + Zeaxanthin	µg	287.6	1224.2	2325.8

1. Poach fish until it flakes easily.
2. Hard-boil eggs. Discard shells and mash coarsely.
3. Prepare oatmeal according to package directions to yield 1¼ cups of cooked oatmeal.
4. Pulse almonds, broccoli, carrots, tomatoes, cod liver oil, safflower oil, and salmon oil to small kernels.
5. Add HILARY'S BLEND™ supplement to the fish and mix thoroughly.
6. Stir all ingredients together.

INGREDIENTS		
APPROX.	INGREDIENT	GRAMS
⅓ cup	Almonds, ground	32
1¼ cups	Broccoli, raw, chopped	114
¾ cup	Carrots, raw, grated	83
1 tsp	Cod liver oil	5
2 large	Eggs, hard-boiled	100
240 g raw	Flatfish/sole, cooked	168
1¼ cups	Oatmeal, cooked	293
5 tsp	Safflower oil	23
4 tsp	Salmon oil	18
1 cup	Tomatoes, cherry, raw	149
1½ scoops	HILARY'S BLEND™ supplement	15
	Total	1000

FEEDING GUIDE				
Body weight		Energy intake	Amount to feed	
lbs	kg	kcal/day	grams/day	
10	4.5	296	238	
20	9.1	497	401	
40	18.2	836	675	
60	27.3	1134	914	
80	36.4	1407	1134	
100	45.5	1663	1341	

METABOLIZABLE ENERGY

124 kcal/100 grams

Hilary's Blend™
Supplement for home-made meals

R100

Low Sodium Recipe 4

1. Thaw frozen peas overnight in the refrigerator.
2. Pan-broil lean (10% fat) beef to brown crumbles.
3. Hard-boil eggs. Discard shells and mash coarsely.
4. Prepare oatmeal according to package directions to yield 1½ cups of cooked oatmeal.
5. Pulse blueberries, broccoli, carrots, peas, spinach, cod liver oil, safflower oil, and salmon oil to small kernels.
6. Add HILARY'S BLEND™ supplement to the beef crumbles and mix thoroughly.
7. Stir all ingredients together.

INGREDIENTS

APPROX.	INGREDIENT	GRAMS
245 g raw	Beef, ground, cooked	183
¼ cup	Blueberries, raw	37
1½ cups	Broccoli, raw, chopped	137
½ cup	Carrots, raw, grated	55
½ tsp	Cod liver oil	2
2 large	Eggs, hard-boiled	100
1½ cups	Oatmeal, cooked	350
½ cup	Peas, thawed from frozen	73
3 tsp	Safflower oil	14
3 tsp	Salmon oil	14
2 leaves	Spinach, raw	20
1½ scoops	HILARY'S BLEND™ supplement	15
	Total	1000

METABOLIZABLE ENERGY

122 kcal/100 grams

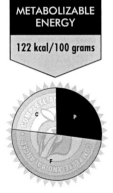

FEEDING GUIDE

Body weight		Energy intake	Amount to feed
lbs	kg	kcal/day	grams/day
10	4.5	296	242
20	9.1	497	408
40	18.2	836	686
60	27.3	1134	929
80	36.4	1407	1153
100	45.5	1663	1363

NUTRITION

		Per 100g As Fed	Per 100g Dry Matter	Per 1000 kcal
PROTEIN	g	8.29	34.34	67.73
Arginine	g	0.54	2.23	4.40
Histidine	g	0.24	1.01	1.99
Isoleucine	g	0.37	1.52	3.00
Leucine	g	0.64	2.63	5.19
Lysine	g	0.61	2.53	4.99
Methionine + Cystine	g	0.32	1.33	2.62
Phenylalanine + Tyrosine	g	0.62	2.55	5.03
Threonine	g	0.34	1.39	2.74
Tryptophan	g	0.07	0.27	0.53
Valine	g	0.42	1.76	3.47
FAT (LIPID)	g	6.73	27.86	54.95
Linoleic acid	g	1.40	5.78	11.40
MINERALS				
Calcium	mg	221.01	915.16	1804.98
Phosphorus	mg	175.83	728.06	1435.96
Calcium to Phosphorus ratio		1.26	1.26	1.26
Potassium	mg	316.65	1311.20	2586.09
Sodium	mg	41.74	172.84	340.89
Magnesium	mg	24.54	101.62	200.43
Iron	mg	4.66	19.31	38.09
Copper	mg	0.34	1.40	2.76
Manganese	mg	0.53	2.20	4.34
Zinc	mg	6.54	27.08	53.41
Iodine	mg	0.09	0.37	0.73
Selenium	µg	10.32	42.72	84.26
VITAMINS				
Vitamin A	IU	1514	6269	12364
Vitamin D	IU	25	105	206
Vitamin E	mg	4.93	20.43	40.29
Thiamin	mg	0.13	0.52	1.03
Riboflavin	mg	0.25	1.03	2.03
Niacin	mg	1.86	7.71	15.21
Pantothenic acid	mg	1.07	4.41	8.70
Pyridoxine	mg	0.19	0.80	1.58
Folic acid	µg	12.00	49.69	98.00
Choline	mg	105.13	435.34	858.62
Vitamin B12	µg	1.81	7.48	14.75
OTHER (non-essential nutrients)				
Total dietary fiber	g	1.99	8.22	16.21
FATTY ACIDS				
Polyunsaturated fatty acids	g	2.04	8.45	16.67
Eicosapentaenoic acid	mg	197	810	1598
Docosahexaenoic acid	mg	281	1160	2288
Omega 6:3 ratio (estimate)		3.3	3.3	3.3
ANTIOXIDANTS				
Vitamin C	mg	16.39	67.85	133.82
Beta-carotene	µg	652.7	2702.8	5330.7
Lycopene	µg	0.1	0.2	0.5
Lutein + Zeaxanthin	µg	732.3	3032.5	5980.9

Supplement for home-made meals

Low Sodium Recipe 5

1. Thaw frozen peas overnight in the refrigerator.
2. Poach chicken until tender. Dice finely.
3. Hard-boil eggs. Discard shells and mash coarsely.
4. Prepare rice according to package directions to yield 1¼ cups of cooked rice.
5. Add HILARY'S BLEND™ supplement to the eggs and mix thoroughly.
6. Pulse broccoli, brussels sprouts, peas, cod liver oil, safflower oil, and salmon oil to small kernels.
7. Stir all ingredients together.

NUTRITION

		Per 100g As Fed	Per 100g Dry Matter	Per 1000 kcal
PROTEIN	g	8.30	31.58	65.96
Arginine	g	0.53	2.01	4.20
Histidine	g	0.22	0.84	1.75
Isoleucine	g	0.41	1.55	3.24
Leucine	g	0.62	2.35	4.91
Lysine	g	0.59	2.25	4.70
Methionine + Cystine	g	0.34	1.28	2.67
Phenylalanine + Tyrosine	g	0.64	2.42	5.05
Threonine	g	0.35	1.34	2.80
Tryptophan	g	0.10	0.36	0.75
Valine	g	0.44	1.66	3.47
FAT (LIPID)	g	5.90	22.44	46.87
Linoleic acid	g	1.48	5.63	11.76
MINERALS				
Calcium	mg	227.02	863.86	1804.26
Phosphorus	mg	179.59	683.36	1427.26
Calcium to Phosphorus ratio		1.26	1.26	1.26
Potassium	mg	300.86	1144.84	2391.11
Sodium	mg	45.47	173.01	361.35
Magnesium	mg	28.55	108.64	226.91
Iron	mg	4.39	16.70	34.88
Copper	mg	0.35	1.31	2.74
Manganese	mg	0.58	2.20	4.59
Zinc	mg	5.60	21.30	44.49
Iodine	mg	0.09	0.34	0.71
Selenium	µg	12.53	47.67	99.56
VITAMINS				
Vitamin A	IU	602	2290	4782
Vitamin D	IU	25	96	201
Vitamin E	mg	4.97	18.91	39.50
Thiamin	mg	0.15	0.55	1.15
Riboflavin	mg	0.29	1.09	2.28
Niacin	mg	2.69	10.24	21.39
Pantothenic acid	mg	1.19	4.53	9.46
Pyridoxine	mg	0.25	0.94	1.96
Folic acid	µg	12.00	45.66	95.37
Choline	mg	112.04	426.32	890.41
Vitamin B12	µg	1.46	5.56	11.61
OTHER (non-essential nutrients)				
Total dietary fiber	g	2.34	8.91	18.61
FATTY ACIDS				
Polyunsaturated fatty acids	g	2.15	8.20	17.13
Eicosapentaenoic acid	mg	198	750	1566
Docosahexaenoic acid	mg	287	1090	2277
Omega 6:3 ratio (estimate)		3.4	3.4	3.4
ANTIOXIDANTS				
Vitamin C	mg	27.71	105.44	220.22
Beta-carotene	µg	168.1	639.5	1335.7
Lycopene	µg	0	0	0
Lutein + Zeaxanthin	µg	803.2	3056.5	6383.7

INGREDIENTS

APPROX.	INGREDIENT	GRAMS
1½ cups	Broccoli, raw, chopped	137
6	Brussels sprouts, raw	114
225 g raw	Chicken breast, cooked	116
½ tsp	Cod liver oil	2
4 large	Eggs, hard-boiled	200
1 cup	Peas, thawed from frozen	145
1¼ cup	Rice, brown, cooked	243
3 tsp	Safflower oil	14
3 tsp	Salmon oil	14
1½ scoops	HILARY'S BLEND™ supplement	15
	Total	1000

FEEDING GUIDE

Body weight		Energy intake	Amount to feed
lbs	kg	kcal/day	grams/day
10	4.5	296	235
20	9.1	497	395
40	18.2	836	664
60	27.3	1134	900
80	36.4	1407	1116
100	45.5	1663	1320

METABOLIZABLE ENERGY

126 kcal/100 grams

Supplement for home-made meals

Appendix 1

Current body weight		Very active young adult dog	Average mature adult dog	Very active mature adult dog
kg	lb			
2	4.4	235	160	219
3	6.6	319	217	296
4	8.8	396	269	368
5	11.0	468	318	435
6	13.2	537	364	498
7	15.4	602	409	559
8	17.6	666	452	618
9	19.8	727	494	675
10	22.0	787	534	731
12	26.4	903	613	838
14	30.8	1013	688	941
16	35.2	1120	760	1040
18	39.6	1223	830	1136
20	44.0	1324	898	1229
22	48.4	1422	965	1321
24	52.8	1518	1030	1410
26	57.2	1612	1094	1497
28	61.6	1704	1156	1582
30	66.0	1795	1218	1666
32.5	71.5	1906	1293	1770
35	77.0	2015	1367	1871
37.5	82.5	2122	1440	1970
40	88.0	2227	1511	2068
42.5	93.5	2330	1581	2164
45	99.0	2432	1651	2259
47.5	104.5	2533	1719	2352
50	110.0	2632	1786	2444
52.5	115.5	2731	1853	2535
55	121.0	2827	1919	2626
57.5	126.5	2923	1984	2715
60	132.0	3018	2048	2803
62.5	137.5	3112	2112	2890
65	143.0	3205	2175	2976
67.5	148.5	3297	2237	3061
70	154.0	3388	2299	3146
72.5	159.5	3478	2360	3230
75	165.0	3568	2421	3313
77.5	170.5	3657	2481	3396
80	176.0	3745	2541	3477

Daily energy requirements (kcal/day) for healthy adult dogs of normal body weight.

Use the chart at left to determine how many kilocalories to feed a healthy adult dog each day. For example, a 143 lb (65 kg) very active mature adult dog needs 2976 kcal/day.

Appendix 2

Daily energy requirements (kcal/day) for healthy senior dogs of normal body weight.

Use the chart at right to determine how many kilocalories to feed a healthy senior dog of normal body weight. For example, a 22 lb (10 kg) very active senior dog needs 590 kcal/day.

Current body weight		Average senior dog	Very active senior dog
kg	lb		
2	4.4	143	177
3	6.6	194	239
4	8.8	240	297
5	11.0	284	351
6	13.2	326	403
7	15.4	366	452
8	17.6	404	499
9	19.8	442	546
10	22.0	478	590
12	26.4	548	677
14	30.8	615	760
16	35.2	680	840
18	39.6	743	918
20	44.0	804	993
22	48.4	863	1067
24	52.8	922	1139
26	57.2	979	1209
28	61.6	1035	1278
30	66.0	1090	1346
32.5	71.5	1157	1429
35	77.0	1223	1511
37.5	82.5	1288	1591
40	88.0	1352	1670
42.5	93.5	1415	1748
45	99.0	1477	1824
47.5	104.5	1538	1900
50	110.0	1598	1974
52.5	115.5	1658	2048
55	121.0	1717	2121
57.5	126.5	1775	2193
60	132.0	1832	2264
62.5	137.5	1889	2334
65	143.0	1946	2404
67.5	148.5	2002	2473
70	154.0	2057	2541
72.5	159.5	2112	2609
75	165.0	2166	2676
77.5	170.5	2220	2743
80	176.0	2274	2809

Appendix 3

Current body weight		Overweight adult dog
kg	lb	
2	4.4	92
3	6.6	125
4	8.8	156
5	11.0	184
6	13.2	211
7	15.4	237
8	17.6	262
9	19.8	286
10	22.0	309
12	26.4	355
14	30.8	398
16	35.2	440
18	39.6	481
20	44.0	520
22	48.4	559
24	52.8	596
26	57.2	633
28	61.6	669
30	66.0	705
32.5	71.5	749
35	77.0	791
37.5	82.5	833
40	88.0	875
42.5	93.5	915
45	99.0	956
47.5	104.5	995
50	110.0	1034
52.5	115.5	1073
55	121.0	1111
57.5	126.5	1148
60	132.0	1186
62.5	137.5	1223
65	143.0	1259
67.5	148.5	1295
70	154.0	1331
72.5	159.5	1367
75	165.0	1402
77.5	170.5	1437
80	176.0	1471

Daily energy requirements (kcal/day) for overweight adult dogs.

Use the chart at left to determine how many kilocalories to feed an overweight adult dog for weight loss. For example, an overweight dog that currently weighs 88 lb (40 kg) should be fed 875 kcal/day. This calorie chart should only be used when feeding Low Calorie Recipes (Recipes R46–R55).

Appendix 4

Daily energy requirements (kcal/day) for dogs suffering from disease conditions that increase energy requirements.

Dogs suffering from a variety of clinical conditions such as kidney disease, gastrointestinal disease, cardiac disease, allergic skin disease and other chronic inflammatory diseases typically have increased energy requirements as a result of their condition. Use the chart at right to determine how many kilocalories to feed an adult dog with disease conditions. For example, a 66 lb (30 kg) dog with kidney disease needs 1602 kcal/day.

Current body weight		Adult dogs with disease conditions
kg	lb	
2	4.4	210
3	6.6	285
4	8.8	354
5	11.0	418
6	13.2	479
7	15.4	538
8	17.6	595
9	19.8	650
10	22.0	703
12	26.4	806
14	30.8	905
16	35.2	1000
18	39.6	1092
20	44.0	1182
22	48.4	1270
24	52.8	1355
26	57.2	1439
28	61.6	1522
30	66.0	1602
32.5	71.5	1701
35	77.0	1799
37.5	82.5	1894
40	88.0	1988
42.5	93.5	2081
45	99.0	2172
47.5	104.5	2262
50	110.0	2350
52.5	115.5	2438
55	121.0	2525
57.5	126.5	2610
60	132.0	2695
62.5	137.5	2779
65	143.0	2862
67.5	148.5	2944
70	154.0	3025
72.5	159.5	3106
75	165.0	3186
77.5	170.5	3265
80	176.0	3344

Appendix 5

Puppy's current body weight		Adult weight of puppy when it reaches maturity in pounds and (kilograms)											
kg	lb	4.4 (2.0)	8.8 (4.0)	13.2 (6.0)	17.6 (8.0)	22.0 (10.0)	26.4 (12.0)	30.8 (14.0)	35.2 (16.0)	39.6 (18.0)	44.0 (20.0)	48.4 (22.0)	52.8 (24.0)
0.25	0.6	117	125	127	128	129	130	130	130	131	131	131	131
0.50	1.1	174	197	205	210	212	214	215	216	217	217	218	218
0.75	1.7	208	251	267	275	281	284	286	288	290	291	292	293
1.00	2.2	228	293	318	332	340	345	349	352	355	357	358	360
1.25	2.8	236	326	361	380	392	400	406	410	414	417	419	421
1.50	3.3	237	351	397	423	438	449	457	463	468	472	475	478
1.75	3.9	232	369	428	460	480	494	504	512	518	523	527	531
2.0	4.4		383	454	493	518	535	548	558	565	571	576	581
2.5	5.5		397	493	547	583	607	625	639	650	659	667	673
3.0	6.6		399	519	589	636	668	692	711	725	737	747	756
3.5	7.7		391	534	621	679	719	750	774	792	808	820	831
4.0	8.8			541	644	713	763	800	829	852	871	887	900
4.5	9.9			541	659	740	799	843	878	906	928	947	963
5.0	11.0			535	668	761	829	880	921	953	980	1002	1021
6.0	13.2				671	787	873	939	991	1034	1069	1098	1124
7.0	15.4				657	795	899	980	1045	1097	1141	1178	1210
8.0	17.6					789	910	1006	1083	1146	1199	1244	1283
9.0	19.8					772	909	1019	1109	1183	1245	1298	1344
10.0	22.0						899	1023	1124	1209	1280	1341	1394
11.0	24.2						881	1017	1130	1225	1306	1375	1435
12.0	26.4							1004	1128	1234	1323	1401	1468
13.0	28.6							985	1120	1235	1333	1418	1493
14.0	30.8								1105	1229	1337	1430	1511
15.0	33.0								1086	1219	1334	1435	1524
16.0	35.2									1203	1326	1435	1531
17.0	37.4									1183	1314	1430	1532
18.0	39.6										1298	1421	1530
19.0	41.8										1278	1407	1523
20.0	44.0											1391	1512
21.0	46.2											1371	1498
22.0	48.4												1481
23.0	50.6												1461

Daily energy requirements (kcal/day) for puppies with mature weights from 4 to 55 lbs (2–25 kg).

Use the chart at left to determine how many kilocalories to feed a puppy that will weigh from 4 to 55 lbs (2–25 kg) as an adult. For example, a 2.2 lb (1 kg) puppy that will weigh 22 lb (10 kg) at maturity needs 340 kcal/day. Use Appendix 8 to estimate the mature adult weight of the puppy.

Appendix 6

Daily energy requirements (kcal/day) for puppies with mature weights from 55 to 121 lbs (25 to 55 kg).

Use the chart at right to determine how many kilocalories to feed a puppy that will weigh from 55 to 121 lbs (25 to 55 kg) as an adult. For example, a 33 lb (15 kg) puppy that will weigh 88 lb (40 kg) at maturity needs 1971 kcal/day. Use Appendix 8 to estimate the mature adult weight of the puppy.

Puppy's current body weight		Adult weight of puppy when it reaches maturity in pounds and (kilograms)											
kg	lb	55.0 (25.0)	60.5 (27.5)	66.0 (30.0)	71.5 (32.5)	77.0 (35.0)	82.5 (37.5)	88.0 (40.0)	93.5 (42.5)	99.0 (45.0)	104.5 (47.5)	110.0 (50.0)	121.0 (55.0)
3.0	6.6	759	768	774	780	785	790	794	797	800	803	805	809
4.0	8.8	906	919	930	939	948	955	961	966	971	976	980	987
5.0	11.0	1030	1048	1064	1078	1089	1100	1109	1117	1124	1130	1136	1146
6.0	13.2	1135	1160	1181	1199	1214	1228	1240	1251	1261	1269	1277	1291
7.0	15.4	1224	1256	1282	1305	1325	1343	1358	1372	1385	1396	1406	1424
8.0	17.6	1300	1338	1371	1399	1424	1446	1465	1482	1497	1511	1524	1546
9.0	19.8	1364	1410	1449	1483	1512	1538	1561	1582	1600	1617	1632	1659
10.0	22.0	1418	1471	1517	1556	1591	1621	1648	1672	1694	1714	1732	1763
11.0	24.2	1462	1523	1575	1621	1660	1695	1727	1755	1780	1803	1824	1860
12.0	26.4	1498	1567	1626	1677	1722	1762	1798	1830	1859	1885	1908	1950
13.0	28.6	1527	1603	1669	1726	1777	1822	1862	1898	1930	1960	1987	2034
14.0	30.8	1549	1632	1705	1769	1825	1875	1919	1960	1996	2029	2059	2112
15.0	33.0	1564	1656	1735	1805	1867	1922	1971	2015	2055	2092	2125	2184
16.0	35.2	1574	1673	1760	1836	1903	1963	2017	2066	2110	2150	2186	2251
17.0	37.4	1579	1686	1779	1861	1934	1999	2058	2111	2159	2203	2243	2313
18.0	39.6	1580	1693	1793	1882	1960	2031	2094	2151	2203	2251	2294	2371
19.0	41.8	1576	1697	1803	1898	1982	2058	2126	2187	2243	2295	2341	2424
20.0	44.0	1568	1696	1809	1910	2000	2080	2153	2219	2279	2334	2385	2474
22.0	48.4	1543	1684	1810	1922	2023	2114	2196	2271	2339	2402	2459	2561
24.0	52.8	1506	1660	1798	1922	2033	2134	2225	2309	2385	2455	2520	2635
26.0	57.2		1625	1775	1909	2031	2141	2242	2334	2418	2496	2568	2696
28.0	61.6			1742	1887	2018	2138	2248	2348	2441	2526	2604	2745
30.0	66.0				1855	1996	2125	2244	2352	2452	2545	2631	2784
32.0	70.4				1817	1967	2104	2231	2347	2455	2555	2648	2814
34.0	74.8					1930	2076	2210	2335	2450	2557	2656	2835
36.0	79.2						2041	2183	2315	2437	2551	2657	2848
38.0	83.6							2149	2288	2417	2538	2650	2854
40.0	88.0								2256	2392	2519	2637	2853
42.0	92.4								2219	2361	2494	2618	2846
44.0	96.8									2325	2464	2594	2833
46.0	101.2										2429	2566	2815
48.0	105.6										2391	2532	2792
50.0	110.0												2765
52.0	114.4												2733

Appendix 7

Puppy's current body weight		Adult weight of puppy when it reaches maturity in pounds and (kilograms)									
kg	lb	126.5 (57.5)	132.0 (60.0)	137.5 (62.5)	143.0 (65.0)	148.5 (67.5)	154.0 (70.0)	159.5 (72.5)	165.0 (75.0)	170.5 (77.5)	176.0 (80.0)
8.0	17.6	1555	1564	1572	1580	1587	1594	1600	1606	1611	1616
10.0	22.0	1777	1790	1801	1812	1823	1832	1841	1849	1857	1864
12.0	26.4	1969	1986	2001	2016	2030	2042	2054	2065	2076	2086
14.0	30.8	2135	2157	2177	2195	2213	2229	2244	2258	2272	2285
16.0	35.2	2280	2306	2331	2354	2375	2395	2414	2431	2448	2464
18.0	39.6	2405	2437	2466	2494	2519	2543	2566	2587	2607	2626
20.0	44.0	2514	2550	2585	2617	2647	2675	2701	2726	2750	2772
22.0	48.4	2607	2649	2689	2725	2760	2792	2823	2851	2878	2904
24.0	52.8	2686	2734	2779	2820	2860	2896	2931	2964	2994	3023
26.0	57.2	2753	2806	2856	2903	2947	2988	3027	3064	3098	3131
28.0	61.6	2809	2868	2923	2975	3023	3069	3112	3153	3192	3228
30.0	66.0	2854	2918	2979	3036	3089	3140	3187	3232	3275	3315
32.5	71.5	2897	2968	3036	3099	3158	3215	3268	3318	3365	3410
35.0	77.0	2926	3005	3079	3148	3214	3276	3335	3390	3443	3492
37.5	82.5	2944	3029	3110	3186	3257	3325	3389	3450	3508	3562
40.0	88.0	2951	3043	3130	3212	3290	3363	3433	3499	3561	3621
42.5	93.5	2948	3047	3140	3228	3312	3391	3466	3537	3605	3669
45.0	99.0	2936	3041	3141	3235	3324	3409	3489	3566	3639	3708
47.5	104.5	2916	3027	3133	3233	3328	3418	3504	3586	3663	3738
50.0	110.0	2889	3006	3118	3223	3324	3420	3511	3597	3680	3759
52.5	115.5	2855	2978	3096	3207	3313	3414	3510	3602	3689	3773
55.0	121.0	2815	2944	3067	3184	3295	3401	3502	3599	3691	3779
57.5	126.5		2905	3033	3155	3271	3382	3488	3590	3687	3779
60.0	132.0			2993	3120	3242	3358	3468	3575	3676	3773
62.5	137.5				3081	3207	3328	3443	3554	3660	3761
65.0	143.0					3168	3293	3413	3528	3638	3744
67.5	148.5						3254	3378	3498	3612	3722
70.0	154.0							3339	3463	3581	3696
72.5	159.5								3424	3547	3665
75.0	165.0									3508	3630
77.5	170.5										3591

Daily energy requirements (kcal/day) for puppies with mature weights over 121 lbs (55 kg).

Use the chart at left to determine how many kilocalories to feed a puppy that will weigh more than 121 lbs (55 kg) as an adult. For example, a 44 lb (20 kg) puppy that will weigh 154 lb (70 kg) as an adult needs 2675 kcal/day. Use Appendix 8 to estimate the mature adult weight of the puppy.

Appendix 8

Average mature adult weight of dogs of various breeds in pounds (lbs).

BREED	Males (lbs)	Females (lbs)	BREED	Males (lbs)	Females (lbs)
Affenpinscher	7–8	7–8	Chihuahua	2–5	2–6
Afghan Hound	60	50	Chinese Shar Pei	45–55	35–45
Airedale Terrier	45–60	40–55	Chow Chow	45–60	40–50
Akita	70–85	65–75	Collie (Rough)	65–75	50–65
Alaskan Malamute	85–95	75–85	Collie (Smooth)	65–75	50–65
American Staffordshire Terrier	45–55	40–50	Dachshund (Miniature)	10	10
Australian Cattle Dog	35–45	35–45	Dachshund (Standard)	16–22	16–22
Australian Shepherd	45–65	45–65	Dalmatian	50–65	45–55
Australian Terrier	12–14	12–14	Dandie Dinmont Terrier	18–24	18–24
Basenji	24–25	22–22	Doberman Pinscher	65–80	55–70
Basset Hound	65–75	50–65	English Toy Spaniel	8–14	8–14
Beagle - 13"	13–18	13–16	Finnish Spitz	25–35	25–30
Beagle - 15"	17–22	15–20	Fox Terrier	17–19	15–17
Bearded Collie	55–65	50–60	Foxhound (American)	65–75	55–65
Bedlington Terrier	17–23	17–23	Foxhound (English)	65–75	50–70
Belgian Malinois	60–70	43–55	French Bulldog	20–28	20–28
Belgian Sheepdog	60–70	43–55	German Shepherd Dog	75–90	65–80
Belgian Tervuren	60–70	43–55	German Shorthair Pointer	55–70	45–60
Bernese Mountain Dog	75–90	65–80	German Wirehair Pointer	60–75	50–65
Bichon Frise	9–12	9–12	Giant Schnauzer	70–85	60–75
Black and Tan Coonhound	70–85	55–70	Great Dane	120–180	100–130
Bloodhound	90–110	80–100	Great Pyrenees	110–125	85–115
Border Terrier	13–15	11–14	Greyhound	65–70	60–65
Borzoi	75–105	70–90	Harrier	40–50	35–45
Boston Terrier	15–24	15–24	Ibizan Hound	50	45
Bouvier des Flandres	70–90	70–90	Irish Terrier	27	25
Boxer	55–70	50–60	Irish Wolfhound	120	105
Briard	65–75	60–70	Italian Greyhound	8–15	5–15
Brittany	35–40	30–40	Japanese Chin	4–20	4–20
Brussels Griffon	10–12	8–10	Keeshond	40–50	40–50
Bull Terrier	52–62	45–55	Kerry Blue Terrier	33–40	30–38
Bull Terrier (Miniature)	15–20	15–20	Komodor	100–130	80–110
Bulldog	45–55	40–50	Kuvasz	100–115	70–90
Bullmastiff	110–130	100–120	Lakeland Terrier	17	17
Cairn Terrier	14	13	Lhasa Apso	13–15	13–15

Appendix 8 (cont'd)

BREED	Males (lbs)	Females (lbs)	BREED	Males (lbs)	Females (lbs)
Maltese	4–6	4–6	Scottish Deerhound	85–110	75–95
Manchester Terrier (Standard)	12–22	12–22	Scottish Terrier	19–22	18–21
Manchester Terrier (Toy)	7–12	7–12	Sealyham Terrier	23–24	21–23
Mastiff	175–190	160–180	Setter - English	60–75	55–65
Miniature Pinscher	10–12	9–11	Setter - Gordon	55–80	45–70
Miniature Schnauzer	16–18	12–16	Setter - Irish	70	60
Newfoundland	130–150	100–120	Shetland Sheepdog	16–22	14–18
Norfolk Terrier	11–12	11–12	Shih Tzu	12–17	10–15
Norweigan Elkhound	55	48	Siberian Husky	45–60	35–50
Norwich Terrier	11–12	11–12	Silky Terrier	8–10	8–10
Old English Sheepdog	60–70	60–70	Skye Terrier	25–30	20–25
Otter Hound	75–115	65–100	Soft-Coated Wheaten Terrier	35–40	30–35
Papillon	8–10	7–9	Spaniel - American Water	28–45	25–40
Pekingese	10–14	10–14	Spaniel - Clumber	70–85	55–70
Petit Basset Griffon Vendeen	40–45	40–45	Spaniel - Cocker (American)	25–30	20–25
Pharaoh Hound	55–70	50–65	Spaniel - Cocker (English)	28–34	26–32
Pointer	55–75	45–64	Spaniel - English Springer	49–54	40–45
Pomeranian	4–7	3–5	Spaniel - Field	35–45	35–45
Poodle (Miniature)	17–20	15–20	Spaniel - Irish Water	55–65	45–58
Poodle (Standard)	50–60	45–55	Spaniel - Sussex	35–45	30–40
Poodle (Toy)	7–10	7–10	Spaniel - Welsh Springer	35–50	35–50
Portuguese Water Dog	42–60	35–50	Staffordshire Bull Terrier	28–38	24–34
Pug	14–18	14–18	Standard Schnauzer	30–40	25–35
Puli	29–33	29–33	Tibetan Spaniel	9–15	9–15
Retriever - Chesapeake Bay	65–80	55–70	Tibetan Terrier	18–30	18–30
Retriever - Curly Coated	65–70	65–70	Vizsla	45–55	40–50
Retriever - Flat Coated	50–65	45–60	Weimaraner	60–75	55–70
Retriever - Golden	65–75	55–65	Welsh Corgi (Cardigan)	30–38	25–34
Retriever - Labrador	65–80	55–70	Welsh Corgi (Pembroke)	27–30	25–28
Rhodesian Ridgeback	75	65	Welsh Terrier	18–22	16–18
Rottweiler	80–95	70–85	West Highland White Terrier	12–14	11–13
Saint Bernard	130–180	120–160	Whippet	20–28	18–23
Saluki	50–70	45–65	Wirehaired Pointing Griffon	55–65	50–60
Samoyed	50–65	45–60	Yorkshire Terrier	4–7	3–6
Schipperke	12–18	12–16			

Appendix 9

2008 AAFCO NUTRIENT PROFILES for adult dogs*

	Units	Per 100g of Food (Dry matter basis)		Per 1000 kcal of Food (Energy basis)	
		minimum	maximum	minimum	maximum
Crude protein	g	18.0		51.4	
Arginine	g	0.51		1.46	
Histidine	g	0.18		0.51	
Isoleucine	g	0.37		1.06	
Leucine	g	0.59		1.69	
Lysine	g	0.63		1.80	
Methionine + Cystine	g	0.43		1.23	
Phenylalanine + Tyrosine	g	0.73		2.09	
Threonine	g	0.48		1.37	
Tryptophan	g	0.16		0.46	
Valine	g	0.39		1.11	
Lipid (fat)	g	5.0		14.3	
Linoleic acid	g	1.0		2.9	
Minerals					
Calcium	mg	600	2500	1700	7100
Phosphorus	mg	500	1600	1400	4600
Calcium:Phosphorus ratio		1:1	2:1		
Potassium	mg	600		1700	
Sodium	mg	60		170	
Chloride	mg	90		260	
Magnesium	mg	40	300	110	860
Iron	mg	8	300	23	857
Copper	mg	0.73	25	2.1	71
Manganese	mg	0.5		1.4	
Zinc	mg	12	100	34	286
Iodine	mg	0.15	5	0.43	14
Selenium	µg	11	200	30	570
Vitamins					
Vitamin A	IU	500	25000	1429	71429
Vitamin D	IU	50	500	143	1429
Vitamin E	mg	5	100	14	286
Thiamin (B1)	mg	0.1		0.29	
Riboflavin (B2)	mg	0.22		0.63	
Niacin (B3)	mg	1.14		3.3	
Pantothenic acid (B5)	mg	1		2.9	
Pyridoxine (B6)	mg	0.1		0.29	
Folic acid	µg	18		50	
Choline	mg	120		343	
Vitamin B12	µg	2.2		6	

Appendix 9 (cont'd)

2008 AAFCO NUTRIENT PROFILES for growing puppies*

	Units	Per 100g of Food (Dry matter basis)		Per 1000 kcal of Food (Energy basis)	
		minimum	maximum	minimum	maximum
Crude protein	g	22.0		62.9	
Arginine	g	0.62		1.77	
Histidine	g	0.22		0.63	
Isoleucine	g	0.45		1.29	
Leucine	g	0.72		2.06	
Lysine	g	0.77		2.20	
Methionine + Cystine	g	0.53		1.51	
Phenylalanine + Tyrosine	g	0.89		2.54	
Threonine	g	0.58		1.66	
Tryptophan	g	0.20		0.57	
Valine	g	0.48		1.37	
Lipid (fat)	g	8.0		22.9	
Linoleic acid	g	1.0		2.9	
Minerals					
Calcium	mg	1000	2500	2900	7100
Phosphorus	mg	800	1600	2300	4600
Calcium:Phosphorus ratio		1:1	2:1		
Potassium	mg	600		1700	
Sodium	mg	300		860	
Chloride	mg	450		1290	
Magnesium	mg	40	300	110	860
Iron	mg	8	300	23	857
Copper	mg	0.73	25	2.1	71
Manganese	mg	0.5		1.4	
Zinc	mg	12	100	34	286
Iodine	mg	0.15	5	0.43	14
Selenium	µg	11	200	30	570
Vitamins					
Vitamin A	IU	500	25000	1429	71429
Vitamin D	IU	50	500	143	1429
Vitamin E	mg	5	100	14	286
Thiamin (B1)	mg	0.1		0.29	
Riboflavin (B2)	mg	0.22		0.63	
Niacin (B3)	mg	1.14		3.3	
Pantothenic acid (B5)	mg	1		2.9	
Pyridoxine (B6)	mg	0.1		0.29	
Folic acid	µg	18		50	
Choline	mg	120		343	
Vitamin B12	µg	2.2		6	

* © The Association of American Feed Control Officials (AAFCO), Official Publication 2008. Reproduced with kind permission. To order a copy of the AAFCO Official Publication, please visit www.AAFCO.org